Business Analytics Using R - A Practical Approach

Dr. Umesh R. Hodeghatta

Umesha Nayak

Apress®

Business Analytics Using R - A Practical Approach

Dr. Umesh R. Hodeghatta
Bangalore, Karnataka
India

Umesha Nayak
Bangalore, Karnataka
India

ISBN-13 (pbk): 978-1-4842-2513-4
DOI 10.1007/978-1-4842-2514-1

ISBN-13 (electronic): 978-1-4842-2514-1

Managing Director: Welmoed Spahr
Lead Editor: Celestin Suresh John
Technical Reviewer: Jojo Moolayil
Editorial Board: Steve Anglin, Pramila Balan, Laura Berendson, Aaron Black,
    Louise Corrigan, Jonathan Gennick, Robert Hutchinson, Celestin Suresh John,
    Nikhil Karkal, James Markham, Susan McDermott, Matthew Moodie, Natalie Pao,
    Gwenan Spearing
Coordinating Editor: Prachi Mehta
Copy Editor: Sharon Wilkey
Compositor: SPi Global
Indexer: SPi Global
Artist: SPi Global

Distributed to the book trade worldwide by Springer Science+Business Media New York, 233 Spring Street, 6th Floor, New York, NY 10013. Phone 1-800-SPRINGER, fax (201) 348-4505, e-mail orders-ny@springer-sbm.com, or visit www.springeronline.com. Apress Media, LLC is a California LLC and the sole member (owner) is Springer Science + Business Media Finance Inc (SSBM Finance Inc). SSBM Finance Inc is a **Delaware** corporation.

For information on translations, please e-mail rights@apress.com, or visit www.apress.com.

Apress and friends of ED books may be purchased in bulk for academic, corporate, or promotional use. eBook versions and licenses are also available for most titles. For more information, reference our Special Bulk Sales–eBook Licensing web page at www.apress.com/bulk-sales.

Any source code or other supplementary materials referenced by the author in this text are available to readers at www.apress.com. For detailed information about how to locate your book's source code, go to www.apress.com/source-code/. Readers can also access source code at SpringerLink in the Supplementary Material section for each chapter.

Printed on acid-free paper

Contents at a Glance

About the Authors... xv

About the Technical Reviewer xvii

Chapter 1: Overview of Business Analytics..................................... 1

Chapter 2: Introduction to R 17

Chapter 3: R for Data Analysis 37

Chapter 4: Introduction to descriptive analytics.......................... 59

Chapter 5: Business Analytics Process and Data Exploration...... 91

Chapter 6: Supervised Machine Learning—Classification 131

Chapter 7: Unsupervised Machine Learning.............................. 161

Chapter 8: Simple Linear Regression 187

Chapter 9: Multiple Linear Regression 207

Chapter 10: Logistic Regression... 233

Chapter 11: Big Data Analysis—Introduction and
Future Trends.. 257

References.. 267

Index... 273

Contents

About the Authors... xv

About the Technical Reviewer xvii

■Chapter 1: Overview of Business Analytics...................................... 1

1.1   Objectives of This Book... 3

1.2   Confusing Terminology.. 4

1.3   Drivers for Business Analytics... 5

    1.3.1   Growth of Computer Packages and Applications 6

    1.3.2   Feasibility to Consolidate Data from Various Sources 7

    1.3.3   Growth of Infinite Storage and Computing Capability 7

    1.3.4   Easy-to-Use Programming Tools and Platforms 7

    1.3.5   Survival and Growth in the Highly Competitive World 7

    1.3.6   Business Complexity Growing out of Globalization 8

1.4   Applications of Business Analytics... 8

    1.4.1   Marketing and Sales.. 8

    1.4.2   Human Resources 9

    1.4.3   Product Design 9

    1.4.4   Service Design 9

    1.4.5   Customer Service and Support Areas.. 9

1.5   Skills Required for a Business Analyst.. 10

    1.5.1   Understanding the Business and Business Problems 10

    1.5.2   Understanding Data Analysis Techniques and Algorithms........................ 10

    1.5.3   Having Good Computer Programming Knowledge 11

1.5.4   Understanding Data Structures and Data Storage/Warehousing
Techniques 11

1.5.5   Knowing Relevant Statistical and Mathematical Concepts 11

1.6   Life Cycle of a Business Analytics Project.................................... 11

1.7   The Framework for Business Analytics 14

1.8   Summary.. 15

Chapter 2: Introduction to R 17

2.1   Data Analysis Tools... 17

2.2   R Installation 21

2.2.1   Installing R... 21

2.2.2   Installing RStudio 23

2.2.3   Exploring the RStudio Interface... 23

2.3   Basics of R Programming.. 25

2.3.1   Assigning Values.. 26

2.3.2   Creating Vectors 27

2.4   R Object Types.. 27

2.5   Data Structures in R 29

2.5.1   Matrices 30

2.5.2   Arrays 31

2.5.3   Data Frames 32

2.5.4   Lists.. 34

2.5.5   Factors 35

2.6   Summary.. 36

Chapter 3: R for Data Analysis 37

3.1   Reading and Writing Data... 37

3.1.1   Reading Data from a Text File... 38

3.1.2   Reading Data from a Microsoft Excel File 42

3.1.3   Reading Data from the Web... 44

3.2   Using Control Structures in R 45

   3.2.1   if-else 46

   3.2.2   for loops 46

   3.2.3   while loops 47

   3.2.4   Looping Functions 48

   3.2.5   Writing Your Own Functions in R 55

3.3   Working with R Packages and Libraries 56

3.4   Summary 58

Chapter 4: Introduction to descriptive analytics 59

4.1   Descriptive analytics 62

4.2   Population and sample 62

4.3   Statistical parameters of interest 63

   4.3.1   Mean 64

   4.3.2   Median 66

   4.3.3   Mode 68

   4.3.4   Range 68

   4.3.5   Quantiles 69

   4.3.6   Standard deviation 70

   4.3.7   Variance 73

   4.3.8   "Summary" command in R 73

4.4   Graphical description of the data 74

   4.4.1   Plots in R 74

   4.4.2   Histogram 77

   4.4.3   Bar plot 77

   4.4.4   Boxplots 78

4.5   Computations on data frames 79

   4.5.1   Scatter plot 81

4.6   Probability 84

   4.6.1   Probability of mutually exclusive events 85

   4.6.2   Probability of mutually independent events 85

   4.6.3   Probability of mutually non-exclusive events: 86

   4.6.4   Probability distributions 86

4.7   Chapter summary 88

Chapter 5: Business Analytics Process and Data Exploration 91

5.1   Business Analytics Life Cycle 91

   5.1.1   Phase 1: Understand the Business Problem 91

   5.1.2   Phase 2: Collect and Integrate the Data 92

   5.1.3   Phase 3: Preprocess the Data 92

   5.1.4   Phase 4: Explore and Visualize the Data 92

   5.1.5   Phase 5: Choose Modeling Techniques and Algorithms 93

   5.1.6   Phase 6: Evaluate the Model 93

   5.1.7   Phase 7: Report to Management and Review 94

   5.1.8   Phase 8: Deploy the Model 94

5.2   Understanding the Business Problem 94

5.3   Collecting and Integrating the Data 95

   5.3.1   Sampling 96

   5.3.2   Variable Selection 97

5.4   Preprocessing the Data 97

   5.4.1   Data Types 97

   5.4.2   Data Preparation 99

   5.4.3   Data Preprocessing with R 100

5.5   Exploring and Visualizing the Data 104

    5.5.1   Tables 105

    5.5.2   Summary Tables 106

    5.5.3   Graphs 106

    5.5.4   Scatter Plot Matrices 112

    5.5.5   Data Transformation 117

5.6   Using Modeling Techniques and Algorithms 118

    5.6.1   Descriptive Analytics 118

    5.6.2   Predictive Analytics 118

    5.6.3   Machine Learning 119

5.7   Evaluating the Model 122

    5.7.1   Training Data Partition 122

    5.7.2   Test Data Partition 122

    5.7.3   Validation Data Partition 122

    5.7.4   Cross-Validation 123

    5.7.5   Classification Model Evaluation 123

    5.7.6   Regression Model Evaluation 127

5.8   Presenting a Management Report and Review 128

    5.8.1   Problem Description 128

    5.8.2   Data Set Used 128

    5.8.3   Data Cleaning Carried Out 128

    5.8.4   Method Used to Create the Model 128

    5.8.5   Model Deployment Prerequisites 128

    5.8.6   Model Deployment and Usage 129

    5.8.7   Issues Handling 129

5.9   Deploying the Model 129

5.10   Summary 130

Chapter 6: Supervised Machine Learning—Classification 131

6.1   What Is Classification? What Is Prediction? 131

6.2   Probabilistic Models for Classification 132

6.2.1   Example 133

6.2.2   Naïve Bayes Classifier Using R 134

6.2.3   Advantages and Limitations of the Naïve Bayes Classifier 136

6.3   Decision Trees 136

6.3.1   Recursive Partitioning Decision-Tree Algorithm 138

6.3.2   Information Gain 138

6.3.3   Example of a Decision Tree 140

6.3.4   Induction of a Decision Tree 142

6.3.5   Classification Rules from Tree 145

6.3.6   Overfitting and Underfitting 145

6.3.7   Bias and Variance 147

6.3.8   Avoiding Overfitting Errors and Setting the Size of Tree Growth 148

6.4   Other Classifier Types 150

6.4.1   K-Nearest Neighbor 150

6.4.2   Random Forests 152

6.5   Classification Example Using R 153

6.6   Summary 160

Chapter 7: Unsupervised Machine Learning 161

7.1   Clustering - Overview 161

7.2   What Is Clustering? 163

7.2.1   Measures Between Two Records 163

7.2.2   Distance Measures for Categorical Variables 164

7.2.3   Distance Measures for Mixed Data Types 165

7.2.4   Distance Between Two Clusters 166

7.3 Hierarchical Clustering 168

   7.3.1 Dendrograms 169

   7.3.2 Limitations of Hierarchical Clustering 169

7.4 Nonhierarchical Clustering 169

   7.4.1 K-Means Algorithm 170

   7.4.2 Limitations of K-Means Clustering 172

7.5 Clustering Case Study 172

   7.5.1 Retain Only Relevant Variables in the Data Set 173

   7.5.2 Remove Any Outliers from the Data Set 173

   7.5.3 Standardize the Data 174

   7.5.4 Calculate the Distance Between the Data Points 175

7.6 Association Rule 182

   7.6.1 Choosing Rules 183

   7.6.2 Example of Generating Association Rules 185

   7.6.3 Interpreting Results 186

7.7 Summary 186

Chapter 8: Simple Linear Regression 187

8.1 Introduction 187

8.2 Correlation 188

   8.2.1 Correlation Coefficient 189

8.3 Hypothesis Testing 192

8.4 Simple Linear Regression 193

   8.4.1 Assumptions of Regression 193

   8.4.2 Simple Linear Regression Equation 193

   8.4.3 Creating Simple Regression Equation in R 194

   8.4.4 Testing the Assumptions of Regression: 197

8.4.5　Conclusion 203

8.4.6　Predicting the Response Variable 203

8.4.7　Additional Notes 204

8.5　Chapter Summary 204

Chapter 9: Multiple Linear Regression 207

9.1　Using Multiple Linear Regression 209

9.1.1　The Data 209

9.1.2　Correlation 210

9.1.3　Arriving at the Model 212

9.1.4　Validation of the Assumptions of Regression 213

9.1.5　Multicollinearity 218

9.1.6　Stepwise Multiple Linear Regression 221

9.1.7　All Subsets Approach to Multiple Linear Regression 221

9.1.8　Multiple Linear Regression Equation 223

9.1.9　Conclusion 224

9.2　Using an Alternative Method in R 224

9.3　Predicting the Response Variable 225

9.4　Training and Testing the Model 225

9.5　Cross Validation 227

9.6　Summary 230

Chapter 10: Logistic Regression 233

10.1　Logistic Regression 235

10.1.1　The Data 235

10.1.2　Creating the Model 236

10.1.3　Model Fit Verification 240

10.1.4　General Words of Caution 241

10.1.5   Multicollinearity 242

10.1.6   Dispersion 242

10.1.7   Conclusion for Logistic Regression 242

10.2   Training and Testing the Model 243

10.2.1   Predicting the Response Variable 245

10.2.2   Alternative Way of Validating the Logistic Regression Model 245

10.3   Multinomial Logistic Regression 248

10.4   Regularization 248

10.5   Summary 254

Chapter 11: Big Data Analysis—Introduction and Future Trends 257

11.1   Big Data Ecosystem 259

11.2   Future Trends in Big Data Analytics 261

11.2.1   Growth of Social Media 261

11.2.2   Creation of Data Lakes 262

11.2.3   Visualization Tools at the Hands of Business Users 262

11.2.4   Prescriptive Analytics 262

11.2.5   Internet of Things 262

11.2.6   Artificial Intelligence 262

11.2.7   Whole Data Processing 263

11.2.8   Vertical and Horizontal Applications 263

11.2.9   Real-Time Analytics 263

11.2.10   Putting the Analytics in the Hands of Business Users 263

11.2.11   Migration of Solutions from One Tool to Another 263

11.2.12   Cloud, Cloud, Everywhere the Cloud 264

11.2.13   In-Database Analytics 264

11.2.14 In-Memory Analytics..264

11.2.15 Autonomous Services for Machine Learning.........................264

11.2.16 Addressing Security and Compliance....................................264

11.2.17 Healthcare 265

References..**267**

Index...**273**

About the Authors

Dr. Umesh Rao Hodeghatta is an acclaimed professional in the field of machine learning, NLP, and business analytics. He has a master's degree in electrical engineering from Oklahoma State University and a PhD from the Indian Institute of Technology (IIT), Kharagpur with a specialization in machine learning and NLP. He has held technical and senior management positions at Wipro Technologies, McAfee, Cisco Systems, and AT&T Bell Laboratories. Dr. Hodeghatta has published many journal articles in international journals and conference proceedings. He is a co-author of *The InfoSec Handbook: An Introduction to Information Security*. Dr. Hodeghatta has contributed to numerous professional organizations and regulatory bodies, including the IEEE Computer Society (India), the Information Systems Audit and Control Association (ISACA) in the United States, the government of Odisha, the International Neural Network Society (INNS) in India, and the Task Force on Business Intelligence & Knowledge Management. He is also a senior member of the IEEE. Further details about Dr. Hodeghatta are available at www.mytechnospeak.com. You may reach him at umesh_hr@yahoo.com.

Umesha Nayak is a director and principal consultant of MUSA Software Engineering, which focuses on systems/process/management consulting. He has 35 years of experience, including 14 years of consulting to IT/manufacturing and other organizations across the globe. He has an MS in software systems and an MA in economics. His certifications include CAIIB, Certified Information Systems Auditor (CISA) and Certified Risk and Information Systems Control (CRISC) professional from ISACA, PGDFM, Certified Lead Auditor for many of the standards, and Certified Coach, among others. He has worked extensively in banking, software development, product design and development, project management, program management, information technology audits, information application audits, quality assurance, coaching, product reliability, human resource management, business analytics, and consultancy. He was vice president and corporate executive council member at Polaris Software Lab, Chennai prior to his current assignment. He started his journey with computers in 1981 with ICL mainframes and continued further with minis and PCs. He was one of the founding members of information systems auditing in the banking industry in India. He has effectively guided many organizations through successful ISO 9001/ISO 27001/ CMMI and other certifications and process/product improvements and business analytics. He has co-authored *The InfoSec Handbook: An Introduction to Information Security*. You may reach him at aum136@rediffmail.com.

About the Technical Reviewer

Jojo Moolayil is a data scientist and author of *Smarter Decisions—The Intersection of Internet of Things and Decision Science*. With over four years of industrial experience in data science, decision science, and IoT, he has worked with industry leaders on high-impact and critical projects across multiple verticals. He is currently associated with General Electric, a pioneer and leader in data science for industrial IoT, and lives in Bengaluru—the Silicon Valley of India

He was born and raised in Pune, India and graduated from the University of Pune with a major in information technology engineering. He started his career with Mu Sigma, the world's largest pure play analytics provider, and worked with the leaders of many Fortune 50 clients. One of the early enthusiasts to venture into IoT analytics, he now focuses on solving decision science problems for industrial IoT use cases. As a part of his role at GE, he also develops data science and decision science products and platforms for industrial IoT. Jojo is also an active data science tutor and maintains a blog at `www.jojomoolayil.com/web/blog/`.

CHAPTER 1

Overview of Business Analytics

Today's world is knowledge based. In the earliest days, knowledge was gathered through observation. Later, knowledge not only was gathered through observation, but also confirmed by actually doing and then extended by experimenting further. Knowledge thus gathered was applied to practical fields and extended by analogy to other fields. Today, knowledge is gathered and applied by analyzing, or deep-diving, into the data accumulated through various computer applications, web sites, and more. The advent of computers complemented the knowledge of statistics, mathematics, and programming. The enormous storage and extended computing capabilities of the cloud, especially, have ensured that knowledge can be quickly derived from huge amounts of data and also can be used for further preventive or productive purposes. This chapter provides you with the basic knowledge of where and how business analytics is used.

Imagine the following situations:

- You visit a hotel in Switzerland and are welcomed with your favorite drink and dish; how delighted you are!

- You are offered a stay at a significantly discounted rate at your favorite hotel when you travel to your favorite destination.

- You are forewarned about the high probability of becoming a diabetic. You are convinced about the reasoning behind this warning and take the right steps to avoid it.

- You are forewarned of a probable riot at your planned travel destination. Based on this warning, you cancel the visit; you later learn from news reports that a riot does happen at that destination!

- You are forewarned of an incompatibility with the person whom you consider making your life partner, based on both of your personal characteristics; you avoid a possible divorce!

© Dr. Umesh R. Hodeghatta and Umesha Nayak 2017
U. R. Hodeghatta and U. Nayak, *Business Analytics Using R - A Practical Approach*,
DOI 10.1007/978-1-4842-2514-1_1

- You enter a grocery store and you find that your regular monthly purchases are already selected and set aside for you. The only decision you have to make is whether you require all of them or want to remove some from the list. How happy you are!

- Your preferred airline reserves tickets for you well in advance of your vacation travels and at a lower rate compared to the market rate.

- You are planning to travel and are forewarned of a possible cyclone in that place. Based on that warning, you postpone your visit. Later, you find that the cyclone created havoc, and you avoided a terrible situation.

We can imagine many similar scenarios that are made possible by analyzing data about you and your activities that is collected through various means—including your Google searches, visits to various web sites, your comments on social media sites, your activities using various computer applications, and more. The use of data analytics in these scenarios has focused on your individual perspective.

Now, let's look at scenarios from a business perspective. Imagine these situations:

- You are in the hotel business and are able to provide competitive yet profitable rates to your prospective customers. At the same time, you can ensure that your hotel is completely occupied all the time by providing additional benefits, including discounts on local travel and local sightseeing offers tied into other local vendors.

- You are in the taxi business and are able to repeatedly attract the same customers based on their earlier travel history and preferences of taxi type and driver.

- You are in the fast-food business and offer discounted rates to attract customers on slow days. These discounts enable you to ensure full occupancy on those days also.

- You are in the human resources (HR) department of an organization and are bogged down by high attrition. But now you are able to understand the types of people you should focus on recruiting, based on the characteristics of those who perform well and who are more loyal and committed to the organization.

- You are in the airline business, and based on data collected by the engine system, you are warned of a potential engine failure in the next three months. You proactively take steps to carry out the necessary corrective actions.

- You are in the business of designing, manufacturing, and selling medical equipment used by hospitals. You are able to understand the possibility of equipment failure well before the equipment actually fails, by carrying out analysis of the errors or warnings captured in the equipment logs.

All these scenarios are possible by analyzing data that the businesses and others collect from various sources. There are many such possible scenarios. The application of data analytics to the field of business is called *business analytics*.

You have likely observed the following scenarios:

- You've been searching for the past few days on Google for adventurous places to visit. You've also tried to find various travel packages that might be available. You suddenly find that various other web sites you visit or the searches you make show a specific advertisement of what you are looking for, and that too at a discounted rate.

- You've been searching for a specific item to purchase on Amazon (or any other site). Suddenly, on other sites you visit, you find advertisements related to what you are looking for or find customized mail landing in your mailbox, offering discounts along with other items you might be interested in.

- You've also seen recommendations that Amazon makes based on your earlier searches for items, your wish list, or previous Amazon purchases. Many times you've also likely observed Amazon offering you discounts or promoting products based on its available data.

All of these possibilities are now a reality because of data analytics specifically used by businesses. This book takes you through the exciting field of business analytics and enables you to step into this field as well.

1.1 Objectives of This Book

Many professionals are becoming interested in learning analytics. But not all of them have rich statistical or mathematical backgrounds. This book is the right place for techies as well as those who are not so techie to get started with business analytics. You'll start with a hands-on introduction to R for beginners. You'll also learn about predictive modeling and big data, which forms a key part of business analytics. This is an introductory book in the field of business analytics using R.

The following are some of the advantages of this book:

- This book covers both R programming and analytics using numerous real-life examples.

- It offers the right mix of theory and hands-on labs. The concepts are explained using business scenarios or case studies where required.

- It is written by industry professionals who are currently working in the field of analytics on real-life problems for paying customers.

This book provides the following:

- Practical insights into the use of data that has been collected, collated, purchased, or available for free from government sources or others. These insights are attained via computer programming, statistical and mathematical knowledge, and expertise in relevant fields that enable you to understand the data and arrive at predictive capabilities.

- Information on the effective use of various techniques related to business analytics.

- Explanations of how to effectively use the programming platform R for business analytics.

- Practical cases and examples that enable you to apply what you learn from this book.

- The dos and don'ts of business analytics.

- The book does *not* do the following:

  - Deliberate on the definitions of various terms related to analytics, which can be confusing

  - Elaborate on the fundamentals behind any statistical or mathematical technique or particular algorithm beyond certain limits

  - Provide a repository of all the techniques or algorithms used in the field of business analytics (but does explore many of them)

1.2   Confusing Terminology

Many terms are used in discussions of this topic— for example, *data analytics, business analytics, big data analytics,* and *data science.* Most of these are, in a sense, the same. However, the purpose of the analytics, the extent of the data that's available for analysis, and the difficulty of the data analysis may vary from one to the other. Finally, regardless of the differences in terminology, we need to know how to use the data effectively for our businesses. These differences in terminology should not come in the way of applying techniques to the data (especially in analyzing it and using it for various purposes including understanding it, deriving models from it, and then using these models for predictive purposes).

In layman's terms, let's look at some of this terminology:

- *Data analytics* is the analysis of data, whether huge or small, in order to understand it and see how to use the knowledge hidden within it. An example is the analysis of the data related to various classes of travelers (as noted previously).

- *Business analytics* is the application of data analytics to business. An example is offering specific discounts to different classes of travelers based on the amount of business they offer or have the potential to offer.

- *Data science* is an interdisciplinary field (including disciplines such as statistics, mathematics, and computer programming) that derives knowledge from data and applies it for predictive or other purposes. Expertise about underlying processes, systems, and algorithms is used. An example is the application of t-values and p-values from statistics in identifying significant model parameters in a regression equation.

- *Big data analytics* is the analysis of huge amounts of data (for example, trillions of records) or the analysis of difficult-to-crack problems. Usually, this requires a huge amount of storage and/or computing capability. This analysis requires enormous amounts of memory to hold the data, a huge number of processors, and high-speed processing to crunch the data and get its essence. An example is the analysis of geospatial data captured by satellite to identify weather patterns and make related predictions.

1.3   Drivers for Business Analytics

The following are the growth drivers for business analytics:

- Increasing numbers of relevant computer packages and applications. One example is the R programming environment with its various data sets, documentation on its packages, and ready-made algorithms.

- Feasibility to consolidate related and relevant data from various sources and of various types (data from flat files, data from relational databases, data from log files, data from Twitter messages, and more). An example is the consolidation of information from data files in a Microsoft SQL Server database with data from a Twitter message stream.

- Growth of seemingly infinite storage and computing capabilities by clustering multiple computers and extending these capabilities via the cloud. An example is the use of Apache Hadoop clusters to distribute and analyze huge amounts of data.

- Availability of many easy-to-use programming tools, platforms, and frameworks (such as R and Hadoop).

- Emergence of many algorithms and tools to effectively use statistical and mathematical concepts for business analysis. One example is the k-means algorithm used for partition clustering analysis.

- The need for business survival and growth techniques in our highly competitive world. The highly competitive nature of business requires each company to deep-dive into data in order to understand customer behavior patterns and take advantage of them.

- Business complexity arising from globalization. An economic or political situation in a particular country can affect the sales in that country, for example.

A note of caution here: not all of these problems require complicated analytics. Some may be easy to understand and to solve by using techniques such as visual depiction of data. Now let's discuss each of these drivers for business analytics in more detail.

1.3.1   Growth of Computer Packages and Applications

Computer packages and applications have completely flooded modern life. This is true at both an individual and business level. This is especially true with our extensive use of smartphones, which enable the following:

- Communication with others through e-mail packages

- Activities in social media and blogs

- Business communications through e-mail, instant messaging, and other tools

- Day-to-day searches for information and news through search engines

- Recording of individual and business financial transactions through accounting packages

- Recording of our travel details via online ticket-booking web sites or apps

- Recording of our various purchases in e-commerce web sites

- Recording our daily exercise routines, calories burned, and diets through various applications

We are surrounded by many computer packages and applications that collect a lot of data about us. This data is used by businesses to make them more competitive, attract more business, and retain and grow their customer base. With thousands of apps on platforms such as Android, iOS, and Windows, the capture of data encompasses nearly all the activities carried out by individuals across the globe (who are the consumers for most of the products and services). This has been enabled further by the reach of hardware devices such as computers, laptops, mobile phones, and smartphones even to remote places.

1.3.2 Feasibility to Consolidate Data from Various Sources

Technology has grown by leaps and bounds over the last few years. It is now easy for us to convert data from one format to another and to consolidate it into a required format. The growth of technology coupled with almost unlimited storage capability has enabled us to consolidate related or relevant data from various sources—right from flat files, to database data, to data in various formats. This ability to consolidate data from various sources has provided a great deal of momentum to effective business analysis.

1.3.3 Growth of Infinite Storage and Computing Capability

The memory and storage capacity of individual computers has increased drastically, whereas external storage devices have provided a significant increase in storage capacity. This has been augmented by cloud-based storage services that can provide a virtually unlimited amount of storage. The growth of cloud platforms has also contributed to virtually unlimited computing capability. Now you can hire the processing power of multiple CPUs, coupled with huge memory and huge storage, to carry out any analysis—however big the data is. This has reduced the need to rely on a sampling of data for analysis. Instead, you can take the entire population of data available with you and analyze it by using the power of cloud storage and computing capabilities.

1.3.4 Easy-to-Use Programming Tools and Platforms

In addition to commercially available data analytics tools, many open source tools or platforms such as R and Hadoop are available. These powerful tools are easy to use and well documented. They do not require high-end programming experience but usually require an understanding of basic programming concepts. Hadoop is especially helpful in effective and efficient analysis of big data.

1.3.5 Survival and Growth in the Highly Competitive World

Businesses have become highly competitive. With the Internet easily available to every business, every consumer has become a target for every business. Each business is targeting the same customer and that customer's spending capability. Each business also can easily reach other dependent businesses or consumers equally well. Using the Internet and the Web, businesses are fiercely competing with each other; often they offer heavy discounts and cut prices drastically. To survive, businesses have to find the best ways to target other businesses that require their products and services as well as the end consumers who require their products and services. Data or business analytics has enabled this effectively.

1.3.6   Business Complexity Growing out of Globalization

Economic globalization that cuts across the boundaries of the countries where businesses produce goods or provide services has drastically increased the complexities of business. Businesses now have the challenge of catering to cultures that may have been previously unknown to them. With the large amount of data now possible to acquire (or already at their disposal), businesses can easily gauge differences between local and regional cultures, demands, and practices including spending trends and preferences.

1.4   Applications of Business Analytics

Business analytics has been applied effectively to many fields, including retail, e-commerce, travel (including the airline business), hospitality, logistics, and manufacturing. Furthermore, business analytics has been applied to a whole range of other businesses, including predictive failure analysis of machines and equipment.

Business analytics has been successfully applied to the fields of marketing and sales, human resources, finance, manufacturing, product design, service design, and customer service and support. In this section, we discuss some of the areas in which data/business analytics is used effectively to the benefit of the organizations. These examples are only illustrative and not exhaustive.

1.4.1   Marketing and Sales

Marketing and sales teams are the ones that have heavily used business analytics to identify appropriate approaches to marketing in order to reach a maximum number of potential customers at an optimized or reduced effort. These teams use business analytics to identify which marketing channel would be most effective (for example, e-mails, web sites, or direct telephone contacts). They also use business analytics to determine which offers make sense to which types of customers (in terms of geographical regions, for instance) and to specifically tune their offers.

A marketing and sales team might, for example, determine whether people like adventurous vacations, spiritual vacations, or historical vacations. That data, in turn, can provide the inputs needed to focus marketing and sales efforts according to those specific interests of the people— thus optimizing the time spent by the marketing and sales team. In the retail business, this can enable retail outlets (physical or online) to market products along with other products, as a bundled offer, based on the purchasing pattern of consumers. In logistics, which logistics company provides the services at what mode sticking to delivery commitments is always an important factor for the businesses to tie up for their services. An airline could present exciting offers based on a customer's travel history, thus encouraging that customer to travel again and again via this airline only, and thereby creating a loyal customer over a period of time.

1.4.2   Human Resources

Retention is the biggest problem faced by an HR department in any industry, especially in the support industry. An HR department can identify which employees have high potential for retention by processing employee data. Similarly, an HR department can also analyze which competence (qualification, knowledge, skill, or training) has the most influence on the organization's or team's capability to deliver quality within committed timelines.

1.4.3   Product Design

Product design is not easy and often involves complicated processes. Risks factored in during product design, subsequent issues faced during manufacturing, and any resultant issues faced by customers or field staff can be a rich source of data that can help you understand potential issues with a future design. This analysis may reveal issues with materials, issues with the processes employed, issues with the design process itself, issues with the manufacturing, or issues with the handling of the equipment installation or later servicing. The results of such an analysis can substantially improve the quality of future designs by any company. Another interesting aspect is that data can help indicate which design aspects (color, sleekness, finish, weight, size, or material) customers like and which ones customers do not like.

1.4.4   Service Design

Like products, services are also carefully designed and priced by organizations. Identifying components of the service (and what are not) also depends on product design and cost factors compared to pricing. The length of warranty, coverage during warranty, and pricing for various services can also be determined based on data from earlier experiences and from target market characteristics. Some customer regions may more easily accept "use and throw" products, whereas other regions may prefer "repair and use" kinds of products. Hence, the types of services need to be designed according to the preferences of regions. Again, different service levels (responsiveness) may have different price tags and may be targeted toward a specific segment of customers (for example, big corporations, small businesses, or individuals).

1.4.5   Customer Service and Support Areas

After-sales service and customer service is an important aspect that no business can ignore. A lack of effective customer service can lead to negative publicity, impacting future sales of new versions of the product or of new products from the same company. Hence, customer service is an important area in which data analysis is applied significantly. Customer comments on the Web or on social media (for example, Twitter) provide a significant source of understanding about the customer pulse as well as the reasons behind the issues faced by customers. A service strategy can be accordingly drawn up, or necessary changes to the support structure may be carried out, based on the analysis of the data available to the industry.

1.5 Skills Required for a Business Analyst

Having discussed drivers and applications of business analytics, let's now discuss the skills required by a business analyst. Typically, a business analyst requires substantial knowledge about the following:

- The business and problems of the business

- Data analysis techniques and algorithms that can be applied to the business data

- Computer programming

- Data structures and data-storage or data-warehousing techniques, including how to query the data effectively

- Statistical and mathematical concepts used in data analytics (for example, regression, naïve Bayes analysis, matrix algebra, and cost-optimization algorithms such as gradient descent or ascent algorithms)

Now let's discuss these knowledge areas in more detail.

1.5.1 Understanding the Business and Business Problems

Having a clear understanding of the business and business problems is one of the most important requirements for a business analyst. If the person analyzing the data does not understand the underlying business, the specific characteristics of that business, and the specific problems faced by that business, that person can be led to the wrong conclusions or led in the wrong direction. Having only programming skills along with statistical or mathematical knowledge can sometimes lead to proposing impractical (or even dangerous) suggestions for the business. These suggestions also waste the time of core business personnel.

1.5.2 Understanding Data Analysis Techniques and Algorithms

Data analysis techniques and algorithms must be applied to suitable situations or analyses. For example, linear regression or multiple linear regression (supervised method) may be suitable if you know (based on business characteristics) that there exists a strong relationship between a response variable and various predictors. You know, for example, that geographical location, proximity to the city center, or the size of a plot (among others) has a bearing on the price of the land to be purchased. Clustering (unsupervised method) can allow you to cluster data into various segments. Using and applying business analytics effectively can be difficult without understanding these techniques and algorithms.

1.5.3   Having Good Computer Programming Knowledge

Good computer knowledge is required for a capable business analyst, so that the analyst doesn't have to depend on other programmers who don't understand the business and may not understand the statistics or mathematics behind the techniques or algorithms. Having good computer programming knowledge is always a bonus capability for business analysts, even though it is not mandatory because analysts can always employ a computer programmer. Computer programming may be necessary to consolidate data from different sources as well as to program and use the algorithms. Platforms such as R and Hadoop have reduced the pain of learning programming, even though at times we may have to use other complementary programming languages (for example, Python) for effectiveness and efficiency.

1.5.4   Understanding Data Structures and Data Storage/ Warehousing Techniques

Knowledge of data structures and of data storage/warehousing techniques eases the life of a business analyst by eliminating dependence on database administrators and database programmers. This enables business analysts to consolidate data from varied sources (including databases and flat files), put them into a proper structure, and store them appropriately in a data repository. The capability to query such a data repository is another additional competence of value to any business analyst. This know-how is not a must, however, because a business analyst can always hire someone else to provide this skill.

1.5.5   Knowing Relevant Statistical and Mathematical Concepts

Data analytics uses many statistical and mathematical concepts on which various algorithms, measures, and computations are based. A business analyst should have good knowledge of statistical and mathematical concepts in order to properly use these concepts to depict, analyze, and present the data and the results of analysis. Otherwise, the business analyst can lead others in the wrong direction by misinterpreting the results because the application of the technique or interpretation of the result itself was wrong.

1.6   Life Cycle of a Business Analytics Project

Figure 1-1 illustrates the typical steps of a business analytics project. These steps are as follows:

1.   Start with a business problem and all the data considered as relevant to the problem.

      or

      Start with the data to understand what patterns you see in the data and what knowledge you can decipher from the data.

11

2. Study the data and then clean up the data for missed data elements or errors.

3. Check for the outliers in the data and remove them from the data set to reduce their adverse impact on the analysis.

4. Identify the data analysis technique(s) to be used (for example, supervised or unsupervised).

5. Analyze the results and check whether alternative technique(s) can be used to get better results.

6. Validate the results and then interpret the results.

7. Publish the results (learning/model).

8. Use the learning from the results / model arrived at.

9. Keep calibrating the learning / model as you keep using it.

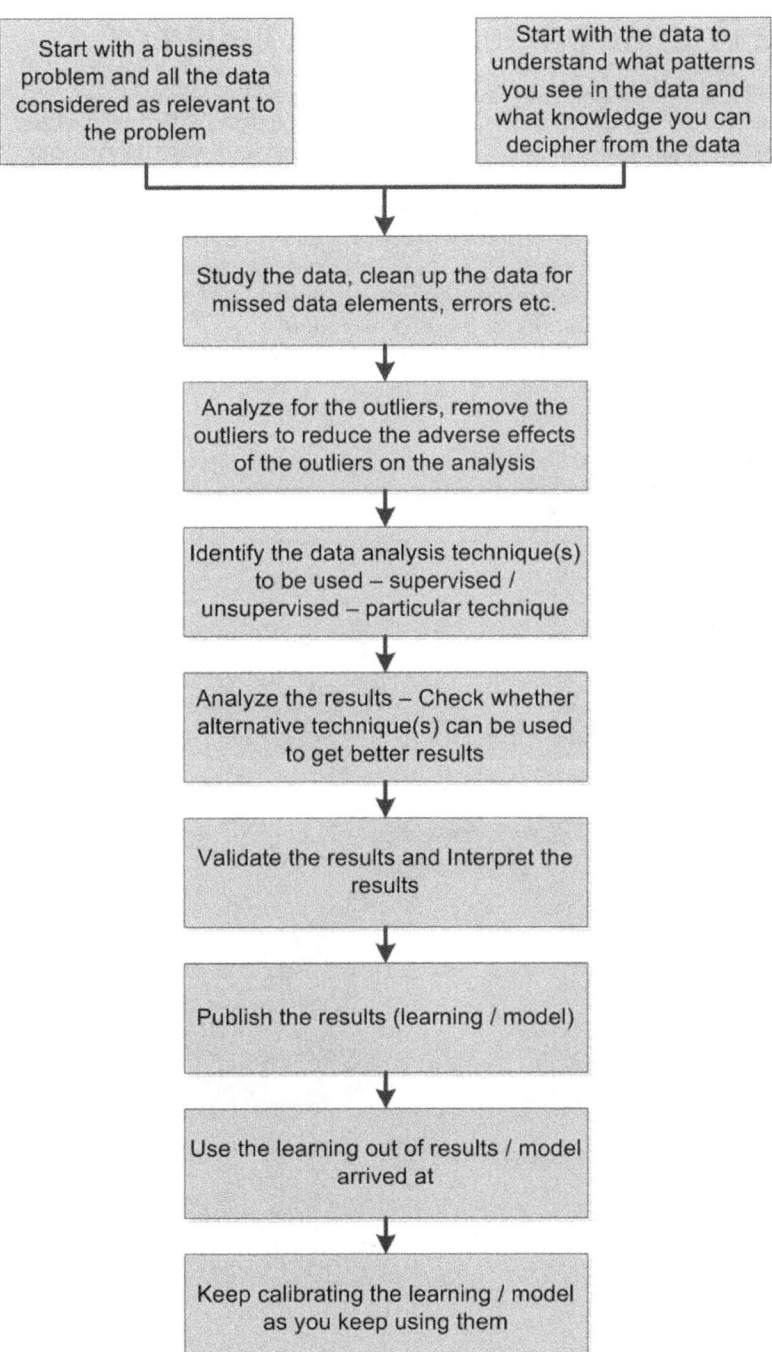

Figure 1-1. *Life cycle of a business analysis project*

1.7   The Framework for Business Analytics

As discussed earlier in this chapter, statistics contributes to a significant aspect of effective business analysis. Similarly, the knowledge discovery enablers such as machine learning have contributed significantly to the application of business analytics. Another area that has given impetus to business analytics is the growth of database systems, from SQL-oriented ones to NoSQL ones. All these combined together, along with easy data visualization and reporting capabilities, have led to a clear understanding of what the data tells us and what we understand from the data. This has led to the vast application of business analytics to solve problems faced by organizations and to drive a competitive edge in business through the application of this understanding.

There are umpteen number of tools available to support each piece of the business analytics framework. Figure 1-2 presents some of these tools, along with details of the framework.

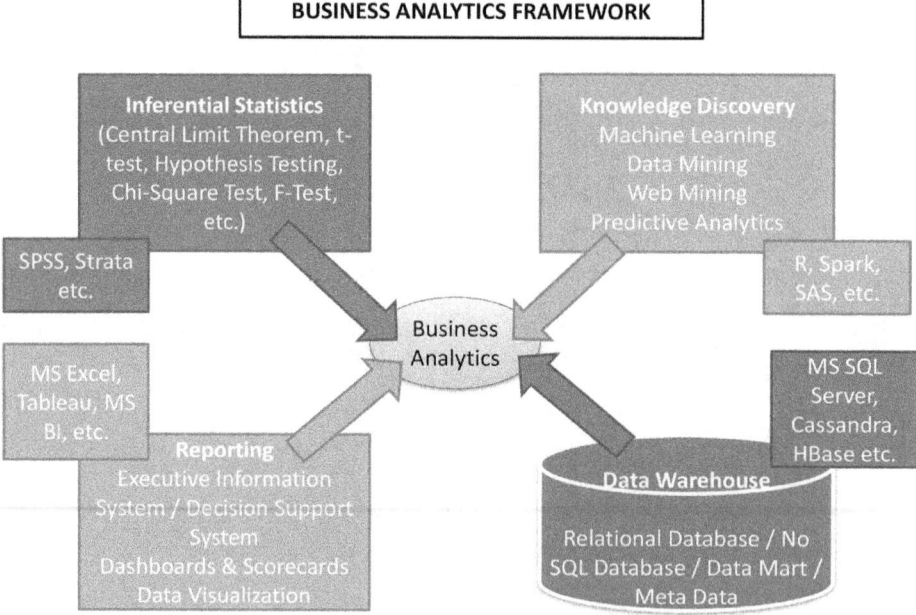

Figure 1-2. Business analytics framework

1.8 Summary

To start with you went through an introduction as to how knowledge has evolved. You also went through many scenarios in which data analytics helps individuals. Many examples of business analytics helping businesses to grow and compete effectively were illustrated to you. You were also provided with examples as to how business analytics results are used by businesses effectively.

Next, you were taken through the objectives of this book. Primarily, this book is intended to be a practical guidebook enabling you to acquire necessary skills. This is an introductory book. You are not going to focus on terminology here but are going to look into the practical aspects. This book will also show how to use R for business analytics.

Next you went through the definitions of data analytics, business analytics, data science, and big data analytics. You were provided with these definitions in layman's terms in order to remove any possible confusion about the terminology.

Then you explored important drivers for business analytics, including the growth of computer packages and applications, the feasibility of consolidating data from various sources, the growth of infinite storage and computing capabilities, the increasing numbers of easy-to-use programming tools and platforms, the need for companies to survive and grow among their competition, and business complexity in this era of globalization. Next you got introduced to the applications of business analytics with examples in certain fields.

You briefly went through the skills required for a business analyst. In particular, you understood the importance of the following: understanding the business and business problems, data analysis techniques and algorithms, computer programming, data structures and data storage/warehousing techniques, and statistical and mathematical concepts required for data analytics.

Finally, you also briefly went through the life cycle of the business analytics project.

CHAPTER 2

Introduction to R

This chapter introduces the R tool, environment, workspace, variables, data types, and fundamental tool-related concepts. This chapter also covers how to install R and RStudio. After reading this chapter, you'll have enough foundational topics to start R programming for data analysis.

2.1 Data Analysis Tools

Many commercial and free tools are available to perform data analysis. In this book, we focus on using R, a software package that is one of the most popular statistical/ analytical tools available. This free tool is widely used by academia and the research community.

Before we begin discussing data analytics, it is important to learn the basic concepts of R. In this chapter, we introduce R as a way to perform data analysis. However, for your benefit, we list some of the *most popular* statistical/data analysis tools available in Table 2-1.

© Dr. Umesh R. Hodeghatta and Umesha Nayak 2017   17
U. R. Hodeghatta and U. Nayak, *Business Analytics Using R - A Practical Approach*,
DOI 10.1007/978-1-4842-2514-1_2

Table 2-1. *Business Analytics and Statistical Tools*

Sl. No	Software Package	Functionality Supported	URL

1	Microsoft Excel	Descriptive statistics.
		
		Hypothesis testing, F-tests, chi-squared tests, t-tests.
		
		Analysis of variance (ANOVA).
		
		Bar graphs, pie charts, linear regression.
			`https://products.`
			`office.com/en-us/`
			`excel`

2	gretl (open source)	Regression and time-series analysis. Least squares, maximum likelihood, GMM; single-equation and system methods. Time-series methods: ARIMA, a wide variety of univariate models.	`http://gretl.` `sourceforge.net/`

3	Octave
	(open source)
		Probability distributions, descriptive statistics, hypothesis testing, t-tests, ANOVA, plots, histograms, clustering analysis.	`http://octave.`
			`sourceforge.net/`
			`statistics/`

4	MathWorks MATLAB	Full set of statistics and machine-learning functionality. Nonlinear optimization, system identification, and financial modeling. MapReduce functionality for Hadoop, and by connecting interfaces to ODBC/JDBC databases.	`http://`
			`uk.mathworks.com/`
			`products/matlab/`
			`http://`
			`uk.mathworks.`
			`com/solutions/`
			`data-analytics/`
			`index-b.html`

5	PSPP (open source alternative for IBM SPSS Statistics)	Comparison of means (t-tests and one-way ANOVA); linear regression, logistic regression, reliability (Cronbach's alpha, not failure or Weibull), and reordering data, nonparametric tests, factor analysis, cluster analysis, principal component analysis, chi-square analysis, and more.	`www.gnu.org/` `software/pspp/`

6	OpenStat
	(open source)
		OpenStat contains a large variety of parametric, nonparametric, multivariate, measurement, statistical process control, financial ,and other procedures.	`http://statpages.`
			`info/miller/`
			`OpenStatMain.htm`

(continued)

Table 2-1. (*continued*)

Sl. No	Software Package	Functionality Supported	URL
7	Salstat (open source)	Descriptive statistics, inferential statistics, parametric and nonparametric analysis, bar charts, box plots, histograms, and more.	www.salstat.com
8	IBM SPSS	Full set of statistical analysis, parametrics, nonparametric analysis, classification, regression, clustering analysis. Bar charts, histograms, box plots. Social media analysis, text analysis, and so forth.	www-01.ibm. com/software/ analytics/spss/
9	Stata by StataCorp	Descriptive statistics, ARIMA, ANOVA, and MANOVA, linear regression, time-series smoothers, generalized linear models (GLMs), cluster analysis. For more details refer to: http://www.stata.com/features/	www.stata.com
10	Statistica	Statistical analysis, graphs, plots, data mining, data visualization, and so forth. For more details refer to: http://www.statsoft.com/ Products/STATISTICA-Featuresdata	www.statsoft.com
11	SciPy (pronounced *Sigh Pie*) (open source)	Python library used by scientists and analysts doing scientific computing and technical computing. SciPy contains modules for optimization, linear algebra, interpolation, digital signal and image processing, machine- learning techniques.	www.scipy.org
12	Weka, or Waikato Environment for Knowledge Analysis (open source)	Contains a collection of visualization tools and algorithms for data analysis and predictive modeling, together with graphical user interfaces for easy access to these functions.	www.cs.waikato. ac.nz/ml/weka/

(*continued*)

Table 2-1. (*continued*)

Sl. No	Software Package	Functionality Supported	URL
13	RapidMiner (open source)	Integrated environment for machine learning, data mining, text mining, predictive analytics, and business analytics.	`https://rapidminer.com/`
14	R (open source)	Full set of functions to support statistical analysis, histograms, box plots, hypothesis testing, inferential statistics, t-tests, ANOVA, machine learning, clustering, and so forth.	`www.r-project.org`
15	Minitab by Minitab Statistical Software	Descriptive statistical analysis, hypothesis testing, data visualization, t-tests, ANOVA, regression analysis, reliability, and survival analysis. `https://www.minitab.com/en-us/products/minitab/`	`www.minitab.com`
16	Tableau Desktop by Tableau Software	Statistical summaries of your data, experiment with trend analyses, regressions, correlations. Connect directly to your data for live, up-to-date data analysis that taps into the power of your data warehouse.	`www.tableau.com/products/desktop`
17	TIBCO Spotfire	Statistical and full predictive analytics. Integration of R, S+, SAS and MATLAB into Spotfire and custom applications. `http://spotfire.tibco.com/discover-spotfire/what-does-spotfire-do/predictive-analytics/tibco-spotfire-statistics-services-tsss`	`http://spotfire.tibco.com/`
18	SAS by SAS	Advance statistical and machine-learning functions and much more.	`www.sas.com`

Data analysis tools help in analyzing data and support handling and manipulating data, statistical analysis, graphical analysis, building various types of models, and reporting. R is an integrated suite of software packages for data handling, data manipulation, statistical analysis, graphical analysis, and developing learning models. This software is an extension of the S software originally developed by Bell Labs. It is open source, free software, licensed under the GNU General Public License (www.gnu.org/licenses/gpl-2.0.html) and supported by large research communities spread all over the world. In the year 2000, R version 1.0.0 was released to the public.

R has following advantages and hence it is the most recommended tool for data scientists today:

- Flexible, easy, and friendly graphical capabilities that can be displayed on the video display of your computer or stored in different file formats.

- Data storage facility to store large amounts of data effectively in the memory for data analysis.

- Large number of free packages available for data analysis.

- Provides all the capabilities of a programming language.

- Supports getting data from a wide variety of sources, including text files, database management systems, web XML files, and other repositories.

- Duns on a wide array of platforms, including Windows, Unix, and macOS.

- Most commercial statistical software platforms cost thousands or even tens of thousands of dollars. R is free! If you're a teacher or a student, the benefits are obvious.

However, most programs in R are written for a single piece of data analysis.

2.2   R Installation

R is available for all the major computing platforms, including macOS, Windows, and Linux. As of 1st of November 2016, the latest R version is 3.3.2.

2.2.1   Installing R

Follow these steps to download the binaries:

1.   Go to the official R site at www.r-project.org.

2.   Click the Download tab.

3.   Select the operating system.

4. Read the instructions to install the software. For example, installing on Linux/Unix requires root/admin permissions, and command-line options are different from those on other platforms. On Windows, you just have to click the installer and follow the instructions provided.

5. Pick your geographic area and mirror site to download.

6. Download the installer and run the installer.

7. Follow the instructions by the installer to successfully install the software.

After the installation, click the 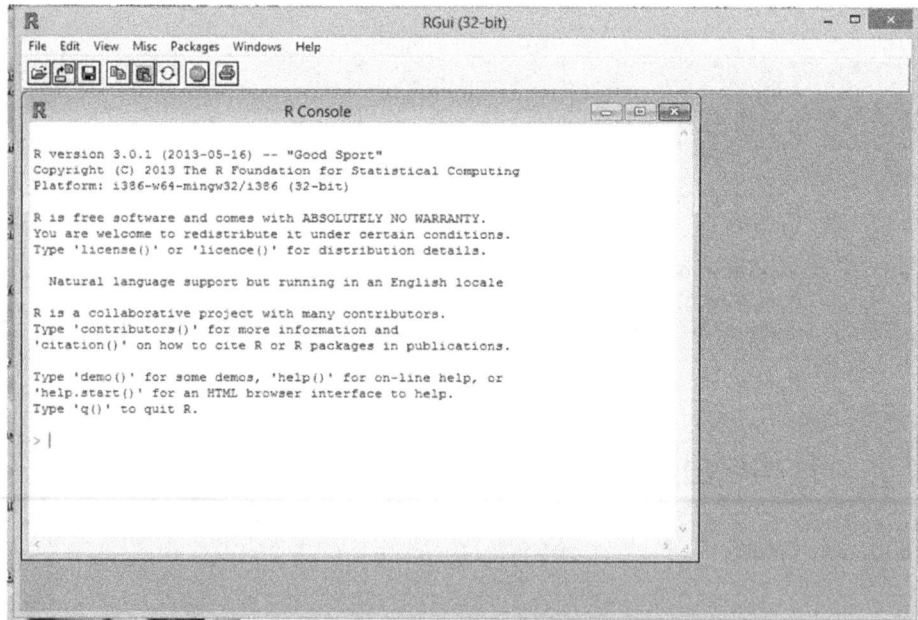 icon to start R. A window appears, showing the R console (as shown in Figure 2-1).

Figure 2-1. R console

2.2.2 Installing RStudio

RStudio provides an integrated development environment (IDE) for R. RStudio is available in two variants: a desktop version and a server version. RStudio Desktop allows RStudio to run locally on the desktop. RStudio Server runs on a web server and can be accessed remotely by using a web browser. RStudio Desktop is available for Microsoft Windows, macOS, and Linux. For more information on RStudio and its support, refer to the RStudio web site at `www.rstudio.com/products/RStudio/#Desktop`.

This section details the installation of RStudio Desktop or RStudio Server for Windows. The installation procedure is similar for other OSs. For more details and procedures for installation, please download RStudio desktop version and follow the instructions given in the web site: `https://www.rstudio.com/products/RStudio/#Desktop` To install RStudio, follow these steps:

1. Go to the official RStudio web site: `www.rstudio.com`.

2. Click the Products option.

3. Select the server version or desktop version, depending on your needs.

4. Click the Downloads option and select the appropriate OS. For Windows, select the installer.

5. After downloading the installer, run the installer and follow its instructions.

Please note that R has to be installed first. If R is not installed, at the end of RStudio installation, an error message will appear and ask you to install R (Figure 2-2).

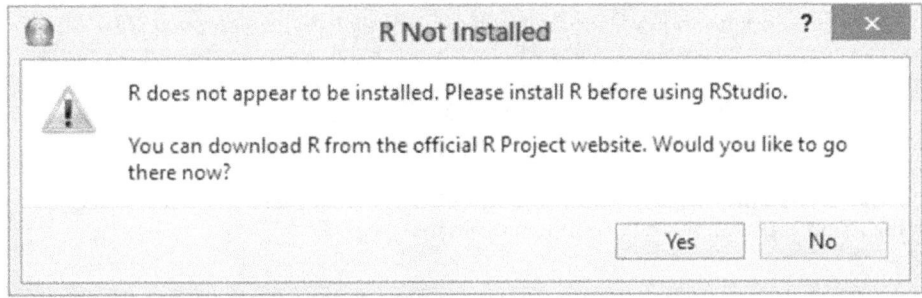

Figure 2-2. *RStudio installation error*

2.2.3 Exploring the RStudio Interface

After the installation is complete, a shortcut ⬛ appears on your desktop. Click this icon to start RStudio. The interface shown in Figure 2-3 appears.

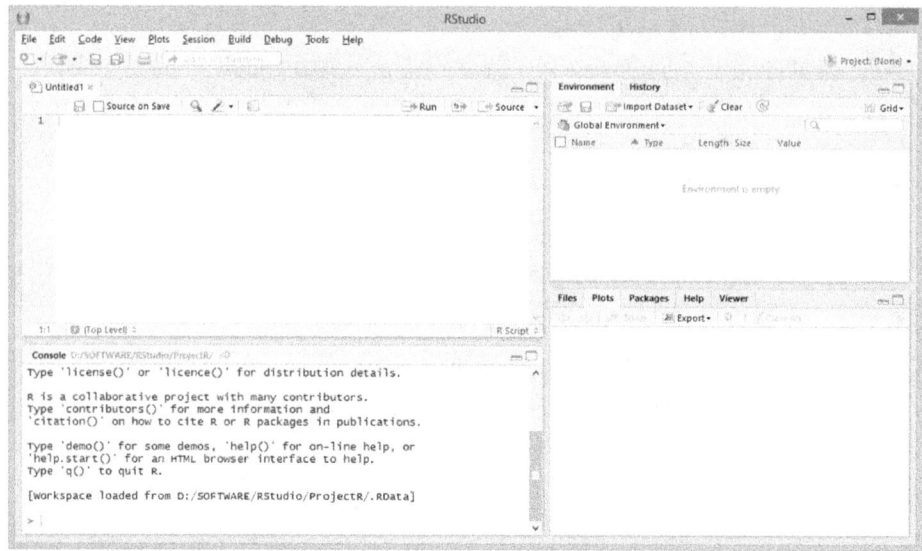

***Figure 2-3.** RStudio window*

RStudio has four windows, which allow you to write scripts, view the output, view the environment and the variables, and view the graphs and plots. The top-left window allows you to enter the R commands or scripts. R scripts provided in the window can be executed one at a time or as a file. The code also can be saved as an R script for future reference. Each R command can be executed by clicking Run at the top-right corner of this window.

The bottom-left window is the R console, which displays the R output results. Also, you can enter any R command in this window to check the results. Because it is a console window, your R commands cannot be stored.

The top-right window lists the environment variable types and global variables. The bottom-right window shows the generated graphs and plots, and provides help information. It also has an option to export or save plots to a file.

Figure 2-4 shows a window with a sample R script, its output in the console, a graph in the graphical window, and environment variable types.

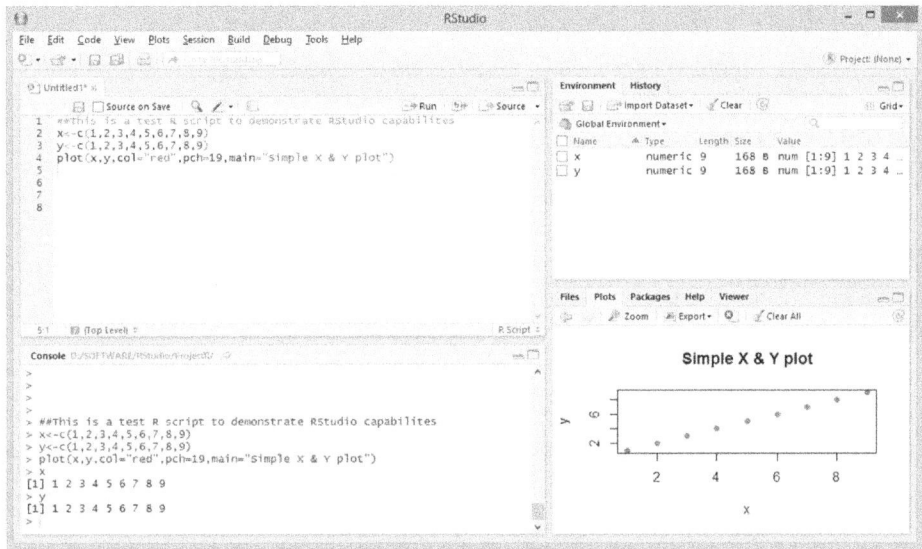

Figure 2-4. *Example of RStudio output*

2.3   Basics of R Programming

R is a programming language specifically for statistical analysis, and there is no need to compile the code. As soon as you hit the Return key after entering the command, the R script executes and the output is displayed in the console. The output also can be redirected to files or printers, which we discuss later in this section.

After you are in the R console window, you are prompted with a greater-than symbol (>), which indicates that R is ready to take your commands. For example, if you type **4 + 3** and hit Return, R displays the results in the console, as shown in Figure 2-5.

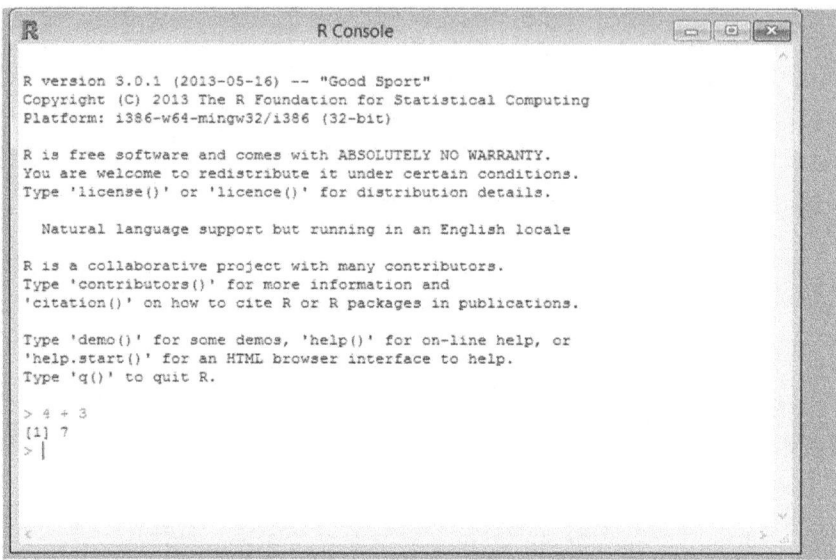

```
R                          R Console                        [□][□][✕]
R version 3.0.1 (2013-05-16) -- "Good Sport"
Copyright (C) 2013 The R Foundation for Statistical Computing
Platform: i386-w64-mingw32/i386 (32-bit)

R is free software and comes with ABSOLUTELY NO WARRANTY.
You are welcome to redistribute it under certain conditions.
Type 'license()' or 'licence()' for distribution details.

  Natural language support but running in an English locale

R is a collaborative project with many contributors.
Type 'contributors()' for more information and
'citation()' on how to cite R or R packages in publications.

Type 'demo()' for some demos, 'help()' for on-line help, or
'help.start()' for an HTML browser interface to help.
Type 'q()' to quit R.

> 4 + 3
[1] 7
> |
```

Figure 2-5. *R console output*

Notice that the results have two parameters: the first part, [1], indicates the index of the first number displayed in row 1 of the vector, and element 7 is the result. In R, any number you enter on the console is interpreted as a vector.

If you type **"Hello World!"**, R prints "Hello World!":

```
> "Hello World!!"
[1] "Hello World!!"
>
```

2.3.1   Assigning Values

The next step is assigning values to variables. In R, you can use the assignment function or just the <- shortcut:

```
> assign("x", 1)
> x
[1] 1
> x<-1
> x
[1] 1

>
```

Direction of the arrow really does not matter. You can use the equals sign (=) as well:

```
>
> 1->y
> y
[1] 1
> z=1
> z
[1] 1
>
```

2.3.2   Creating Vectors

In R, everything is represented as a vector. *Vectors* are one-dimensional arrays that can hold numeric data, character data, or logical data. To create a vector, you use the function c(). Here are examples of creating vectors:

```
a <- c(1, 2, 5, 3, 6, -2, 4)
b <- c(TRUE, FALSE, TRUE, FALSE)
c <- c("one", "two", "three")
```

Here, a is a numeric vector, b is a logical vector, and c is a character vector. Note that the data stored in a vector can be of only one type.

2.4   R Object Types

There are five types of objects in R:

- Numeric
- Character
- Integer
- Complex
- Logical

Numbers are generally treated as numeric objects in R. For example, the digit 1 is represented as 1.00, and the digit 2 is represented as 2.00, and so forth. The class() command gives you information about the class of the object:

```
> x<-c(1,2)
> x
[1] 1 2
> class(x)
[1] "numeric"
>
```

To create a vector in R, you use the c() function. Alternatively, You can also use the vector() function to create a vector of type numeric:

```
> y<-vector ("numeric",length=1)
> y
[1] 0
> class(y)
[1] "numeric"
>
```

Character objects are used in the same way as numeric vectors:

```
> a<-c("one","two","three")
> a
[1] "one"  "two"  "three"
> class(a)
[1] "character"
>
```

To create an integer variable in R, invoke the as.integer() function:

```
> d<-as.integer(3)
> d
[1] 3
> class(d)
[1] "integer"
>
```

Complex and logical vectors are created as follows:

```
> z<-c(1+2i,2+3i)   ##Complex
> z
[1] 1+2i 2+3i
> class(z)
[1] "complex"
>
> w<-c(TRUE,FALSE)   #Logical
> class(w)
[1] "logical"
> w
[1]  TRUE FALSE
>
```

2.5   Data Structures in R

Data structures in R are known as *objects*. Each object can hold vectors, scalars, matrices, arrays, data frames, and lists. A list is a special type of object that can hold any or all object types. Figure 2-6 shows the data structure representation in R. Let's take a look at each of the data structure types now.

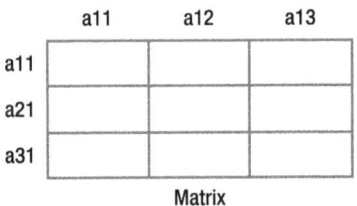

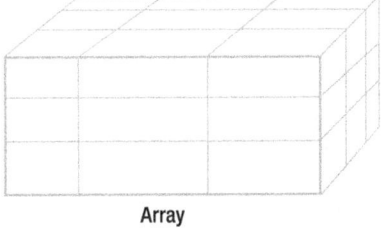

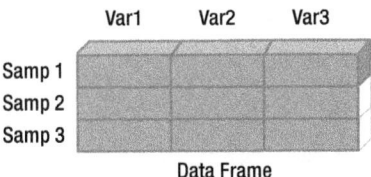

Figure 2-6. *Data structures in R*

2.5.1 Matrices

R uses two terms to refer to two-dimensional data sets: *matrix* and *array*. Software engineers working with application development and images call a two-dimensional data set an array, whereas mathematicians and statisticians refer the same two-dimensional data set as a matrix. The two-dimensional array can function exactly like a matrix. The terms *matrix* and *array* are interchangeable, but the different conventions assumed by different people may sometimes cause confusion.

In R, *matrices* are created using the matrix() function. The general format is as follows:

mymatrix <- matrix(*vector*, nrow=*number_of_rows*, ncol=*number_of_columns*, byrow=*logical_value*, dimnames=list(*char_vector_rownames*, *char_vector_colnames*))

Here, vector contains the elements for the matrix, using nrow and ncol to specify the row and column dimensions of the matrix, respectively; dimnames contains row and column labels stored in character vectors, which is optional. The byrow indicates whether the matrix should be filled in by row (byrow=TRUE) or by column (byrow=FALSE). The default is by column.

The following example in R shows how to create a matrix by using the matrix() function:

```
> x<-matrix(1:9,nrow=3,ncol=3)
> x
     [,1] [,2] [,3]
[1,]   1    4    7
[2,]   2    5    8
[3,]   3    6    9
```

You can access each row, each column, or an element of the matrix as shown by the following example:

```
> x
     [,1] [,2] [,3]
[1,]   1    4    7
[2,]   2    5    8
[3,]   3    6    9
> x[,1]
[1] 1 2 3
> x[1,]
[1] 1 4 7
> x[1,1]
[1] 1
> x[2,3]
[1] 8
> x[3,3]
[1] 9
>
```

To identify rows, columns, or elements of a matrix, use subscripts and brackets—for example, X[i,] refers to the ith row of matrix X, X[, j] refers to the jth column, and X[i, j] refers to the ith row, j^{th} column element, respectively.

2.5.2 Arrays

Arrays can have more than two dimensions. In R, they're created by using the array() function:

```
myarray <- array(vector, dimensions, dimnames)
```

Here, vector contains the data for the array, dimensions is a numeric vector giving the maximal index for each dimension, and dimnames is a list of dimension labels.

The following example shows how to create a three-dimensional (2 × 3 × 2) array:

```
> dim1 <- c("A1","A2")
> dim2 <- c("B1","B2","B3")
> dim3 <- c("C1","C2")
> dim1
[1] "A1" "A2"
> dim2
[1] "B1" "B2" "B3"
> dim3
[1] "C1" "C2"
> z<-array(1:12,c(2,3,2),dimnames=list(dim1,dim2,dim3))
> z
, , C1

   B1 B2 B3
A1  1  3  5
A2  2  4  6

, , C2

   B1 B2 B3
A1  7  9 11
A2  8 10 12
>
```

Arrays are extensions of matrices. They can be useful in programming some of the statistical methods. Identifying elements of an array is similar to what you've seen for matrices. For the previous example, the z[2, 3, 2] element is 12:

```
> z
, , C1

   B1 B2 B3
A1  1  3  5
A2  2  4  6

, , C2

   B1 B2 B3
A1  7  9 11
A2  8 10 12

> z[1,2,1]
[1] 3
> z[2,3,2]
[1] 12
> z[,1,]
   C1 C2
A1  1  7
A2  2  8
> z[1,,]
   C1 C2
B1  1  7
B2  3  9
B3  5 11
>
```

2.5.3   Data Frames

Data frames are important object types and the most common data structure you will use in R. They are similar to data storage in Microsoft Excel, Stata, SAS, or SPSS.

You can have multiple columns of different types; columns can be integer or character or logical types. Though a data frame is similar to a matrix or an array, unlike a matrix or an array you can store multiple data types in data frames. Data frames are a special type of list, and every element of the list has to have the same length. Each column can be named, indicating the names of the variables or predictors. Data frames also have an attribute named row.names(), which indicates the information in each row.

When you read files by using read.csv(), data frames are automatically created.

A data frame is created with the data.frame() function:

```
mydframe <- data.frame(col1, col2, col3,...)
```

Here, col1, col2, and col3, are column vectors of any type (such as character, numeric, or logical). Names for each column can be provided by using the names function. The following example makes this clear:

Creating a data frame

```
> strID <- c(1,2,3,4)
> month<-c("Jan","Feb","March","Apr")
> sales<-c(15000,20000,125000,40000)
> region<-c("east","west","south","north")
> salesData<-data.frame(strID,month,sales,region)
> salesData
  strID month  sales region
1   1   Jan   15000   east
2   2   Feb   20000   west
3   3  March 125000  south
4   4   Apr   40000  north
>
```

You can access the elements of the data set in several ways. You can use the subscript notation you used before in the matrices or you can specify column names. The following example demonstrates these approaches:

Identifying elements of the data frame

```
> salesData[2]
  month
1  Jan
2  Feb
3 March
4  Apr
> salesData[4]
  region
1  east
2  west
3 south
4 north
> salesData[c("month","region")]
  month region
1  Jan   east
2  Feb   west
3 March  south
4  Apr   north
> salesData$sales
[1] 15000  20000 125000  40000
>> salesData[1:2]
  strID month
1   1   Jan
2   2   Feb
3   3  March
4   4   Apr
>
>
```

2.5.4   Lists

Lists are the most complex of the R data types. Lists allow you to specify and store any data type object. A list can contain a combination of vectors, matrices, or even data frames under one single object name. You create a list by using the list() function:

```
mylist <- list(object1, object2, ...)
```

Here, object1 and object2 are any of the structures seen so far. Optionally, you can name the objects in a list:

```
mylist <- list(name1=object1, name2=object2, ...)
```

The following example shows how to create a list. In this example, you use the list() function to create a list with four components: a string, a numeric vector, a character, and a matrix. You can combine any number of objects and save them as a list. To access the list, specify the list type you want to access—for example, accessing the second element, myFirstList[[2]] and myFirstList[["ID"]], both refer to the numeric vector you are trying to access.

Creating a List

```
> a<- "My First List"
> b <- c(10,20,30,40)
> c <- c("one","Two","Three")
> d <- matrix(1:8,nrow=4)
> myFirstList = list(title=a, ID=b, c, d)
> myFirstList
$title
[1] "My First List"

$ID
[1] 10 20 30 40

[[3]]
[1] "one"  "Two"  "Three"

[[4]]
     [,1] [,2]
[1,]   1   5
[2,]   2   6
[3,]   3   7
[4,]   4   8

>
```

Accessing List

```
> myFirstList[["ID"]]
[1] 10 20 30 40
> myFirstList[[3]]
[1] "one"  "Two"  "Three"
>
```

2.5.5   Factors

Factors are special data types used to represent categorical data, which is important in statistical analysis. A *factor* is an integer vector; each integer type has a label. For example, if your data has a variable by name "sex" with values Male or Female, then factor automatically assigns values 1 for Male and 2 for Female. With these assignments, it is easy to identify values and performstatistical analysis. In the previous example, if we have have another variable by name "Performance" and is defined as "Excellent", "Average", "Poor". This is an example of ordinal type. You know that if a specific region is doing excellent sales, then it's performance is "Excellent". In R, categorical (ordinal) variables are called *factors* and they play crucial role in R determining how data will be analyzed and presented visually.

Factor objects can be created using the factor() function that stores the categorical values as a vector of integers in the range [1... j], and automatically assigns an internal vector of character strings (the original values) mapped to these integers.

For example, assume that you have the vector performance <- c("Excellent", "Average", "Poor", "Average"):

The statement performance <- factor(performance) stores this vector as (1, 2, 3, 2) and associates it with 1= Excellent, 2 = Average, 3= Poor internally (the assignment is alphabetical).

Any analysis performed on the vector performance will treat the variable as nominal and select the statistical methods appropriate for this measurement.

```
Factors

> strID <- c(1,2,3,4)
> month<-c("Jan","Feb","March","Apr")
> sales<-c(15000,20000,125000,40000)
> region<-c("east","west","south","north")
> performance = c("Poor","Poor","Excellent","Average")
> salesData<-data.frame(strID,month,sales,region,performance)
> performance<-factor(performance,order=TRUE)
> salesData<-data.frame(strID,month,sales,region,performance)
> salesData
  strID month  sales region performance
1   1  Jan  15000   east       Poor
2   2  Feb  20000   west       Poor
3   3 March 125000  south    Excellent
4   4  Apr  40000  north     Average
> str(salesData)
'data.frame':  4 obs. of  5 variables:
 $ strID   : num  1 2 3 4
 $ month   : Factor w/ 4 levels "Apr","Feb","Jan",..: 3 2 4 1
 $ sales   : num  15000 20000 125000 40000
 $ region  : Factor w/ 4 levels "east","north",..: 1 4 3 2
 $ performance: Ord.factor w/ 3 levels "Average"<"Excellent"<..: 3 3 2 1
 >
```

First, you enter the data as vectors viz. strID, month, sales, region, and performance. Then you specify that performance is an ordered factor. Finally, you combine the data into a data frame. The function str(object) provides information on an object in R (the data frame, in this case). It clearly shows that performance is an ordered factor and also region as a factor, along with how it's coded internally.

2.6 Summary

In this chapter, you looked at various statistical and data analysis tools available in the market as well as the strengths of R that make it an attractive option for students, researchers, statisticians, and data scientists. You walked through the steps of installing R and RStudio. You also learned about the basics of R, including various data types like vectors, arrays, matrices, and lists—including one of the most important data structures, the data frame.

Now that you have R up and running, it's time to get your data for the analysis. In the next chapter, you'll look at performing file manipulations, reading various types of files, and using functions, loops, plots, and graphs; you'll also see other aspects of R that are required to perform effective data analysis. We don't want to make you wait any longer. In the next chapter, you'll jump directly into the basics of analysis using R.

CHAPTER 3

▮ ▮ ▮

R for Data Analysis

In the previous chapter, we introduced R and how to start using R programming to analyze data. In this chapter, we further explain some of the important concepts required for data analysis, including reading various types of data files, storing data, and manipulating data. We also discuss how to create your own functions and R packages. After reading this chapter, you will have a good introduction to R and can get started with data analysis.

3.1   Reading and Writing Data

Data is available from a variety of sources and in a variety of formats. As a data scientist, your task is to read data from different sources and different formats, analyze it, and report the findings. A data source can be an Oracle database, a SAP management system, the Web, or a combination of these. The data format can be a simple flat file in a comma-delimited format, Excel format, or Extensible Markup Language (XML) format. R provides a wide range of tools for importing data. Figure 3-1 shows the various interfaces of R. More information about importing and exporting R data is available in the R manual online at `https://cran.r-project.org/doc/manuals/R-data.pdf`.

© Dr. Umesh R. Hodeghatta and Umesha Nayak 2017
U. R. Hodeghatta and U. Nayak, *Business Analytics Using R - A Practical Approach*,
DOI 10.1007/978-1-4842-2514-1_3

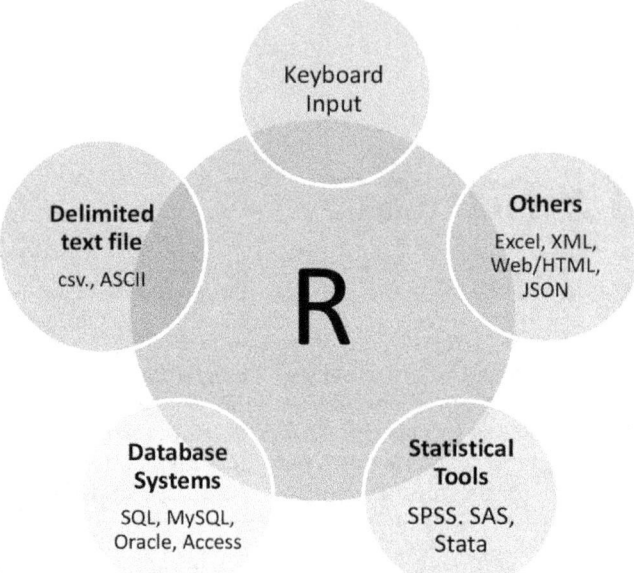

Figure 3-1. *Various interfaces to R*

As you can see, R supports data from the following sources:

- Various databases, including MS SQL Server, MySQL, Oracle, and Access

- Simple flat files such as TXT files

- Microsoft Excel

- Other statistical packages such as SPSS and SAS

- XML and HTML files

- Other files such as JavaScript Object Notation (JSON) files

We cover some of these important data formats in later sections of this chapter and in later chapters.

3.1.1   Reading Data from a Text File

The read.table() and read.csv() functions are the two functions supported by R to import data from a text file. The read.csv() function is specifically used to read comma-delimited files, whereas read.table() can be used to read any delimited file, but the delimiter must be mentioned as the parameter.

One of the most popular input formats to R is Comma-Separated Values (CSV). To read CSV files in R, you can use read.csv(),which imports data from a CSV file and creates a data frame. The syntax for read.csv() is as follows (from the R help file):

```
myCSV <- read.csv(file, header = TRUE, sep = ",", quote = "\"",
         dec = ".", fill = TRUE, comment.char = "", ...)
```

file: The name of the file. The full path of the file should be specified (use getwd() to check the path). Each line in a file is translated as each row of a data frame. file can also be a complete URL.

header: A logical variable (TRUE or FALSE) indicating whether the first row of the file contains the names of variables. This flag is set to TRUE if the first line contains the names of the variables. By default, it is set to FALSE.

sep: The separator is by default a comma. There's no need to set this flag.

fill: If the file has an unequal length of rows, you can set this parameter to TRUE so that blank fields are implicitly added.

dec: The character used in the file for decimal points.

The only parameter you have to worry about is file with a proper PATH. The file separator is set as a comma by default. Set the header parameter appropriately, depending on whether the first row of a file contains the names of variables.

Figure 3-2 shows a sample text file with each element of a row separated by a comma.

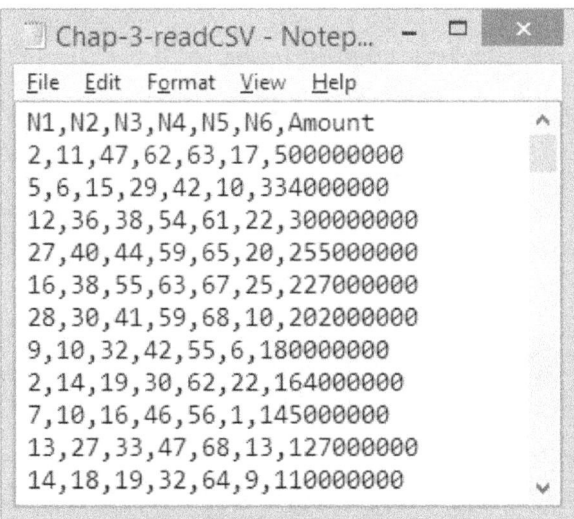

Figure 3-2. *Sample CSV file*

You can read this CSV file into R, as shown in the following example:

```
> myCSV<-read.csv("c31.csv",header=TRUE)
> str(myCSV)
'data.frame':  104 obs. of  7 variables:
 $ N1    : int  2 5 12 27 16 28 9 2 7 13 ...
 $ N2    : int  11 6 36 40 38 30 10 14 10 27 ...
 $ N3    : int  47 15 38 44 55 41 32 19 16 33 ...
 $ N4    : int  62 29 54 59 63 59 42 30 46 47 ...
 $ N5    : int  63 42 61 65 67 68 55 62 56 68 ...
 $ N6    : int  17 10 22 20 25 10 6 22 1 13 ...
 $ Amount: int  500000000 334000000 300000000 255000000 227000000
202000000 180000000 164000000 145000000 127000000 ...
>
```

In this CSV file, the first line contains headers, and the actual values start from the second line. When you read the file by using read.csv(), you must set the header option to TRUE so R can understand that the first row contains the names of the variables and can read the file in a proper data-frame format.

This example demonstrates how read.csv() automatically reads the CSV-formatted file into a data frame. R also decides the type of the variable based on the records present in each column. Seven variables are present in this file, and each parameter is an integer type. To view the data-set table, you can simply use the View() command in R:

```
>
> View(myCSV)
>
```

Using View() opens the data table in another window, as shown in Figure 3-3.

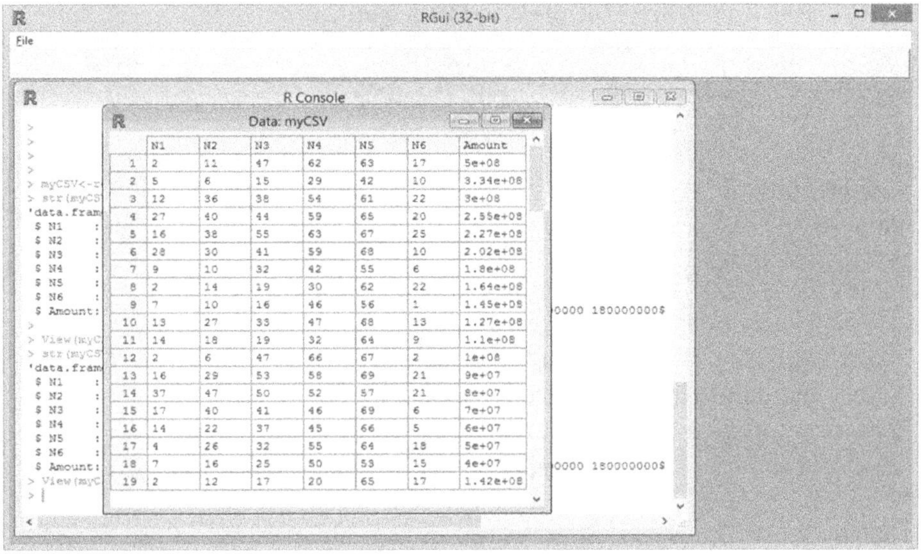

Figure 3-3. *Viewing a CSV file*

The read.table() command is similar to read.csv() but is used to read any text file. The contents of the text file can be separated by a space, comma, semicolon, or colon, and you do have to specify a separator. The command has other optional parameters. For more details, type help(read.table). Figure 3-4 shows an example file containing values separated by a tab.

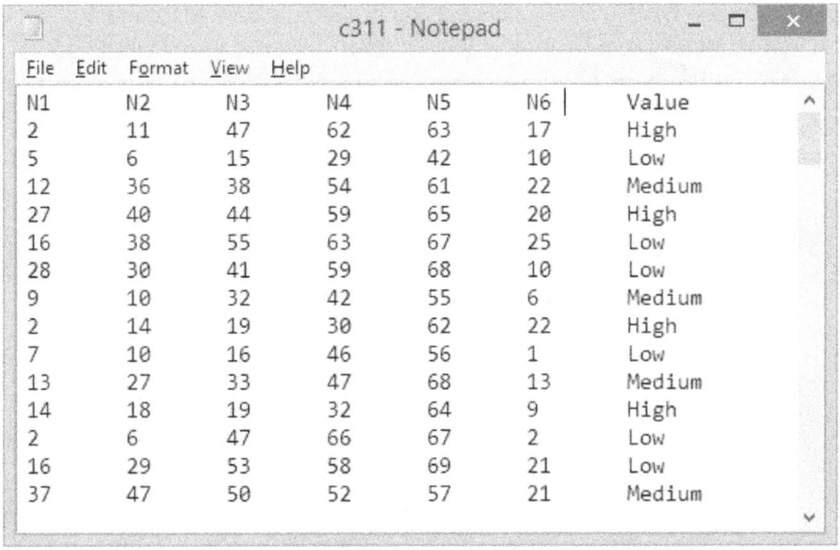

N1	N2	N3	N4	N5	N6	Value
2	11	47	62	63	17	High
5	6	15	29	42	10	Low
12	36	38	54	61	22	Medium
27	40	44	59	65	20	High
16	38	55	63	67	25	Low
28	30	41	59	68	10	Low
9	10	32	42	55	6	Medium
2	14	19	30	62	22	High
7	10	16	46	56	1	Low
13	27	33	47	68	13	Medium
14	18	19	32	64	9	High
2	6	47	66	67	2	Low
16	29	53	58	69	21	Low
37	47	50	52	57	21	Medium

Figure 3-4. *Example file*

Here is the read.table() command and its output:

```
> myTabl <- read.table("c311.txt", sep="\t", header = TRUE)


> str(myTabl)
'data.frame':  108 obs. of  7 variables:
 $ N1   : Factor w/ 35 levels "","1","10","11",..: 12 29 5 17 9 18 33 12 31 6 ...
 $ N2   : int  11 6 36 40 38 30 10 14 10 27 ...
 $ N3   : int  47 15 38 44 55 41 32 19 16 33 ...
 $ N4   : int  62 29 54 59 63 59 42 30 46 47 ...
 $ N5   : int  63 42 61 65 67 68 55 62 56 68 ...
 $ N6   : int  17 10 22 20 25 10 6 22 1 13 ...
 $ Value: Factor w/ 3 levels , "High","Low",..: 2 3 4 2 3 3 4 2 3 4 ...
>
```

In this example, the text file is in a tab-separated format. The first line contains the names of the variables. Also, note that read.table() reads the text file as a data frame, and the Value is automatically recognized as a factor.

3.1.2   Reading Data from a Microsoft Excel File

Several packages are available for reading an Excel file. For Windows, use an Open Database Connectivity (ODBC) connection with the RODBC package. XLConnect is another package that is a Java-based solution. The gdata package is available for Windows, macOS, and Linux platforms. Often, the xlsx package is also used.

The following example shows how to install the RODBC package (for Windows). The first row of the Excel file should contain the variable names. The first step is to download the package by using install.packages ("RODBC"). The procedure is shown in detail here:

```
> install.packages("RODBC")
Installing package into 'C:/Users/user/Documents/R/win-library/3.0'
(as 'lib' is unspecified)
--- Please select a CRAN mirror for use in this session ---

There is a binary version available (and will be installed) but the source
version is later:
     binary source
RODBC 1.3-11 1.3-12

trying URL 'http://cran.utstat.utoronto.ca/bin/windows/contrib/3.0/RODBC_1.3-11.zip'
Content type 'application/zip' length 828930 bytes (809 Kb)
opened URL
downloaded 809 Kb

package 'RODBC' successfully unpacked and MD5 sums checked

The downloaded binary packages are in
     C:\Users\user\AppData\Local\Temp\Rtmp8SzMCi\downloaded_packages
>
```

Once the package is installed successfully, import an Excel file into R by executing the following set of commands:

```
> library(RODBC)
> myodbc<-odbcConnectExcel("c311Lot1.xls")
> mydataframe<-sqlFetch(myodbc,"LOT")
```

First, you establish an ODBC connection to the XLS database by specifying the file name. Then you call the table. Here, c311Lot1.xls is an Excel file in XLS format, LOT is the name of the worksheet inside the Excel file. myodbc is the ODBC object that opens the ODBC connection, and mydataframe is the data frame. The entire process is shown in Figure 3-5. A similar procedure can be used to import data from a Microsoft Access database.

```
> myodbc<-odbcConnectExcel("c311Lot1.xls")
mydataframe<-sqlFetch(myodbc,"LOT")
> str(mydataframe)
'data.frame':   108 obs. of  7 variables:
 $ N1    : num  2 5 12 27 16 28 9 2 7 13 ...
 $ N2    : num  11 6 36 40 38 30 10 14 10 27 ...
 $ N3    : num  47 15 38 44 55 41 32 19 16 33 ...
 $ N4    : num  62 29 54 59 63 59 42 30 46 47 ...
 $ N5    : num  63 42 61 65 67 68 55 62 56 68 ...
 $ N6    : num  17 10 22 20 25 10 6 22 1 13 ...
 $ Value: Factor w/ 3 levels "High","Low","Medium": 1 2 3 1 2 2 3 1
2 3 ...
> View(mydataframe)
```

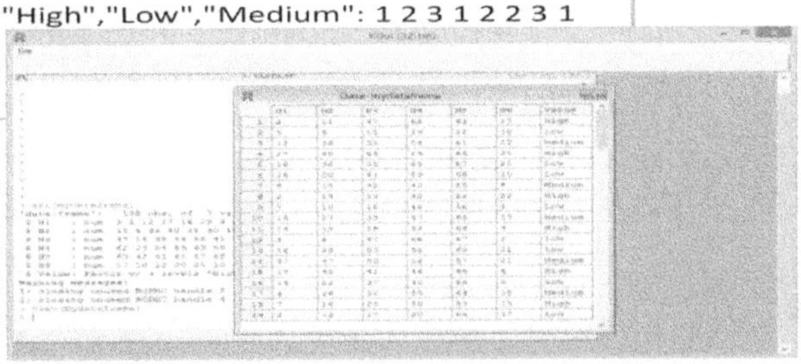

Figure 3-5. *Working with imported data*

43

To read the Excel 2007 XLSX format, you can install the xlsx package using install. packages ("xlsx") and use the read.xlsx() command as follows:

```
> library(xlsx)
> myxlsx<- "c311Lot.xlsx"
> myxlsxdata<-read.xlsx(myxlsx,1)
```

The first argument of read.xlsx() is the Excel file; 1 refers to the first worksheet in Excel, which is saved as a data frame. Numerous packages are available to read the Excel file, including gdata, xlsReadWrite, and XLConnect, but the xlsx package is the most popular. However, it is recommended to convert the Excel file into a CSV file and use read.table() or read.csv() rather than the others. The following code provides examples of using other packages and the reading of the file:

```
> install.packages("XLConnect")
> library(XLConnect)
> myEl <- loadWorkbook("c311Lot1.xls")
> mydata < - readWorksheet(myEl, sheet = "Lot", header = TRUE


> install.packages("gdata")
> Data <- read.xls("c311Lot1.xls", sheet = 1, header = TRUE)
```

3.1.3   Reading Data from the Web

These days, we often want to read data from the Web. You can download a web page by using the readLines() command and save it as an R structure for further analysis. Remember that web data can be unstructured data, and it needs further preprocessing before the analysis. You can use grep() and other regular expressions to manipulate web data. For more information, you can refer to the ProgrammingR web site at www.programmingr.com.

An example of web scraping is shown here:

```
> myCon <- url("http://www.mytechnospeak.com")
> htmlData<- readLines(myCon)
Warning message:
In readLines(myCon) :
  incomplete final line found on 'http://www.mytechnospeak.com'
> close(myCon)
> htmlData[10]
[1] "<link href='http://www.mytechnospeak.com/favicon.ico' rel='icon'
type='image/x-icon'/>"
>
```

3.2   Using Control Structures in R

Similar to other programming languages, R supports control structures that allow you to control the flow of execution. Control structures allow a program to execute with some "logic." However, many times these control structures tend to slow the system. Instead, other built-in functions are used while manipulating the data (which we discuss later in this chapter). Some of the commonly supported control structures are as follows:

> if and else: Test a condition

> while: Executes a loop when a condition is true

> for: Loops a fixed number of times

> repeat: Executes a loop continuously (must break out of loop to exit)

> next: Option to skip an iteration of a loop

> break: Breaks the execution of a loop

3.2.1   if-else

The if-else structure is the most common function used in any programming language, including R. This structure allows you to test a true or false condition. For example, say you are analyzing a data set and have to plot a graph of x vs. y based on a condition—for example, whether the age of a person is greater than 65. In such situations, you can use an if-else statement. The common structure of if-else is as follows:

```
If (< condition >) {
        ## do something
}
else {
        ## do nothing
}
```

You can have multiple if-else statements. For more information, you can look at the R help pages. Here is a demonstration of the if-else function in R:

```
> # Generate uniform random number
> x<-runif(1,0,20)
> x
[1] 17.03558
> if (x>10) {
+ print(x)
+ } else {
+ print("x is less than 10")
+ }
[1] 17.03558
>
```

3.2.2   for loops

for loops are similar to other programing structures. During data analysis, for loops are mostly used to access an array or list. For example, if you are accessing a specific element in an array and performing data manipulation, you can use a for loop. Here is an example of how a for loop is used:

```
> x <- c("John","Banya","George","David")
> x
[1] "John"  "Banya"  "George" "David"
> for (i in 2:3) {
+ ##Print out only 2 elements
+ print(x[i])
+ }
[1] "Banya"
[1] "George"
>
```

Sometimes, the seq_along() function is used in conjunction with the for loop. The seq_along() function generates an integer based on the length of the object. The following example uses seq_along() to print every element of x:

```
> x
[1] "John"  "Banya"  "George" "David"
> for(i in seq_along(x))
+ {
+ print(x[i])
+ }
[1] "John"
[1] "Banya"
[1] "George"
[1] "David"
>
```

3.2.3   while loops

The R while loop has a condition and a body. If the condition is true, the control enters the loop body. The loop continues execution until the condition is true; it exits after the condition fails. Here is an example:

```
> count = 0
> while (count <10) {
+ print(count)
+ count = count + 1
+ }
[1] 0
[1] 1
[1] 2
[1] 3
[1] 4
[1] 5
[1] 6
[1] 7
[1] 8
[1] 9
>
```

repeat() and next() are not commonly used in statistical or data analysis, but they do have their own applications. If you are interested to learn more, you can look at the R help pages.

3.2.4   Looping Functions

Although for and while loops are useful programming tools, using curly brackets and structuring functions can sometimes be cumbersome, especially when dealing with large data sets. Hence, R has some functions that implement loops in a compact form to make data analysis simpler and effective. R supports the following functions, which we'll look at from a data analysis perspective:

> apply(): Evaluates a function to a section of an array and returns the results in an array

> lapply(): Loops over a list and evaluates on each element or applies the function to each element

> sapply(): A user-friendly application of lapply() that returns a vector, matrix, or array

> tapply(): Usually used over a subset of a data set

These functions are used to manipulate and slice data from matrices, arrays, lists, or data frames. These functions traverse an entire data set, either by row or by column, and avoid loop constructs. For example, these functions can be called to do the following:

- Calculate mean, sum, or any other manipulation on a row or a column

- Transform or perform subsetting

The apply() function is simpler in form, and its code can be very few lines (actually, one line) while helping to perform effective operations. The other, more-complex forms are lapply(), sapply(), vapply(), mapply(), rapply(), and tapply(). Using these functions depends on the structure of the data and the format of the output you need to help your analysis.

To understand how the looping function works, you'll look at the *Cars data set*, which is part of the R library. This data set contains the speed of cars and the distances taken to stop. This data was recorded in the 1920s. This data frame has two variables: speed and dist. Both are numeric and contain a total of 50 observations.

3.2.4.1 apply( )

Using the apply() function, you can perform operations on every row or column of a matrix or data frame or list without having to write loops. The following example shows how to use apply() to find the average speed and average distance of the cars:

```
> apply(cars,2,mean)
speed  dist
15.40 42.98
> head(cars)
  speed dist
1   4   2
2   4  10
3   7   4
4   7  22
5   8  16
6   9  10
>
```

The apply() function is used to evaluate a function over an array[] and is often used for operations on rows or columns:

```
> str(apply)
function (X, MARGIN, FUN, ...)
>
```

The apply() function takes the following:

X: An array

MARGIN: An integer vector to indicate a row or column

FUN: The name of the function you are applying

In the preceding example, we calculated the mean of each row and column. But the function could be anything; it can be SUM or average or your own function. The concept is that it loops through the entire array and provides results in the same format. This function eliminates all the cumbersome loops, and results are achieved in one line.

The following example calculates a quantile measure for each row and column:

```
> apply(cars,2,quantile)
     speed dist
0%     4   2
25%   12  26
50%   15  36
75%   19  56
100%  25 120
>
```

3.2.4.2   lapply( )

The lapply() function outputs the results as a list. lapply() can be applied to a list, data frame, or vector. The output is always a list that has the same number of elements as the object that was passed to lapply():

```
> str(lapply)
function (X, FUN, ...)
>
```

It takes following arguments:

X: Data set

FUN: Function

The following example demonstrates the lapply() function for the same Cars data set. The Cars data set is a data frame with two variables dist and speed; both are numeric. To find the mean of speed and dist, you can use lapply(), and the output is a list:

```
>
> str(cars)
'data.frame':    50 obs. of  2 variables:
 $ speed: num  4 4 7 7 8 9 10 10 10 11 ...
 $ dist : num  2 10 4 22 16 10 18 26 34 17 ...
> lap<-lapply(cars,mean)
> lap
$speed
[1] 15.4
```

```
$dist
[1] 42.98

> str(lap)
List of 2
 $ speed: num 15.4
 $ dist : num 43
>
```

3.2.4.3   sapply( )

The main difference between sapply() and lapply() is the output result. The result for sapply() can be a vector or a matrix, whereas the result for lapply() is a list. Depending on the kind of data analysis you are doing and the result format you need, you can use the appropriate functions. As we solve many analytics problems in later chapters, you will see the use of different functions at different times. The following example demonstrates the use of sapply() for the same Car data set example:

```
> sap<-sapply(cars,mean)
> sap
speed  dist
15.40 42.98
> str(sap)
 Named num [1:2] 15.4 43
 - attr(*, "names")= chr [1:2] "speed" "dist"
```

3.2.4.4   tapply( )

tapply() is used over subsets of a vector. The function tapply() is similar to other apply() functions, except it is applied over a subset of a data set:

```
> str(tapply)
function (X, INDEX, FUN = NULL, ..., simplify = TRUE)
```

X: A vector

INDEX: A factor or a list of factors (or they are coerced into factors)

FUN: A function to be applied

- ... contains other arguments to be passed to FUN

- simplify, TRUE or FALSE to simplify result

To demonstrate the function of tapply(), let's consider the Mtcars data set. This data set was extracted from a 1974 *Motor Trend* magazine. The data comprises details of fuel consumption and 10 aspects of automobile design and performance for 32 automobiles (1973–1974 models). Table 3-1 shows the data-set parameters.

51

Table 3-1. *Mtcars Data Set*

[, 1]	mpg	Miles per gallon
[, 2]	cyl	Number of cylinders
[, 3]	disp	Displacement (in cubic inches)
[, 4]	hp	Gross horsepower
[, 5]	drat	Rear-axle ratio
[, 6]	wt	Weight (lb/1000)
[, 7]	qsec	quarter-mile time
[, 8]	vs	V/S
[, 9]	am	Transmission (0 = automatic, 1 = manual)
[,10]	gear	Number of forward gears
[,11]	carb	Number of carburetors

Data source: Henderson and Velleman, "Building Multiple Regression Models Interactively," Biometrics, 37 (1981), pp. 391–411.

Figure 3-6 shows some of the data from the Mtcars data set.

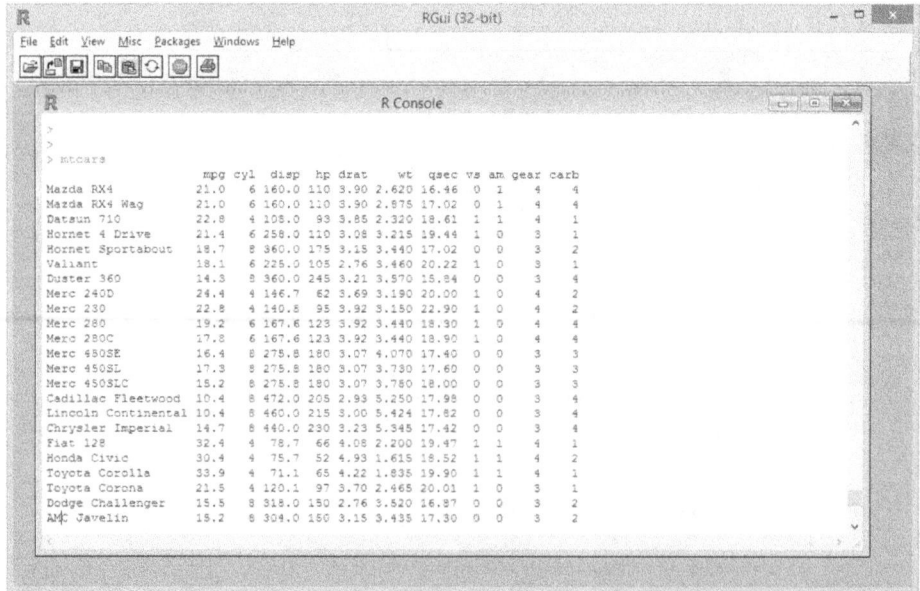

Figure 3-6. *Some sample data from the Mtcars data set*

Let's say that you need to find out the average gasoline consumption (mpg) for each cylinder. Using the tapply() function, the task is executed in one line, as follows:

```
> tapply(mtcars$mpg,mtcars$cyl,mean)
     4       6       8
26.66364 19.74286 15.10000
>
>
```

Similarly, if you want to find out the average horsepower (hp) for automatic and manual transmission, simply use tapply() as shown here:

```
> tapply(mtcars$hp,mtcars$am,mean)
     0       1
160.2632 126.8462
>
```

As you can see from this example, the family of apply() functions is powerful and enables you to avoid traditional for and while loops. Depending on the type of data analysis you want to achieve, you can use the respective functions.

3.2.4.5 cut( )

Sometimes in data analysis, you may have to break up continuous variables to put them into different bins. You can do this easily by using the cut() function in R. Let's take the Orange data set; our task is to group trees based on age. This can be achieved by using cut() as shown here:

```
> Orange
   Tree  age circumference
1    1  118        30
2    1  484        58
3    1  664        87
4    1 1004       115
5    1 1231       120
6    1 1372       142
7    1 1582       145
8    2  118        33
9    2  484        69
10   2  664       111
11   2 1004       156
12   2 1231       172
13   2 1372       203
14   2 1582       203
15   3  118        30
16   3  484        51
```

Next, you create four groups based on the *age* of the trees. The first parameter is the data set and the age, and second parameter is the number of groups you want to create. In this example, the Orange trees are grouped into four categories based on age, and there are five trees between ages 117 and 483:

```
> c1<-cut(Orange$age, breaks=4)
> table(c1)
c1
     (117,483]        (483,850]    (850,1.22e+03] (1.22e+03,1.58e+03]
          5               10             5               15
>
```

The intervals are automatically defined by cut() and may not be the ones you anticipated. However, using the seq() command, you can specify the intervals:

```
> seq(100,2000, by=300)
[1] 100 400 700 1000 1300 1600 1900
> c2<-cut(Orange$age,breaks=seq(100,2000,by=300))
> table(c2)
c2
     (100,400]        (400,700]     (700,1e+03]  (1e+03,1.3e+03] (1.3e+03,1.6e+03]
          5               10            0             10             10
(1.6e+03,1.9e+03]
          0
>
```

3.2.4.6   split( )

Sometimes in data analysis, you may need to split the data set into groups. This can be conveniently accomplished by using split() function. This function divides the data set into groups defined by the argument. The unsplit() function reverses the split() results.

The general syntax of split() is as follows; x is the vector, and f is the split argument:

```
> str(split)
function (x, f, drop = FALSE, ...)
```

In the following example, the Orange data set is split based on the age. The difference is that the data set is grouped based on *age*. There are seven age groups, and the data set is split into seven groups:

```
> c3<-split(Orange,OrangeSage)
> c3
$`118`
  Tree age circumference
1    1 118          30
8    2 118          33
15   3 118          30
22   4 118          32
29   5 118          30

$`484`
   Tree age circumference
2    1 484          58
9    2 484          69
16   3 484          51
23   4 484          62
30   5 484          49

$`664`
   Tree age circumference
3    1 664          87
10   2 664         111
17   3 664          75
24   4 664         112
31   5 664          81

$`1004`
```

3.2.5 Writing Your Own Functions in R

Just as in any other programming language, you can write your own functions in R. Functions are written if a sequence of tasks needs to be repeated multiple times in the program. Functions are also written if code needs to be shared with others or to the general public. Functions are also written if there are no functions already defined as part of the programming language commands. A function reduces programming complexity by creating an abstraction of the code, and only a set of parameters needs to be specified. Functions in R can be treated as an object. In R, functions can be passed as an argument to other functions, such as apply() or sapply().

Functions in R are stored as an object, just like data types, and defined as function(). Function objects are data types with a class object defined as a function. This example shows how to define a simple function:

```
>
> myFunc <- function() {
+ print("My first function")
+ }
> myFunc()
[1] "My first function"
>
```

This function does not take any arguments. To make it more interesting, you can add a function argument. In the body of this function, let's add a for loop, to print as many times as the user wants. The user determines the number of times to loop by specifying the argument in the function. This is illustrated through the following two examples:

```
myFun <- function(num)
{
  for (i in seq_len(num))
  {
    cat("My FUnction: ", i, "\n")
  }
}


myFun(2)
```

```
> myFun(2)
My FUnction: 1
My FUnction: 2
>
```

In this example, myFun() is a function that takes one argument. You can pass the parameter when calling the function. In this case, as you can see from the output, the function prints the number of times it has looped based on the number passed to the function as an argument.

3.3 Working with R Packages and Libraries

R is open source. More than 2,500 users have contributed various functions, known as *packages*, to R. Some functions are part of the installation by default, and others need to be explicitly downloaded and installed from http://cran.r-project.org/web/packages. These packages contain various features or functions developed in R and made available to the public. They are R functions that are already compiled and are available in binary format (or R format). The directory where these codes reside is called a *library*. After installing the packages, you call these functions by loading the library() function so that this is available in your working session.

To see which libraries are installed in your R environment, you can execute library() on the command line. To see the path where these libraries are installed, you can execute the libPaths() command. Here are the executed commands:

```
> .libPaths()
[1] "C:/Users/user/Documents/R/win-library/3.0" "C:/Program Files/R/R-3.0.1/library"
> library()
>
```

Figure 3-7 shows the output, listing the installed libraries.

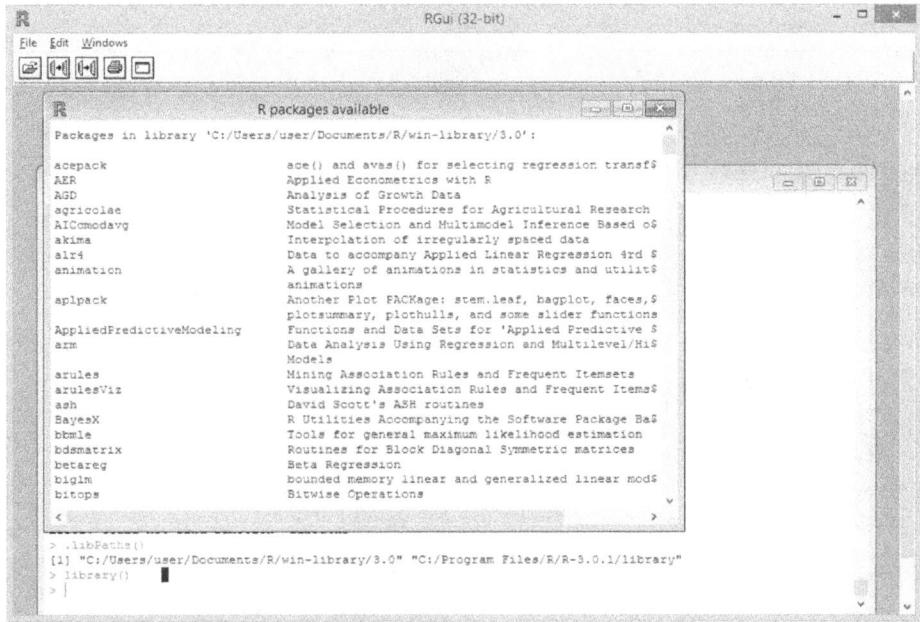

Figure 3-7. *List of libraries installed*

You can install packages by executing the install.packages() command. This example installs the rattle package:

```
> install.packages("rattle")
Installing package into 'C:/Users/user/Documents/R/win-library/3.0'
(as 'lib' is unspecified)

  There is a binary version available (and will be installed) but the source version is later:
    binary source
rattle 3.4.1 4.1.0

trying URL 'http://cran.stat.sfu.ca/bin/windows/contrib/3.0/rattle_3.4.1.zip'
Content type 'application/zip' length 3327234 bytes (3.2 Mb)
opened URL
downloaded 3.2 Mb

package 'rattle' successfully unpacked and MD5 sums checked

The downloaded binary packages are in
    C:\Users\user\AppData\Local\Temp\Rtmpeywag2\downloaded_packages
>
```

■ **Note**   Google's R style guide is available at https://google.github.io/styleguide/ Rguide.xml.

3.4 Summary

Data has to be read effectively into R before any analysis can begin. In this chapter, you started with examples showing that various file formats from diverse sources can be read into R (including database files, text files, XML files, and files from other statistical and analytical tools).

You further explored how various data-file formats can be read into R by using such simple commands as read.csv() and read.table(). You also looked at examples of importing data from MS Excel files and from the Web.

You explored through detailed examples the use of looping structures such as if-else, while, and for. You also learned about simple recursive functions available in R, such as apply(), lapply(), sapply(), and tapply(). These functions can extensively reduce code complexity and potential mistakes that can occur with traditional looping structures such as if-else, while, and for. Additionally, you looked at the use of cut() and split() functions.

User-defined functions are useful when you need to share code or reuse a function again and again. You saw a simple and easy way to build user-defined functions in R.

Finally, you looked at packages. You saw how to use the library() function to determine which packages are already installed in R and how to use the install.packages() function to install additional packages into R.

CHAPTER 4

Introduction to descriptive analytics

Imagine you are traveling and have just reached the bank of a muddy river, but there are no bridges or boats or anybody to help you to cross the river. Unfortunately, you do not know to swim. When you look around in this confused situation where there is no help available to you, you notice a sign board as shown in Figure 4-1:

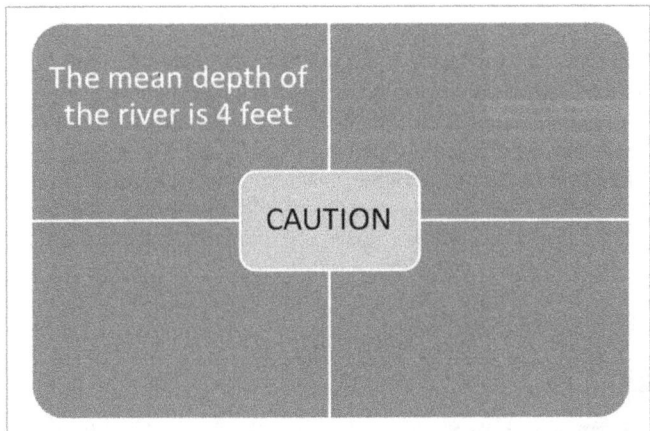

Figure 4-1. *A signson the bank of a river*

The sign says, "The mean depth of the river is 4 feet." Say this value of mean is calculated by averaging the depth of the river at each square-foot area of the river. This leads us to the following question: "What is average or mean?" Average or mean is the quantity arrived at by summing up the depth at each square foot and dividing this sum by the number of measurements (i.e., number of square feet measured).

Your height is 6 feet. Does Figure 4-1 provide enough information for you to attempt to cross the river by walking? If you say, "Yes," definitely I appreciate your guts. I would not dare to cross the river because I do not know whether there is any point where the

© Dr. Umesh R. Hodeghatta and Umesha Nayak 2017   59
U. R. Hodeghatta and U. Nayak, *Business Analytics Using R - A Practical Approach*,
DOI 10.1007/978-1-4842-2514-1_4

depth is more than my height. If there are points with depths like 7 feet, 8 feet, 10 feet, or 12 feet, then I will not dare to cross as I do not know where these points are, and at these points I am likely to drown.

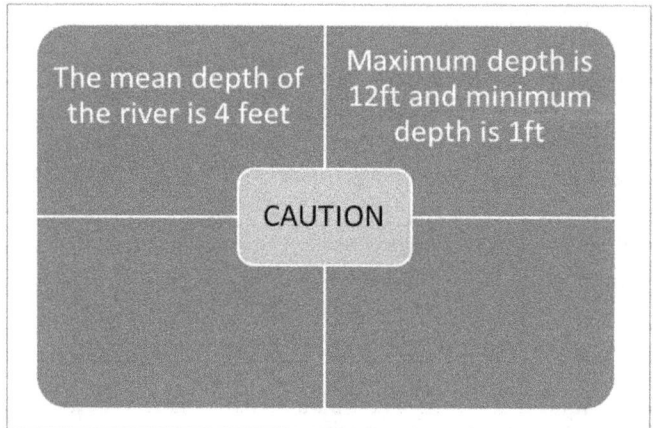

Figure 4-2. *The sign indicating mean, maximum, and minimum depths*

Suppose, the sign board also says, "Maximum depth is 12ft and minimum depth is 1ft" (see Figure 4-2). I am sure this additional information will scare you since you now know that there are points where you can get drowned. Maximum depth is the measure at one or more points that are the largest of all the values measured. Again, with this information you may not be sure that the depth of 12 feet is at one point or at multiple points. Minimum sounds encouraging (this is the lowest of the values observed) for you to cross the river, but again you do not know whether it is at one point or multiple points.

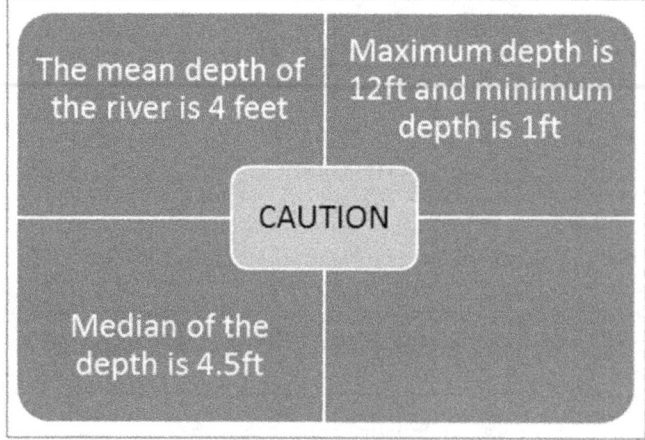

Figure 4-3. *The sign indicating mean, maximum, minimum, and median depths*

Suppose, in addition to the above information the sign board (shown in Figure 4-3) also says, "Median of the depth is 4.5ft." Median is the middle point of all the measured depths if all the measured depths are arranged in ascending order. This means 50% of the depths measured are less than this and also 50% of the depths measured are above this. You may not still dare to cross the river as 50% of the values are above 4.5 feet and maximum depth is 12 feet.

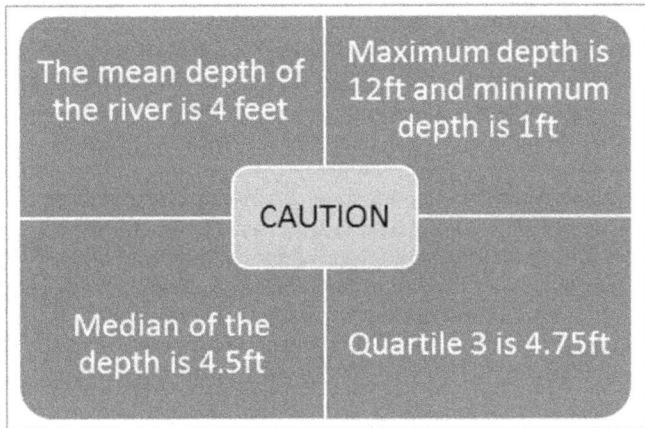

Figure 4-4. *The sign adds a quartile measurement*

Suppose, in addition to the above information the sign board (shown in Figure 4-4) also says, "Quartile 3 is 4.75ft." Quartile 3 is the point below which 75% of the measured values fall when the measured values are arranged in ascending order. This also means there are 25% of the measured values that have greater depth than this. You may not be still comfortable crossing the river as you know the maximum depth is 12 feet and there are 25% of the points above 4.75 feet.

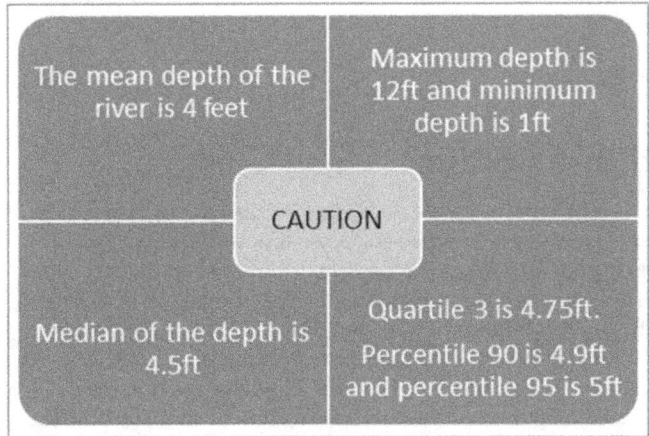

Figure 4-5. *The sign completes its percentile measurements*

Suppose, in addition to the above information, the sign board (shown in Figure 4-5) also says, "Percentile 90 is 4.9ft and percentile 95 is 5ft." Suppose this is the maximum information available. You now know that only 5% of the measured points are of depth more than 5ft. You may now want to take a risk if you do not have any other means other than crossing the river by walking or wading through as now you know that there are only 5% of the points with depth more than 5ft. Your height is 6ft. You may hope that 98 or 99 percentile may be still 5.5ft. You may now believe that the maximum points may be rare and you can by having faith in God can cross the river safely.

In spite of the above cautious calculations you may still drown if you reach rare points of depth of more than 6 feet (like the maximum point of depth). But, with the foregoing information you know that your risk is substantially less compared to your risk at the initial time when you had only limited information (that the mean depth of the river is 4 feet).

This is the point I wanted to drive through the river analogy: with one single parameter of measurement you may not be able to describe the situation clearly and may require more parameters to elaborate the situation. Each additional parameter calculated may increase the clarity required to make decisions or to understand the phenomenon clearly. Again, another note of caution: there are many other parameters than the ones discussed earlier that are of interest in making decisions or understanding any situation or context.

Later in this chapter we will discuss how to calculate all these parameters using R. Before that we need to understand the important aspect—the meaning of "population" and "sample."

4.1   Descriptive analytics

In simple terms, descriptive analysis or descriptive analytics is the analysis of the data to provide the description of the data in various ways to enable users to understand the situation or context or data in a clear way.

Statistical parameters such as mean or average, median, quartile, maximum, minimum, range, variance, and standard deviation describe the data very clearly. As seen in the example discussed earlier, one aspect of the data may not provide all the clarity necessary, but many related parameters provide better clarity with regard to data or situation or context.

4.2   Population and sample

In simple terms, "population" means the complete set of data. In the case of river example, it means that measurements have been taken across the river at each and every square foot without leaving out any area. This also means that the entire possible values are taken into consideration. When we consider the entire possible set of values, we say that we are considering the "population." Following are examples of population: the population of all the employees of entire IT (information technology) industry, population of all the employees of a company, population of all the transaction data of an application, population of all the people in a country, population of all the people in a state, population of all the Internet users, and population of all the users of ecommerce sites. The list of examples is unlimited.

However, when we have to analyze the data, it is difficult to analyze the entire population especially when the data size is huge. This is because

- It takes substantial time to process the data and the time taken to analyze may be prohibitively high in terms of the requirements related to the application of the data. For example, if the entire transaction data related to all the purchases of all the users has to be analyzed before you recommend a particular product to a user, the amount of processing time taken may be so huge that you may miss the opportunity to suggest the product to the user who has to be provided the suggestions quickly when he is in session on the Internet.

- It takes substantial processing power (i.e., memory or CPU power) to hold the data and process it; not everyone has the capability to deploy such a huge processing capability.

In simple terms "sample" means a section or subset of the population selected for analysis. Examples of samples are the following: randomly selected 100, 000 employees from the entire IT industry or randomly selected 1, 000 employees of a company or randomly selected 1, 000, 000 transactions of an application or randomly selected 10, 000, 000 Internet users or randomly selected 5, 000 users each from each ecommerce site, and so on. Sample can also be selected using stratification (i.e., based on some rules of interest). For example, all the employees of the IT industry whose income is above $100,000 or all the employees of a company whose salary is above $50,000 or top 100, 000 transactions by amount per transaction (e.g., minimum $1,000 per transaction or all Internet users who spend more than two hours per day, etc.).

The benefits of sampling are:

- Data is now less and focused on the application. Hence, data can be processed quickly and the information from analysis can be applied quickly.

- The data can be processed easily with lesser requirement for the computing power.

However, of late, we have higher computing power at our hands because of the cloud technologies and the possibility to cluster computers for better computing power. Though such large computing power allows us, in some cases, to use the entire population for analysis, sampling definitely helps carry out the analysis relatively easily and faster in many cases. However, sampling has a weakness: if the samples are not selected properly, then the analysis results may be wrong. For example, for analyzing the data for the entire year only this month's data is taken. This sample selection may not give the required information as to how the changes have happened over the months.

4.3 Statistical parameters of interest

Now, let us dive into the world of statistical parameters and derive a more in-depth understanding. At the same time, we will use R to calculate these statistical parameters.

4.3.1   Mean

"Mean" is also known as "average" in general terms. This is a very useful parameter. If we have to summarize any data set quickly, then the common measure used is "mean." Some examples of the usage of mean are the following:

- For a business, mean profitability over the last five years may be one good way to represent the organization's profitability in order to judge its success.

- For an organization, mean employee retention over last five years may be a good way to represent employee retention in order to judge the success of the HR (human resources) policies.

- For a country, mean GDP (Gross Domestic Product) over the last five years may be a good way to represent the health of the economy.

- For a business mean growth in sales or revenue over a period of the last five years may be a good way to represent growth.

- For a business, mean reduction in cost of operations over a period of the last five years may be a good way to understand operational efficiency improvement.

Normally, a mean or average figure gives a sense of what the figure is likely to be for the next year based on the performance for the last number of years. However, there are limitations of using or relying only on this parameter.

Let us look into few examples to understand more about using mean or average:

- Good Luck Co. Pvt. Ltd earned a profit of $1,000,000; $750,000; $600,000; $500,000; and $500,000 over the last five years. Mean or average profit over the last five years is calculated as sum(all the profits over the last 5 years)/No. of years i.e. ($1,000,000 + $750,000 + $600,000 + $500,000 + $500,000) / 5 = $670,000. This calculation is depicted in Figures 4-6 and 4-7.

```
>
> #GoodLuck Co. Pvt. Ltd - Profit figures for last 5 years
> Year1Prof <- 1000000
> Year2Prof <- 750000
> Year3Prof <- 600000
> Year4Prof <- 500000
> Year5Prof <- 500000
> #To calculate Mean or Average Profit you require the sum of profits of all the years
> Sum5YrsProf <- Year1Prof + Year2Prof + Year3Prof + Year4Prof + Year5Prof
> #To calculate Mean you need to divide Sum of profits of years by number of years
> MeanProf <- Sum5YrsProf / 5
> MeanProf
[1] 670000
>
```

Figure 4-6. *How to calculate mean in R*

```
> #Easier way to calculate the mean of the profit of
> #GoodLuck Co. Pvt. Ltd for the last 5 years
> Prof5Yrs <- c(1000000,750000,600000,500000,500000)
> #The above command will list the profits of 5 years in a single statement
> MeanProf <- mean(Prof5Yrs)
> #Above command "mean" will calculate the mean of the values from the list of profits
> MeanProf
[1] 670000
>
```

Figure 4-7. *Alternative and simple way for calculating mean in R*

The mean for the above example is calculated using R as given in figure 4-6:

Alternative simple way of capturing the data and calculating mean in R is shown in Figure 4-7:

Similarly, for the other examples we can work out the mean or average value if we know the individual figures for the years.

The problem with the mean or average as a single parameter is as follows:

- Any extreme high or low figure in one or more of the years can skew up the mean and thus the mean may not appropriately represent the likely figure next year. For example, consider that there was very high profit in one of the years because of a volatile international economy which led to severe devaluation of the local currency. Profits for five years of a company were, respectively, €6,000,000, €4,000,000, €4,500,000, €4,750,000, and €4,250,000. The first year profit of €5,000,000 was on account of steep devaluation of the Euro in the international market. If the effective value of profit without taking into consideration devaluation during the first year is €4,000,000, then the average or mean profit on account of increased profit would be €400,000 as shown in Figure 4-8.

```
>
> #Duck&Duck LLP
> #Data for 5 years profit - first year profit significantly increased on account
> #of increased foreign exchange rate due to devaluation of local currency
> Prof5Yrs <- c(6000000,4000000,4500000,4750000,4250000)
> MeanProf <- mean(Prof5Yrs)
> MeanProf
[1] 4700000
> #If we remove the extra profit not due to company operations but only due to
> #currency devaluation then the mean profit will be as follows
> Prof5Yrs <- c(4000000,4000000,4500000,4750000,4250000)
> MeanProf <- mean(Prof5Yrs)
> MeanProf
[1] 4300000
>
```

Figure 4-8. *Actual mean profit and effective mean profit example*

- Using mean or average alone will not show the volatility in the figure over the years effectively. Also, mean or average does not depict the trend as to whether it is decreasing or increasing. Let us take an example. Suppose the revenue of a company over the last five years is, respectively, $22,000,000, $15,000,000, $32,000,000, $18,000,000, and $10,000,000. The average revenue of the last five years is $19,400,000. If you notice the figures, the revenue is quite volatile; that is, compared to first year, it decreased significantly in the second year then jumped up by a huge number during the third year, and then decreased significantly during the fourth year, and continued to decrease further significantly during the fifth year. The average or mean figure does not depict either this volatility in revenue or trending downwardness in revenue. Figure 4-9 shows this downside of mean as a measure.

```
>
> #Sam&George LLP
> #Data for 5 years revenue - large variations over the years
> Rev5Yrs <- c(22000000,15000000,32000000,18000000,10000000)
> MeanRev <- mean(Rev5Yrs)
> MeanRev
[1] 19400000
>
```

Figure 4-9. *Downside of mean as a statistical parameter*

4.3.2   Median

Median finds out the middle value by ordering the values in either ascending order or descending order. In many circumstances, median may be more representative than mean. It clearly divides the data set at the middle into two equal partitions; that is, 50% of the values will be below the median and 50% of the values will be above the median. Examples are as follows:

- Age of workers in an organization to know the vitality of the organization.

- Productivity of the employees in an organization.

- Salaries of the employees in an organization pertaining to a particular skill set.

Let us consider the age of 20 workers in an organization as 18, 20, 50, 55, 56, 57, 58, 47, 36, 57, 56, 55, 54, 37, 58, 49, 51, 54, 22, and 57. From a simple examination of these figures, you can make out that the organization has more aged workers than youngsters and there may be an issue of knowledge drain in a few years if the organizational retirement age is 60. Let us also compare mean and median for this data set. The following figure shows that 50% of the workers are above 54 years of age and are likely to retire early (i.e., if we take 60 years as retirement age, they have only 6 years to retirement) which may depict the possibility of significant knowledge drain. However, if we use the average figure of 47.35 it shows a better situation (i.e., about 12.65 years to retirement).

But, it is not so if we look at the raw data: 13 of the 20 employees are already at the age of 50 or older, which is of concern to the organization. Figure 4-10 shows a worked-out example of median using R.

```
>
> #Sam&George LLP
> #Data of employee age of 20 workers
> WorkAge <- c(18, 20, 50, 55, 56, 57, 58, 47, 36, 57, 56, 55, 54, 37, 58, 49, 51, 54, 22, 57)
> #Worker age if arranged in increasing order will be
> #18, 20, 22, 36, 37, 47, 49, 50, 51, 54, 54, 55, 55, 56, 56, 57, 57, 57, 58, 58
> #Mid numbers will be 10th and 11th i.e. 54 each
> #Hence, median age of worker is 54 years
> MedWorkAge <- median(WorkAge)
> MedWorkAge
[1] 54
> MeanWorkAge <- mean(WorkAge)
> MeanWorkAge
[1] 47.35
>
```

Figure 4-10. *How to calculate median using R*

However, if the 10th value had been 54 and 11th value had been 55, respectively, then the median would have been (54+55)/2 i.e., 54.5.

Let us take another example of a productivity of a company. Let the productivity per day in terms of items produced per worker be 20, 50, 55, 60, 21, 22, 65, 55, 23, 21, 20, 35, 56, 59, 22, 23, 25, 30, 35, 41, 22, 24, 25, 24, and 25 respectively. The median productivity is 25 items per day, which means that there are 50% of the workers in the organization who produce less than 25 items per day and 50% of the employees who produce more than 25 items per day. Mean productivity is 34.32 items per day because some of the workers have significantly higher productivity than the median worker, which is evident from the productivity of some of the workers; that is, 65 items per day, 60 items per day, 59 items per day, 56 items per day, 56 items per day, 55 items per day, etc. The analysis from R in Figure 4-11 clearly shows the difference between mean and median.

```
>
> #George&George Inc.
> #Productivity of 25 employees on a particular day
> ProdWorkDay <- c(20, 50, 55, 60, 21, 22, 65, 55, 23, 21, 20, 35, 56, 59, 22, 23, 25, 30, 35, 41, 22, 24, 25, 24, 25)
> MedProd <- median(ProdWorkDay)
> MedProd
[1] 25
> MeanProd <- mean(ProdWorkDay)
> MeanProd
[1] 34.32
> |
```

Figure 4-11. *Difference between mean and median highlighted*

If you have to work out median through hand calculations, you have to arrange the data points in ascending or descending order and then select the value of the middle term if there are an odd number of values. If there are an even number of values, then you have to sum up the middle two terms and then divide the sum by 2 as mentioned in the above discussions.

If you notice from the above discussion, instead of only mean or median alone, looking at both mean and median gives a better idea of the data.

4.3.3   Mode

Mode is the highest times occurring data point in the data set. For example, in our data set related to age of workers, 57 occurs the maximum number of times (i.e., three times). Hence, 57 is the mode of the workers' age data set. This shows the pattern of repetition in the data.

There is no inbuilt function in R to compute mode. Hence, we have written a function and have computed the mode as shown in Figure 4-12. We have used the same data set we used earlier (i.e., WorkAge).

```
> WorkAge
 [1] 18 20 50 55 56 57 58 47 36 57 56 55 54 37 58 49 51 54 22 57
> #We are creating a function by name CalMode to calculate Mode
> #This function is used to compute highest number of occurrences
>  #of the same term
> CalMode <- function(dataset)
+ {
+     UniDataSet <- unique(dataset)
+     UniDataSet[which.max(tabulate(match(dataset,UniDataSet)))]
+ }
> #Using CalMode function on WorkAge data
> CalMode(WorkAge)
[1] 57
>
```

Figure 4-12.   *Calculation of mode using a function created in R*

In the above function **unique()** creates a set of unique numbers from the data set. In the case of WorkAge example unique numbers are: 18, 20, 50, 55, 56, 57, 58, 47, 36, 54, 37, 49, 51, and 22. The **match()** function matches the numbers between the ones in the data set and the unique numbers set we got and provides the position of each unique number in the original data set. The function **tabulate()** returns the number of times each unique number is occurring in the data set. The function **which.max()** returns the position of the maximum times repeating number in the unique numbers set.

4.3.4   Range

Range is a simple but important statistical parameter. It depicts the distance between the end points of the data set arranged in ascending or descending order (i.e., between the maximum value in the data set and the minimum value in the data set). This provides the measure of overall dispersion of the dataset.

The R command **range(dataset)** provides the minimum and maximum values (see Figure 4-13) on the same data set used earlier (i.e., WorkAge).

```
>
> RangeWorkAge <- range(WorkAge)
> RangeWorkAge
[1] 18 58
>
```

Figure 4-13.   *How to calculate range using R*

The difference between maximum and minimum values is the range.

4.3.5 Quantiles

"Quantiles" are also known as "percentiles." Quantiles divide the data set arranged in ascending or descending order into equal partitions. The "median" is nothing but the data point dividing the data arranged in ascending or descending order into two sets of equal number of elements. Hence, it is also known as the 50th percentile. On the other hand, "quartiles" divide the data set arranged in ascending order into four sets of equal number of data elements. First quartile (also known as Q1 or as 25th percentile) will have 25% of the data elements below it and 75% of the data elements above it. Second quartile (also known as Q2 or 50th percentile or median) will have 50% of the data elements below it and 50% of the data elements above it. The third quartile (also known as Q3 or 75th percentile) has 75% of the data elements below it and 25% of the data elements above it. "Quantile" is a generic word whereas "quartile" is specific to a particular percentile. For example, Q1 is 25th percentile. Quartile 4 is nothing but the 100th percentile.

Quantiles, quartiles, or percentiles provide us the information which mean is not able to provide us. In other words, quantiles, quartiles, or percentiles provide us additional information about the data set in addition to mean.

Let us take the same two data sets as given in the section "Median" and work out quartiles. Figures 4-14A and 4-14B show the working of the quartiles.

```
>
> #Sam&George LLP
> #Data of Employee Age of 20 Workers
> WorkAge <- c(18, 20, 50, 55, 56, 57, 58, 47, 36, 57, 56, 55, 54, 37, 58, 49, 51, 54, 22, 57)
> WorkAge
 [1] 18 20 50 55 56 57 58 47 36 57 56 55 54 37 58 49 51 54 22 57
> #Let us now calculate the quartiles.  However, there is no function in R like quartile()
> #Instead we have to use the function quantile() only
> QuartWorkAge <- quantile(WorkAge, probs = seq(0, 1, 0.25))
> QuartWorkAge
   0%   25%   50%   75%  100%
18.00 44.50 54.00 56.25 58.00
> #Now let us calculate median using the median() function as we used earlier
> MedWorkAge <- median(WorkAge)
> MedWorkAge
[1] 54
> #Now let us calculate median of WorkAge using quantile() function
> MediWorkAge <- quantile(WorkAge, probs = 0.50)
> MediWorkAge
50%
 54
```

Figure 4-14A. *Calculating quantiles or percentiles using R*

```
>
> #If we want to divide the data set into 5 partitions
> #Or we want to find out the 20th, 40th, 60th, 80th and 100th percentile
> #We will do the same as follows
> PercentWorkAge <- quantile(WorkAge, probs = seq(0, 1, 0.20))
> PercentWorkAge
   0%   20%   40%   60%   80%  100%
18.0 36.8 50.6 55.0 57.0 58.0
>
```

Figure 4-14B. *Calculating quantiles or percentiles using R*

Similarly, you can divide the data set into 20 sets of equal number of data elements by using the quantile function with ***probs = seq(0, 1, 0.05)***, as shown in Figure 4-15.

```
> #SamiGeorge LLP
> #Data of employee age of 20 workers
> WorkAge <- c(18, 20, 50, 55, 56, 57, 58, 47, 36, 57, 56, 55, 54, 37, 58, 49, 51, 54, 22, 57)
> TwentySplitsWorkAge <- quantile(WorkAge, probs = seq(0, 1, 0.05))
> TwentySplitsWorkAge
    0%    5%   10%   15%   20%   25%   30%   35%   40%   45%   50%   55%   60%   65%   70%   75%   80%   85%   90%   95%  100%
18.00 19.90 21.80 33.90 36.80 44.50 48.40 49.65 50.60 52.65 54.00 54.45 55.00 55.35 56.00 56.25 57.00 57.00 57.10 58.00 58.00
>
```

Figure 4-15. *Partitioning the data into a set of 20 sets of equal number of data elements*

As you can observe from Figure 4-15, the minimum value of the data set is seen at 0 percentile and maximum value of the data set is seen at 100 percentile. As you can observe, typically between each 5 percentiles you can see one data element.

As evident from this discussion, quartiles and various quantiles provide additional information about the data distribution in addition to that information provided by mean or median (even though median is nothing but second quartile).

4.3.6 Standard deviation

The measures mean and median depict the center of the data set or distribution. On the other hand, standard deviation specifies the spread of the data set or data values.

The standard deviation is manually calculated as follows:

1. First mean of the data set or distribution is calculated

2. Then the distance of each value from the mean is calculated (this is known as the deviation)

3. Then the distance as calculated above is squared

4. Then the squared distances are summed up

5. Then the sum of the squared distances arrived at as above is divided by the number of values minus 1 to adjust for the degrees of freedom

The squaring in step 3 is required to understand the real spread of the data as the negatives and positives in the data set compensate for each other or cancel out the effect of each other when we calculate or arrive at the mean.

Let us take the age of the workers example shown in Figure 4-16 to calculate the standard deviation.

Worker	Age	Deviation from the Mean	Square of the Deviation
1	18	=47.35-18=29.35	861.4225
2	20	=47.35-20=27.35	748.0225
3	50	=47.35-50=02.65	7.0225
4	55	=47.35-55=-7.65	58.5225
5	56	=47.35-56=-8.65	74.8225
6	57	=47.35-57=-9.65	93.1225
7	58	=47.35-58=-10.65	113.4225
8	47	=47.35-47=-0.35	0.1225
9	36	=47.35-36=11.35	128.8225
10	57	=47.35-57=-9.65	93.1225
11	56	=47.35-56=-8.65	74.8225
12	55	=47.35-55=-7.65	58.5225
13	54	=47.35-54=-6.65	44.2225
14	37	=47.35-37=10.35	107.1225
15	58	=47.35-58=-10.65	113.4225
16	49	=47.35-49=-1.65	2.7225
17	51	=47.35-51=-3.65	13.3225
18	54	=47.35-54=-6.65	44.2225
19	22	=47.35-22=25.35	642.6225
20	57	=47.35-57=-9.65	93.1225
		Total	3372.55
		Standard Deviation	=squre root(3372.55/(20-1)) =13.32301

Figure 4-16. *Manual calculation of standard deviation using WorkAge data set*

In R, this calculation can be done easily through a simple command: *sd(dataset)*. Figure 4-17A shows the example of finding standard deviation using R.

```
>
> WorkAge
 [1] 18 20 50 55 56 57 58 47 36 57 56 55 54 37 58 49 51 54 22 57
> #Standard Deviation in R is calculated using sd command
> StdDevWorkAge <- sd(WorkAge)
> StdDevWorkAge
[1] 13.32301
>
```

Figure 4-17A. *Calculating standard deviation using R*

Normally, as per the rules of the normal curve (a data set which consists of large number of items is generally said to have a normal distribution or normal curve)

- +/- 1 standard deviation denotes that 68% of the data falls within it

- +/- 2 standard deviation denotes that 95% of the data falls within it

- +/- 3 standard deviation denote that 99.7% of the data falls within it.

In total, around 99.7% of the data will be within +/- 3 standard deviations.

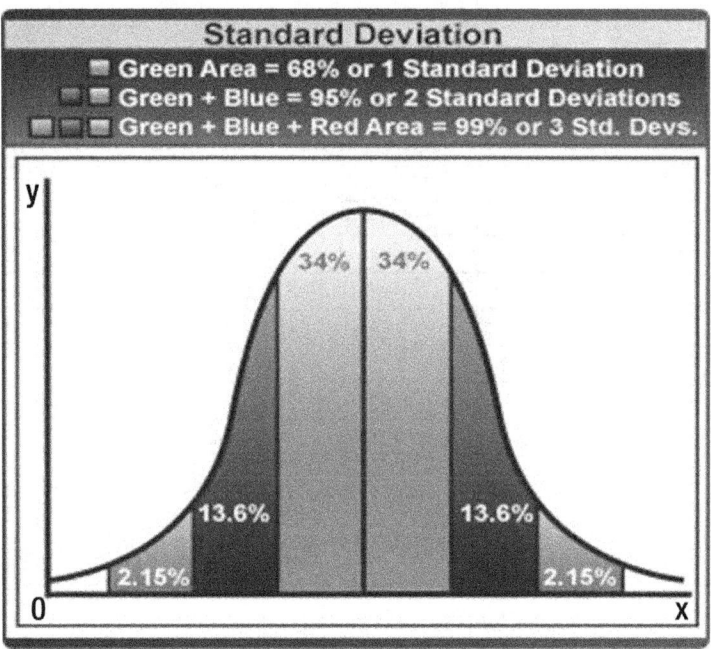

Figure 4-17B. *Bell curve showing data coverage within various standard deviations*

As you can see from Figure 4-17B, in the case of a normally distributed data (where the number of data points is typically greater than 30 (i.e., more the better)) it is observed that about 68% of the data falls within +/- one standard deviation from the center of the distribution (i.e., mean). Similarly, about 95% (or around 95.2% as shown in Figure 4-17B) data values fall within +/- two standard deviations from the center. About 99.7% of the data values fall within +/- three standard deviations from the center. A curve shown here is known as typically a "bell curve" or "normal distribution curve." For example, Profit or Loss of all the companies in a country is normally distributed around the center value (i.e., mean of the profit or loss).

The higher the standard deviation, the higher is the spread from the mean—i.e. it indicates that the data points vary from each other significantly and shows the heterogeneity of the data. The lower the standard deviation, the lower is the spread from the mean—i.e. it indicates that the data points vary less from each other and shows the homogeneity of the data.

However, standard deviation along with other factors such as mean, median, quartiles, and percentiles give us substantial information about the data or explain the data more effectively.

4.3.7 Variance

Variance is another way of depicting the spread. In simple terms, it is the square of the standard deviation as shown in Figure 4-18. Variance provides the spread of squared deviation from the mean value. It is another way of representing the spread compared to the standard deviation. Mathematically, as mentioned earlier, the variance is the square of the standard deviation. We are continuing to use the WorkAge data set we used earlier in this chapter.

```
>
> WorkAgeStdDev <- sd(WorkAge)
> WorkAgeStdDev
[1] 13.32301
> WorkAgeVar <- var(WorkAge)
> WorkAgeVar
[1] 177.5026
>
> WorkAgeStdDev * WorkAgeStdDev
[1] 177.5026
>
```

Figure 4-18. *Calculating variance using R*

4.3.8 "Summary" command in R

The command: ***summary(dataset))*** provides the following information on the data set which covers most of statistical parameters discussed. This command gives us the output viz., minimum value, first quartile, median (i.e., the second quartile), mean, third quartile, maximum value. This is an easy way of getting the summary information through a single command (see Figure 4-19, which has a screenshot from R).

```
>
> #summary command in R provides you the 6 important aspects
> #of data i.e. Min value, 1st quartile, Median (2nd Quartile),
> #Mean, 3rd quartile and Max value
> summary(WorkAge)
   Min. 1st Qu.  Median    Mean 3rd Qu.    Max.
  18.00   44.50   54.00   47.35   56.25   58.00
>
```

Figure 4-19. *Finding out major statistical parameters in R using summary() command*

If you use the ***summary(dataset)*** command then if required you can use additional commands, like ***sd(dataset)***, ***var(dataset),*** etc., to obtain additional parameters of interest related to the data.

4.4 Graphical description of the data

Statistical parameters such as mean, median, quantiles (quartiles, percentiles), standard deviation, and variance provide us complementary and important information about the data and enable us to understand the data set in a better way. On the other hand, graphical description presents the same information in a different way. According to brain theories, graphical representation is more intuitive to more than 50% of the persons than using quantitative figures.

4.4.1   Plots in R

Plotting in R is very simple. The command plot(dataset) provides you the simple plot of the data set. Taking the earlier example of workers' age, the simple command plot(WorkAge) in R will create a good graphical plot (see Figures 4-20 and 4-21).

```
> plot(WorkAge)
>
```

Figure 4-20. *Code for creating a simple plot using R*

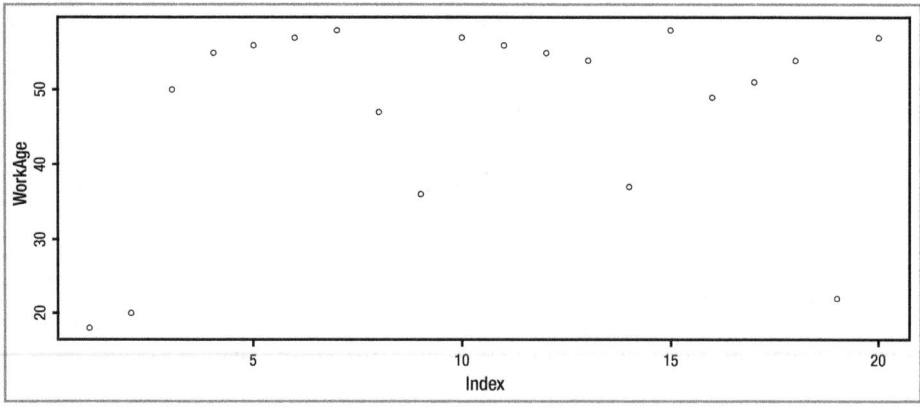

Figure 4-21. *Creating a simple plot using R*

As we have not given any information about the employee other than the age of the worker through a data set named WorkAge, the y-axis is named after the data set it represents. Since the data set provides no additional information about the employee, the data set index is represented in the x-axis.

With a slight variation in the command (as shown in Figure 4-22), we will create a better graphical representation of the age of the workers in the WorkAge data set.

```
> plot(WorkAge, col = "red", main = "Distribution of Workers' Age", xlab = "Employee Sequence", ylab = "Age of the Worker in Years")
> |
```

Figure 4-22. *Getting a better plot using additional parameters in* plot() *command*

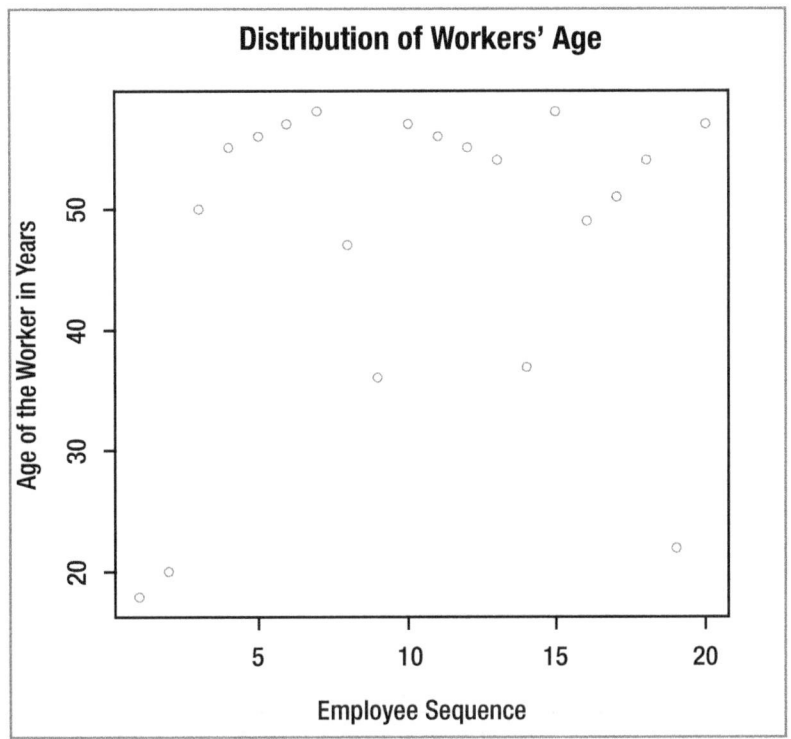

Figure 4-23. *Plot from R adding additional arguments to plot() command*

In the above command, col = "red" defines the color of the data points, xlab = " " specifies the label we want to provide to the x-axis, ylab = " " specifies the label we want to provide to the y-axis and main = " " (with labels / titles provided within the " ") specifies the title we want to provide to the entire graph. We can have subtitles included if required using sub = " " within the plot command. Plotting graphs in R is as simple as this (see Figure 4-23).

A simple addition of type = "l" will provide the following variant of the graph shown in Figures 4-24A and 4-24B.

```
> #Addition of type = "l" will provide the line graph
> #Addition of type = "b" will provide the graph with points connected with lines
> #Addition of type = "h" will provide the graph in the histogram format
> #Addition of type = "s" will provide the step type of graph
> plot(WorkAge, xlab = "Employee Sequence", ylab = "Age of the Workers' in Years", type = "l")
```

Figure 4-24A. How to get variants of the graph in R

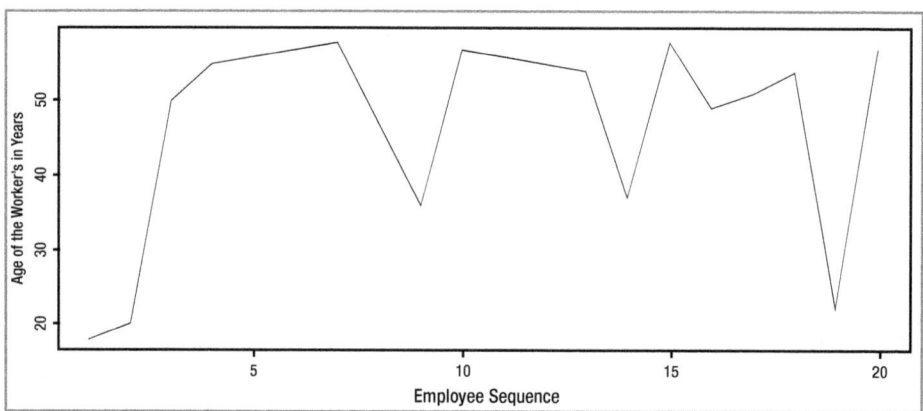

Figure 4-24B. How to get variants of the graph in R

Another small variant of type = "h" will provide the following variant of the graph in a histogram type of format. Figure 4-25 is a bar graph where the bars are represented by lines.

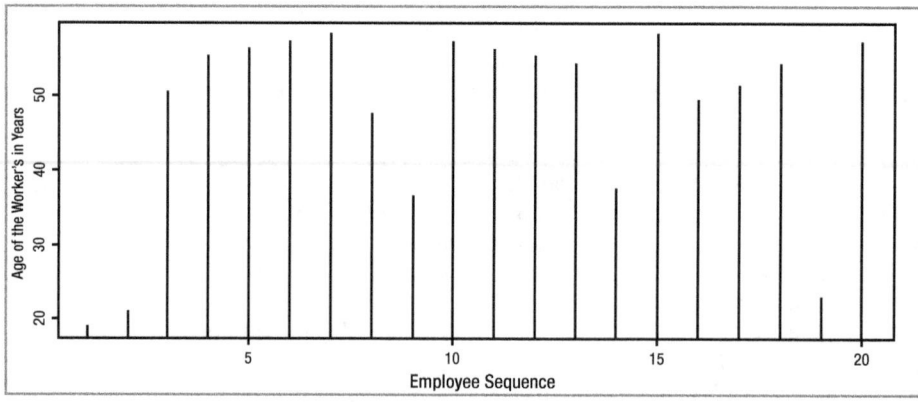

Figure 4-25. Histogram type of graph in R

4.4.2   Histogram

A histogram will provide the data grouped over a range of values. This is very useful for visualizing and understanding more about the data. The simple command in R: hist(dataset) produces a simple histogram as shown in Figures 4-26A and 4-26B.

```
>
> hist(WorkAge)
> |
```

Figure 4-26A. *Code to create a histogram using R*

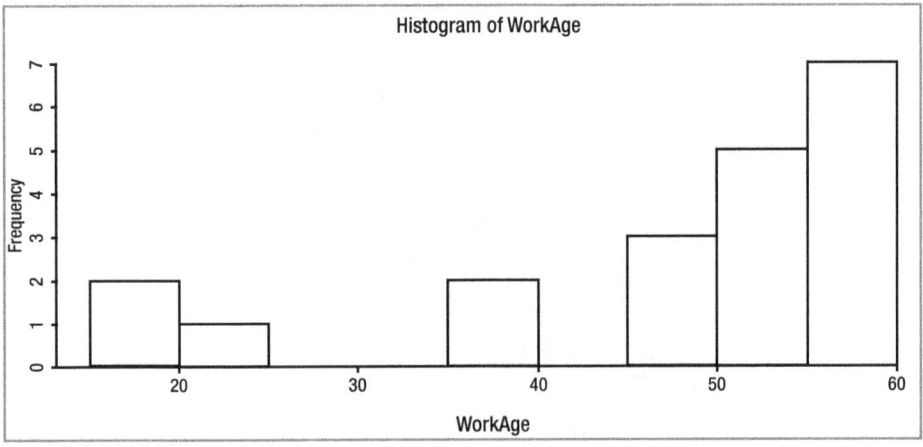

Figure 4-26B. *Simple histogram created using R*

In the graph shown in Figure 4-26B, the x-axis shows the range of age from 15+ to 20, 20+ to 25, and 25+ to 30 .until 55+ to 60. As you can see, we have not specified the range over which various range of values in this case age group has to be depicted. However, R has scanned through the data and decided the age group over which the data has to be depicted taking into consideration the minimum age and the maximum age.

As mentioned earlier, you can use main = " ", xlab = " ", ylab = " ", sub = " " to specify the main title, label for x-axis, label for y-axis, subtitle, respectively.

4.4.3   Bar plot

A bar plot is an easy way to depict the distribution of the data. In Figure 4-27A, we have provided the bar chart of the WorkAge data set. Worker age for each employee is provided on the x-axis. The difference in the length of the bar will denote the difference between the ages of the workers. The usage of the bar plot and corresponding bar plot generated is shown in Figures 4-27A and 4-27B.

```
> barplot(WorkAge, col = "red", xlab = "Worker Index", ylab = "Worker Age", main = "Bar Chart of the Worker Age")
>
```

Figure 4-27A. *Creating a simple bar plot in R*

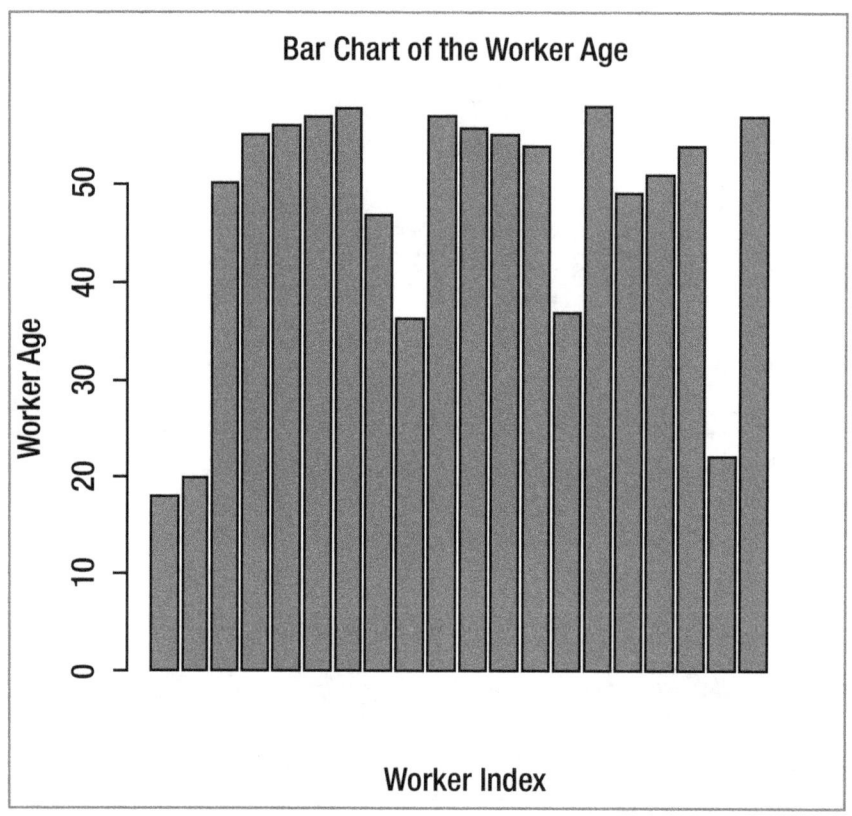

Figure 4-27B. *A bar plot created in R*

4.4.4   Boxplots

The boxplot is a popular way of showing the distribution of the data. Figure 4-28B, shows a boxplot created in R using WorkAge data set in R. The command used is boxplot(dataset) with label for the axis along with the title as shown in Figure 4-28A.

```
> boxplot(WorkAge, xlab="Age of the Worker", main = "Boxplot of Worker Age")
```

Figure 4-28A. *Command used in R to create a boxplot*

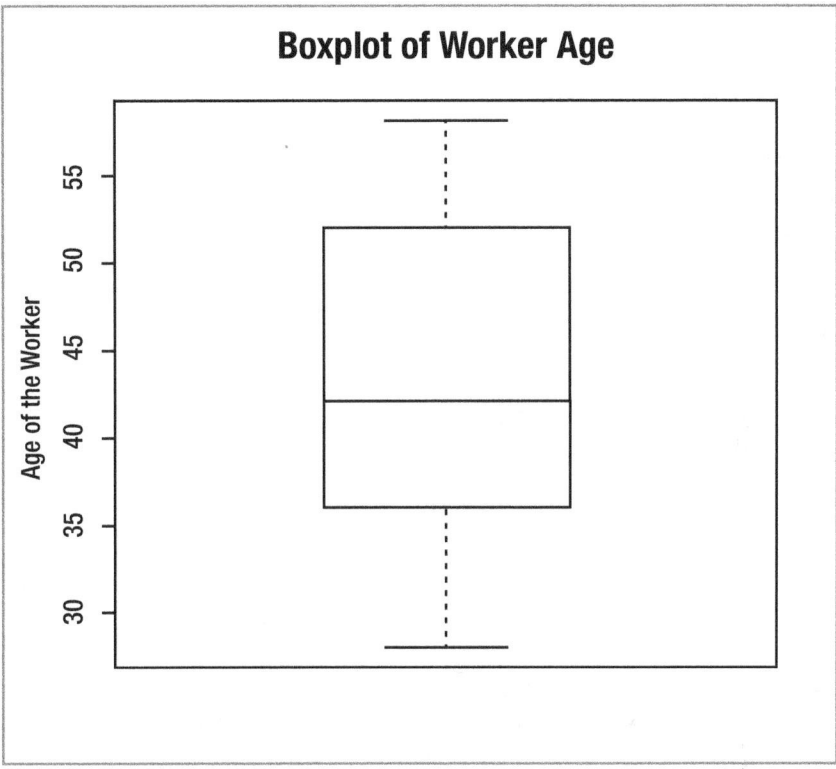

Figure 4-28B. *Boxplot created in R*

4.5 Computations on data frames

All our discussions in the previous paragraphs were focused on single-dimensional data—for example, a vector with a single feature of the workers such as the age of workers.

But most of the data we need to analyze is multidimensional and requires thorough knowledge of how to do this. Often you will encounter two-dimensional data with rows of data pertaining to various features represented through columns.

```
>
> #Here I have a data frame which is
> #a 2 dimensional matix with 10 rows
> #and 3 columns or features
> #3 features are: Name, Age, Salary of
> #the employees
> EmpData
   EmpName EmpAge EmpSal
1      John     18  18000
2     Craig     28  28000
3      Bill     32  32000
4      Nick     42  42000
5     Umesh     50  50000
6      Rama     55  55000
7       Ken     57  57000
8       Zen     58  58000
9   Roberts     59  59000
10     Andy     59  59000
> summary(EmpData)
    EmpName        EmpAge              EmpSal
 Andy   :1   Min.   :18.00   Min.   :18000
 Bill   :1   1st Qu.:34.50   1st Qu.:34500
 Craig  :1   Median :52.50   Median :52500
 John   :1   Mean   :45.80   Mean   :45800
 Ken    :1   3rd Qu.:57.75   3rd Qu.:57750
 Nick   :1   Max.   :59.00   Max.   :59000
 (Other):4
>
```

Figure 4-29. *Dataframe in R*

The data set depicted in Figure 4-29 is a data frame. The data frame is nothing but a table structure in R where each column represents the values of a variable and each row represents data related to a case or an instance. In this data frame, we have data related to name, age, and salary of ten employees. The data of each employee is depicted through a row and the features or aspects of the employee are depicted through the labels of the columns, and this type of data is captured in the corresponding columns.

As you can see in the figure, the command summary(dataset) can be used here also to obtain the summary information pertaining to each feature (i.e., the data in each column).

You can now compute additional information required if any (as shown in Figure 4-30).

```
> StdDevEmpAge <- sd(EmpData$EmpAge)
> StdDevEmpAge
[1] 14.97999
> StdDevEmpSal <- sd(EmpData$EmpSal)
> StdDevEmpSal
[1] 14979.99
>
```

Figure 4-30. *Computation of standard deviation in R on EmpData data frame features*

As seen above, any column from the data set can be accessed using datasetname followed by $column_name.

4.5.1   Scatter plot

Scatter plots are one of the important kinds of plots in the analysis of data. These plots depict the relationship between two variables. Scatter plots are normally used to show the "cause and effect relationships," but any relationship seen in the scatter plots need not be always a "cause and effect relationship." Figure 4-31A shows how to create a scatter plot in R and Figure 4-31B shows the actual scatter plot generated. The underlying concept of correlation has been explained in detail in Chapter 8.?.

```
> EmpData
   EmpName EmpAge EmpSal
1     John     18  18000
2    Craig     28  28000
3     Bill     32  32000
4     Nick     42  42000
5    Umesh     50  50000
6     Rama     55  55000
7      Ken     57  57000
8      Zen     58  58000
9   Roberts    59  59000
10     Andy     59  59000
> plot(EmpData$EmpSal ~ EmpData$EmpAge, type = "b")
>
```

Figure 4-31A. *Code for creating a scatter plot in R*

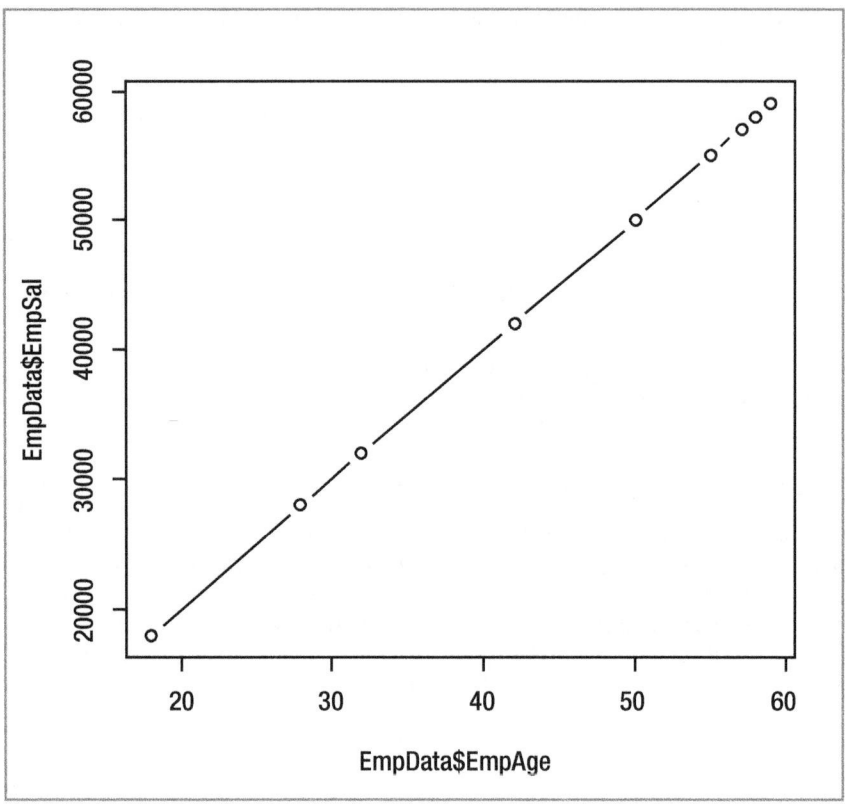

Figure 4-31B. *Scatter plot created in R (using the method specified in Figure 4-31A)*

As you can see from this example, there is a direct relationship between employee age and employee salary. The salary of the employees grows in direct proportion to their age. This may not be true in a real scenario. Figure 4-31A shows that the salary of the employee increases proportionate to his or her age and that too linearly. Such a relationship is known as "linear relationship." Please note that type = "b" along with the plot(dataset) command has created both point and line graph.

Let me now get another data frame named EmpData1 with one more additional feature (also known as column or field) and with different data in it. In Figure 4-32 you can see the data and summary of the data in this data frame. As you can see in Figure 4-32, I have added one more feature namely EmpPerGrade, and also have changed the values of salary from the earlier data frame, that is EmpData. EmpData1 has the following data now.

```
>
> EmpData1 <- data.frame(EmpName1, EmpAge1, EmpSal, EmpPerGrade)
> EmpData1
   EmpName1 EmpAge1 EmpSal EmpPerGrade
1      John      28  28000           0
2    George      32  34000           5
3    Jaison      36  40000           5
4   Roberts      38  42000           4
5    Ronnie      40  44000           4
6    Rajesh      44  46000           4
7    Raghav      48  47000           3
8    Sherry      52  48000           3
9      Bill      56  48500           2
10  William      58  49000           1
> summary(EmpData1)
   EmpName1      EmpAge1            EmpSal         EmpPerGrade
 Bill   :1   Min.   :28.0   Min.   :28000   Min.   :0.00
 George :1   1st Qu.:36.5   1st Qu.:40500   1st Qu.:2.25
 Jaison :1   Median :42.0   Median :45000   Median :3.50
 John   :1   Mean   :43.2   Mean   :42650   Mean   :3.10
 Raghav :1   3rd Qu.:51.0   3rd Qu.:47750   3rd Qu.:4.00
 Rajesh :1   Max.   :58.0   Max.   :49000   Max.   :5.00
 (Other):4
> plot(EmpData1$EmpSal ~ EmpData1$EmpAge1, type = "b")
```

Figure 4-32. *Data from data frame EmpData1*

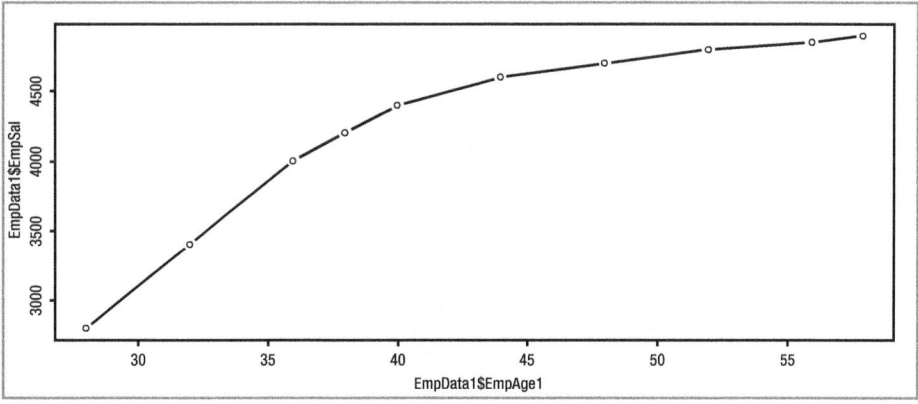

Figure 4-33. *Scatter plot from R showing the changed relationship between two features of data frame EmpData1*

Now, as you can see from Figure 4-33, the relationship between employee age and the employee salary has changed; as you can observe, as the age grows, the increase in employee salary is not proportional but tapers down. This is normally known as a "quadratic relationship."

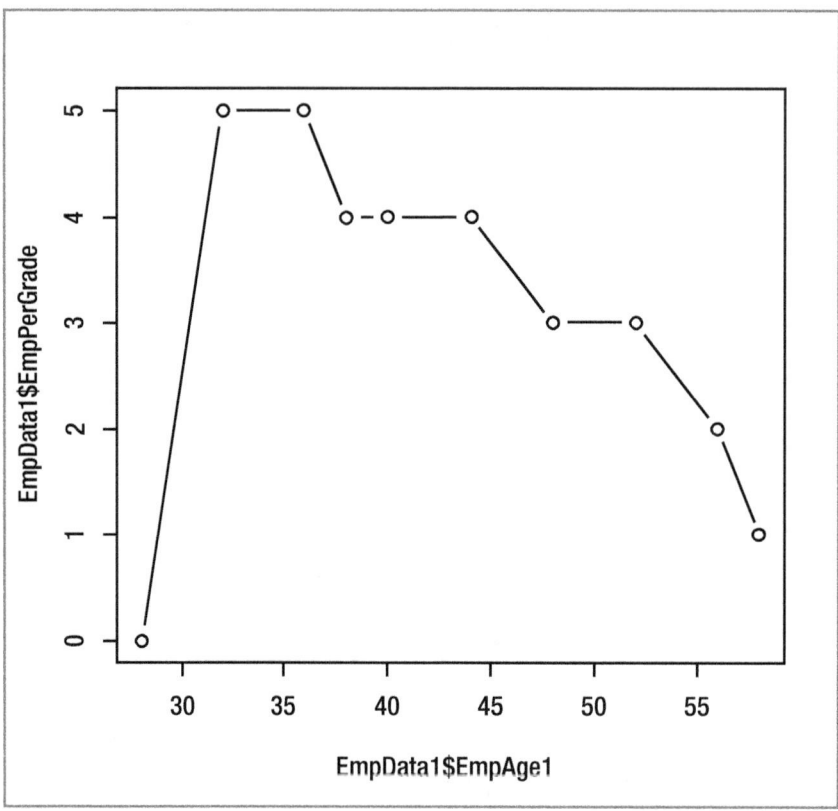

Figure 4-34. *Scatter plot from R showing the changed relationship between two features of data frame EmpData1*

In the Figure 4-34, you can see the relationship plotted between employee age and employee performance grade. Ignore the first data point as it was for a new employee joined recently and he was not graded. Hence, the data related to performance grade is 0. Otherwise, as you can observe, as the age progresses (as per the data above), the performance has come down. In this case there is an inverse relationship between employee age and employee performance (i.e., as the age progresses, performance is degrading). This is again not a true data and is given only for illustration.

4.6   Probability

Concepts of probability and related distributions are as important to business analytics as to the field of pure statistics. Some of the important concepts used in business analytics such as Bayesian theory and decision trees etc. are based on the concepts of probability.

As you are aware, probability in simple terms is the chance of an event happening. In some cases, we may have some prior information related to the event; in other cases, the event may be random—that is, we may not have prior knowledge of the outcome. A popular way to describe the probability is with the example of tossing a coin or tossing a die. A coin has two sides and when it is tossed, the probability of either the head or the tail coming up is 1/2 as in any throw either it can be the head or the tail that comes up. You can validate the same by tossing up the coin many times and observing that the probability of either the head or the tail coming up is around 50% (i.e., 1/2). Similarly, the probability of any one of the numbers being rolled using the die is 1/6, which can be again validated by tossing the die many times.

If an event is not likely to happen, the probability of the same is 0. However, if an event is sure to happen, the probability of the same is 1. However, probability of an event is always between 0 and 1 and depends upon the chance of it happening or the uncertainty associated with its happening.

Any given two or more events can happen independent of each other. Similarly, any two or more events can happen exclusive of each other.

Example 1: Can you travel at the same time to two destinations in opposite directions. If you travel toward the west direction you can't travel toward the east direction at the same time.

Example 2: If we are making profit in one of the client accounts we cannot make loss in the same account.

Examples 1 and 2 are types of events that exclude the happening of a particular event when the other event happens; they are known as mutually exclusive events.

Example 3: A person "tossing a coin" and "raining" can happen at the same, but neither impacts the outcome of the other.

Example 4: A company may make profit and at the same time have legal issues. One event (of making profit) does not have an impact on the other event (of having legal issues).

Examples 3 and 4 are types of events that do not impact the outcome of each other; they are known as mutually independent events. These are also the examples of mutually non-exclusive events as both outcomes can happen at the same time.

4.6.1   Probability of mutually exclusive events

The probability of two mutually exclusive events (say X and Y) happening at the same time is 0 as by definition both do not happen at the same time: $P(X \text{ and } Y) = P(X \cap Y) = 0$.

The probability of n mutually exclusive events (say A1, A2.....AN) happening at the same time is 0 as by definition all these events do not happen at the same time: $P(A1 \text{ and } A2 \text{ and}......AN) = P(A1 \cap A2 \cap.... \cap AN) = 0$.

However, the probability of one of the two mutually exclusive events (say X or Y) happening is the sum of the probability of each of these events happening: $P(X \text{ or } Y) = P(X \cup Y) = P(X) + P(Y)$.

4.6.2   Probability of mutually independent events

The probability of two mutually independent events happening at the same time is $P(X \text{ and } Y) = P(X) * P(Y)$.

4.6.3   Probability of mutually non-exclusive events:

Mutually non-exclusive events are the ones that are not mutually exclusive.

The probability of two mutually non-exclusive events (i.e., the sum of the probability of each of these events happening minus the probability of both of these events happening at the same time (or in other words together)) is $P(X \text{ or } Y) = P(X \cup Y) = P(X) + P(Y) - P(X \cap Y)$.

The probability of n mutually non-exclusive events is $P(A1 \text{ or } A2 \text{ or } \ldots\ldots \text{ or } AN) = P(A1 \cup A2 \cup \ldots\ldots\cup AN) = P(A1) + P(A2) + \ldots\ldots + P(AN) - P(A1 \cap A2 \cap A3 \cap \ldots\ldots\ldots \cap AN)$.

4.6.4   Probability distributions

Random variables are important in analysis. Probability distributions depict the distribution of the values of a random variable. Some important probability distributions are:

- Normal distribution

- Binomial distribution

- Poisson distribution

- Uniform distribution

- Chi-squared distribution

- Exponential distribution

We will not be discussing all of the foregoing. There are many more types of distributions possible including F-distribution, hypergeometric distribution, joint and marginal probability distributions, and conditional distributions. We will discuss only normal distribution, binomial distribution, and Poisson distribution in this chapter. We will discuss more on these distributions and other relevant distributions in later chapters.

4.6.4.1   Normal distribution

A huge amount of data is considered to be normally distributed as the distribution is normally centered around the mean. Normal distribution is observed in real life in many situations. On account of the bell shape of the distribution, the normal distribution is also called "bell curve." The properties of normal distribution typically having 68% of the values within + / - 1 standard deviation, 95% of the values within + / - 2 standard deviation, and 99.7% of the values within + / - 3 standard deviation are the ones heavily used in most of the analytical techniques and so are also the properties of standard normal curve. The standard normal curve has a mean of 0 and a standard deviation of 1. Z-score, used to normalize the values of the features in a regression, is based on the concept of standard normal distribution. Normal distribution can be used in case of other distributions as well as the distribution of the means of random samples is typically a normal distribution in case of large sample size.

One of the important examples of the application of the normal distribution is a statistical process control which is applied in most of the industries to understand the process performance and control it. Another important example is of the distribution of the performance of the employees to identify a few employees as high performers and some as low performers whereas most of the employees perform around the average.

Consider that an organization has 150 employees and the average grade of the employees is 3 and the minimum grade is 1 and the maximum is 5. The standard deviation is 1.5. The percentage of employees getting a grade of 4 and above is calculated using R, as shown in Figure 4-35.

```
>
> pnorm(4, mean = 3, sd = 1.5, lower.tail = FALSE)
[1] 0.2524925
>
```

Figure 4-35. *Example of a normal distribution problem solved in R*

Please note that we are interested in the upper tail as we want to know the percentage of employees who have received a grade of 4 or 5. The answer here is 25.25%.

4.6.4.2   Binomial distribution

Binomial distribution normally follows where success or failure is measured. In a cricket match, tossing a coin is an important event at the beginning of the match to decide which side bats (or fields) first. Tossing a coin and calling for "head" wins you the toss if "head" is the outcome. Otherwise, if the "tail" is the outcome you lose the toss.

As the sales head of an organization you have submitted responses to fifteen tenders. There are five contenders in each tender. You may be successful in some or all or may be successful in none. As there are five contenders in each tender and each tender can be won by only one company the probability of winning the tender is 0.2 (i.e., 1/5). You want to win more than four of the fifteen tenders. You can find out the probability of winning four or less tenders employing binomial distribution using R (see Figure 4-36).

```
>
> pbinom(4, size = 15, prob = 0.2)
[1] 0.8357663
>
```

Figure 4-36. *Example of a binomial distribution problem solved in R*

Please note that pbinom() function uses the cumulative probability distribution function for binomial distribution as we are interested to know the chance of winning four or more tenders. As you can see, the probability of winning four or less tenders is 83.58%. The probability of winning more than four tenders is (100 – 83.58) = 16.42%.

4.6.4.3   Poisson distribution

Poisson distribution represents the independent events happening in a time interval. The arrival of calls at a call center or the arrival of customers in a banking hall or the arrival of passengers at an airport/bus terminus follow Poisson distribution.

Let us take an example of the number of customers arriving at a particular bank's specific branch office. Suppose an average of 20 customers are arriving per hour. We can find out the probability of 26 or more customers arriving at the bank's branch per hour using R and Poisson distribution (see Figure 4-37).

```
> ppois(25, lambda = 20, lower = FALSE)
[1] 0.112185
>
```

Figure 4-37. *Example of a Poisson distribution problem solved in R*

Please note that we have used `lower = FALSE` as we are interested in the upper tail and we want to know the probability of 26 or more customers arriving at the bank's branch per hour.The answer here is 11.22%.

4.7   Chapter summary

- You have looked at how relying only on one of the descriptive statistics can be dangerous. In fact, if you have to get a holistic view of anything you may require multiple statistical functions to understand the context/situation.

- You also understood various statistical parameters of interest in descriptive analytics (mean, median, quantiles, quartiles, percentiles, standard deviation, variance, and mode). You understood how to compute these using R. You also came to know how most of these parameters can be gotten through a simple command like ***summary(dataset)*** using R.

- You explored plotting the data in graphical representation using R. You also understood how graphical representation can provide more information to the users than can descriptive statistics. You understood how you can create histograms, bar charts, and boxplots using R.

- You learnt one of the important data structures of R (i.e., data frames). You understood how to get the summary data from the data contained in these data frames.

- You explored how scatter plots can show the relationship between various features of the data frame and hence enable us to better understand these relationships graphically and easily.

- You explored another important aspect of business analytics known as probability, which has a bearing on many of the techniques used in business analytics (Bayesian techniques, decision trees etc.).

- You learnt the important probability distributions and what they are. You also looked at a few examples of probability distributions, and also how to solve business problems employing some popular distributions like normal distribution, binomial distribution, and Poisson distribution, using R.

CHAPTER 5

Business Analytics Process and Data Exploration

This chapter covers data exploration, validation, and cleaning required for data analysis. You'll learn the purpose of data cleaning, why you need data preparation, how to go about handling missing values, and some of the data-cleaning techniques used in the industry.

5.1 Business Analytics Life Cycle

The purpose of business analytics is to derive information from data in order to make appropriate business decisions. Data can be real-time or historical. Typically, you build a business model from historical data, and once you are satisfied with the accuracy of the model, you can deploy it in production for real-time data analysis. Though there are many standards referenced by various industry experts and tool manufacturers, the process is more or less the same. In this section, we present the basic business analytics process with the help of a flow chart. The same process is followed in all case studies that are discussed in this book.

The life cycle of a business analytics project consists of eight phases. The sequence of phases is shown in Figure 5-1. This sequence may change at times, depending on the business problem and data. The outcome of each phase determines the next phase and the tasks to be performed in that phase. The whole process does not end after the model is deployed. After the deployment, a new set of data that was not seen before can trigger a new set of problems that is addressed as a new model, and the same set of processes is followed once again, with additional inputs learned during previous deployment of the model. Subsequent processes will benefit from the experiences of the previous ones. The following sections describe the functions of each phase.

5.1.1 Phase 1: Understand the Business Problem

In this initial phase of the project, the focus is to understand the problem, objectives, and requirements from the perspective of the business. This understanding is then converted into a data analytics problem with the aim of solving it by using appropriate methods to achieve the objective. The details are discussed in the next section.

© Dr. Umesh R. Hodeghatta and Umesha Nayak 2017
U. R. Hodeghatta and U. Nayak, *Business Analytics Using R - A Practical Approach*,
DOI 10.1007/978-1-4842-2514-1_5

5.1.2   Phase 2: Collect and Integrate the Data

In this important phase, data is collected from various sources. Once you understand the business problem, you can define the process of collecting data, including the parameters required to solve the business problem. If the data is not available in a current database or data warehouse, a survey may be required. This survey needs to be designed as a proper questionnaire via proper research methodology. In some cases, data may be available in an internal database, and proper methods can be designed to extract data from the database.

5.1.3   Phase 3: Preprocess the Data

Most of the time, the raw data received or collected may not be applied to building the model. The raw data may contain errors such as formatting conflicts, wrong data types, and missing values. In this step, data is cleaned and normalized. You fix any missing values in the data, and data is then prepared for further analysis. This process may be repeated several times, depending on the quality of data you get and the accuracy of the model obtained.

5.1.4   Phase 4: Explore and Visualize the Data

The next step is to understand the characteristics of the data, such as its distribution, trends, and relationships among variables. This exploration enables you to get a better understanding of the data. You can become familiar with the types of data you collected, identifying outliers and various data types, and discovering your first insights into the data. The information you uncover in this phase can help form the basis of later hypotheses regarding hidden information in the sample.

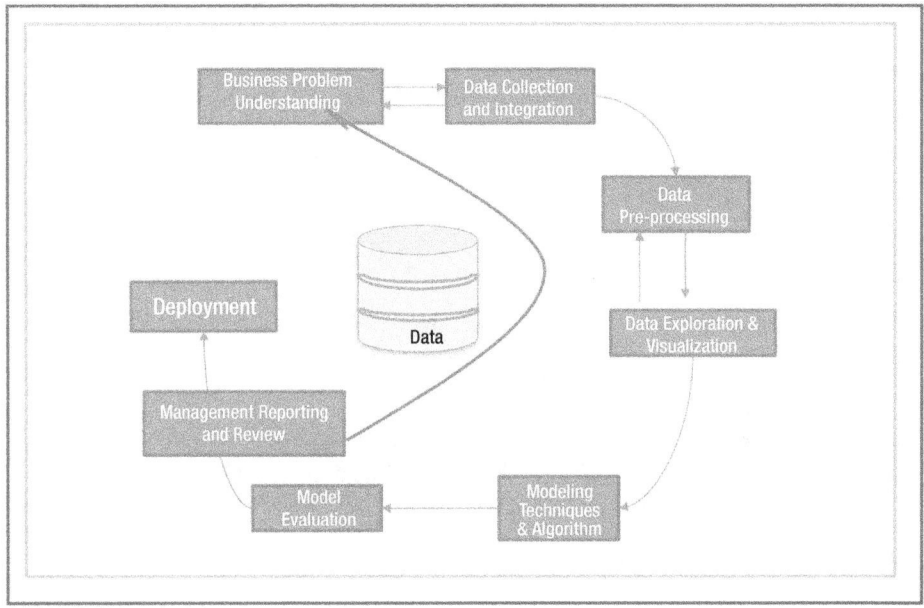

Figure 5-1. *Business analytics process*

5.1.5   Phase 5: Choose Modeling Techniques and Algorithms

In this phase, you decide whether to use unsupervised or supervised machine-learning techniques. Is it a classification problem or a regression problem? Will you use a descriptive or predictive technique? Will you use linear regression or logistic regression methods? These choices depend on both the business requirements and the data you have. A proper training set is created in this stage, and various parameters are calibrated for optimal values and the model. The tools are also chosen in this phase. This may require programming skills or specific tool skills. Once you choose a model, the next step is to build the model and then evaluate its performance.

5.1.6   Phase 6: Evaluate the Model

At this point, you have a model, but how do you know that it will work for you? What is the performance of the model? In this phase, you evaluate the model by using standard methods that measure the accuracy of the model and its performance in the field. It is important to evaluate the model and to be certain that the model achieves the business objectives specified by business leaders. This requires in-depth knowledge of statistics, machine learning, algorithms, and interpreting results. Generally, an advanced education such as a PhD may be useful.

5.1.7   Phase 7: Report to Management and Review

In this phase, you present your mathematical model to the business leaders. It is important to align your mathematical output of the model with the business objectives and to be able to communicate that alignment to the management and business leaders. Once management is satisfied with the results and the model, the model is ready for deployment. If there are any changes to be made, the preceding cycle is repeated.

5.1.8   Phase 8: Deploy the Model

This is a challenging phase of the project. The model is now deployed for end users and is in a production environment, analyzing the live data. Depending on the deployment scenario and business objectives, the model can perform predictive analytics or simple descriptive analytics and reporting. The model also may behave differently in the production environment, as it may see a totally different set of data from the actual model. In such scenarios, the model is revisited for improvements. In many cases, the analysis is carried out by end customers, and they need to be trained properly.

The process of business analytics defined in this book is similar to other data-mining processes followed in the industry. For example, the *Cross-Industry Standard Process for Data Mining* (*CRISP-DM*) consists of six phases: Business Understanding, Data Understanding, Data Preparation, Modeling, Evaluation, and Deployment. This model was launched by Daimler Chrysler, SPSS, and NCR in 1996. Similarly, SEMAA, developed by SAS, has five phases: Sample (obtain a subset of data that is a representative sample, but not too large a data set to process easily), Explore (explore the data for patterns), Modify (transform variables if necessary), Model (apply a data model that best fits the data), and Assess (determine whether the model meets the requirements).

The next sections examine each phase in greater detail. Though each phase could be a separate chapter by itself, we cover only the important steps and solutions required to achieve the goal.

5.2   Understanding the Business Problem

The key purpose of analytics is to solve a business problem. Before you solve the problem, you need to thoroughly understand the problem from a business perspective, so you know what the client really wants you to solve. For example, is the client trying to find a pattern in the data, predict the price of a product to be launched, predict a customer segment to target, figure out who is defaulting on a loan, optimize a software development cycle, or improve the quality of operations? This should be clarified at the beginning of the process and should be documented. Also, it is important to determine the availability of the data, whether you have access to the data source or internal data warehouse, the data format, the data quality, the amount of data available, and the data stream for the final model deployment.

Documentation is an equally important task, as our memories are not very good at recalling every detail. As a part of this task, you need to document the business objective, data source, risks, and limitations of the project. Define the timeline, the infrastructure needed to support the model, and the expertise required to support the project.

5.3   Collecting and Integrating the Data

Getting quality data is the most important factor determining the accuracy of the results. Data can be either from a primary source or secondary source. A *primary source* is your own source—data from an internal database or data from your own research. You have full control of the data collected. A *secondary source* is data from other, secondary places that sell the data or data that already exists apart from the business database. Some examples of secondary sources include official reports from government, newspaper articles, and census data. Depending on the type of business problem being solved, you might use data from a primary source or secondary source or from both the sources. The advantage of using primary data is that you are designing the type of information required for solving the problem, so the data is of good quality, and less time is required to prepare the data for further analysis. An abundance of data may exist inside the organization in various databases. For example:

> *Operational database*: Data related to day-to-day business transactions such as vendor management, supply chains, customer complaints, and customer feedback.

> *Manufacturing and production database*: Data related to the manufacturing process, production details, supply-chain management, production schedule, and repair and maintenance of machinery.

> *HR and finance database*: Data related to HR and finance functions such as employee leave, personnel data, job skills, attrition, and salaries.

> *IT database*: Data related to information systems such as IT assets inventory, licensing details, software and various logs.

> *Data warehouse*: A data warehouse is an integrated database created from multiple databases within the organization. Data warehouse technology typically cleans, normalizes, and preprocesses data before it is stored. This helps in analysis, reporting, and the decision-making process. Data warehouse technology also supports online analytical processing (OLAP) and other functionalities such as data summarization and multidimensional analysis (slice and dice).

> *Metadata*: This is data about the data. It is descriptive information about a particular data set, object, or resource, including how it is formatted, and when and by whom it was collected (or example, web metadata, XML, and JSON format).

> *NoSQL database*: NoSQL databases are developed to overcome the limitations of relational databases and to meet the challenges of the enormous amounts of data being generated on the Web. A NoSQL database can store both structured and unstructured data. Also, NoSQL databases need not have a schema before storing the data.

Most organizations have data spread across various databases. Pulling data from multiple sources is a required part of solving business analytics tasks. Sometimes, data may be stored in databases for different purposes than the objective you are trying to solve. Thus, the data has to be prepared to ensure it addresses the business problem prior to any analytics process. This process is sometimes referred to as *data munging* or *data wrangling*, which is covered in the next section.

5.3.1   Sampling

Many times, unless you have a big data infrastructure, only a sample of the population is used to build analytical modeling. A sample is "a smaller collection of units from a population used to determine truths about that population" (Field, 2005). The sample should be representative of the population. Choosing a sampling technique depends on the type of business problem.

For example, you might want to study the annual gross domestic product (GDP) per capita for several countries over a period of time and the periodic behavior of such series in connection with business cycles. Monthly housing sales over a period of 6–10 years show cyclic behavior, but for 6–12 months, the sales data may show seasonal behavior. Stock market data over a period of 10–15 years may show a different trend than over a 100-day period. Similarly, forecasting sales based on previous data over a period of time, or analyzing Twitter sentiments and trends over a period of time, is cyclic data. If the fluctuations are not of a fixed period, they are cyclic. If the changes are in a specific period of the calendar, the pattern is seasonal. Time-series data is data obtained through repeated measurements over a particular time period.

For time-series data, the sample should contain the time period (date or time or both) and only a sample of measurement records for that particular day or time instead of the complete data collected. For example, the Dow Jones volume is traded over 18 months. The data is collected for every millisecond, so the volume of this data for a day is huge. Over a 10-month period, this data can be in terabytes.

The other type of data is not time dependent. It can be continuous or discrete data, but time has no significance in such data sets. For example, you might be looking at the income or job skills of individuals in a company, or the number of credit transactions in a retail store, or age and gender information. There is no relationship between the two data records.

Unless you have big data infrastructure, for any analysis you can just take a sample of records. Use a randomization technique and take steps to ensure that all the members of a population have an equal chance of being selected. This method is called *probability sampling*. There are several variations on this type of sampling:

> *Random sampling*: A sample is picked randomly, and every member has an equal opportunity to be selected.
>
> *Stratified sampling*: The population is divided into groups, and data is selected randomly from a group, or strata.
>
> *Systematic sampling*: You select members systematically—say, every tenth member—in that particular time or event.

The details of calculating sample sizes is beyond the scope of this book and is covered extensively in statistics and other research methodology books. However, to enhance your understanding, here is a simple formula for calculating a sample:

If the population standard deviation is known, then

$$n = (z \times sigma/E)^{\wedge 2}$$

If standard deviation is unknown,

$$n = (p)(1 - p)* (z/E)^{\wedge 2}$$

5.3.2   Variable Selection

Having more variables in the data set may not always provide desired results. However, if you have more predictor variables, you need more records. For example, if you want to find out the relationship between one Y and one single predictor X, then 15 data points may give you results. But if you have 10 predictor variables, 15 data points is not enough. Then how much is enough? Statisticians and many researchers have worked on this and given a rough estimate. For example, a procedure by Delmater and Hancock (2001), indicates that you should have $6 \times m \times p$ records for any predictive models, where p is number of variables and m is the number of outcome classes. The more records you have, the better the prediction results. Hence, in *big* data processing, you can eliminate the need for sampling and try to process all the available data in order to get better results.

5.4   Preprocessing the Data

As described in the previous phase, data can be collected from various sources, including an internal database or data warehouse. Data in a database may be susceptible to noise and inconsistencies because its data is collected from various end-user applications developed and handled by different people over a period of time. Sometimes, multiple databases may be queried to get data for the business analytics process. In this query process, data may be merged, may contain missing values or junk characters, may be of different data types, and may represent different types of observations or the same observations multiple times. Thus, prior to performing any data analysis, it is essential to understand the data in terms of its data types, variables and characteristics of variables, and data tables.

5.4.1   Data Types

Data can be either qualitative or quantitative. *Qualitative data* is not numerical—for example, type of car, favorite color, or favorite food. *Quantitative data* is numeric. Additionally, quantitative data can be divided into categories of *discrete* or *continuous* data (described in more detail later in this section).

Quantitative data is often referred to as *measurable data*. This type of data allows statisticians to perform various arithmetic operations, such as addition and multiplication, to find parameters of a population, such as mean or variance.

The observations represent counts or measurements, and thus all values are numerical. Each observation represents a characteristic of the individual data points in a population or a sample.

Discrete: A variable can take a certain value that is separate and distinct. Each value is not related to any other value. Some examples of discrete types of data include the number of cars per family, the number of times a person drinks water during a day, or the number of defective products on a production line.

Continuous: A variable that can take numeric values within a specific range or interval. Continuous data can take any possible value that the observations in a set can take. For example, with temperature readings, each reading can take on any real number value on a thermometer.

Nominal data: The order of the data is arbitrary, or no order is associated with the data. For example, race or ethnicity has the values black, brown, white, Indian, American, and so forth; no order is associated with the values.

Ordinal data: This data is in a certain defined order. Examples include Olympic medals—Gold, Silver, and Bronze, and Likert scale surveys—disagree, agree, strongly agree. With ordinal data, you cannot state with certainty whether the intervals between values are equal.

Interval data: This data has meaningful intervals between measurements, but there is no true starting zero. A good example is the measurement of temperature in Kelvin or the height of a tsunami. Interval data is like ordinal data, except the intervals between values are equally split. The most common example is temperature in degrees Fahrenheit. The difference between 29 and 30 degrees is the same magnitude as the difference between 58 and 59 degrees.

Ratio data: The difference between two values has the same meaning of measurement. For example, the height above sea level for two cities can be expressed as a ratio. The difference in water level of two reservoirs can be expressed as a ratio, such as twice as much as X reservoir.

The concept of scale types later received the mathematical rigor that it lacked at its inception with the work of mathematical psychologists Theodore Alper (1985, 1987), Louis Narens (1981a, b), and R. Duncan Luce (1986, 1987, 2001).

Before the analysis, understand the variables you are using and prepare all of them with the right data type. Many tools support the transformation of variable types.

5.4.2   Data Preparation

After the preliminary data type conversions, the next step is to study the data. You need to check the values and their association with the data. You also need to find missing values, null values, empty spaces, and unknown characters so they can be removed from the data before the analysis. Otherwise, this can impact the accuracy of the model. This section describes some of the criteria and analysis that can be performed on the data.

5.4.2.1   Handling Missing Values

Sometimes a database may not contain values for some variables as the values weren't recorded. There may be several records with no values recorded in the database. When you perform analysis with the missing values, the results you obtain may not represent the truth. Missing values have to be addressed properly before the analysis. Following are some of the methods used to resolve this issue:

> *Ignore the values*: This is not a very effective method. This is usually recommended when the label is missing and you're not able to interpret the value's meaning. Also, if there are only one or two records of many variables of the same row is missing, then are you can delete this row of records and ignore the values. If the size of the sample is large, and deleting one or two sample values does not make a difference, then you can delete the record.

> *Fill in the values with average value or mode*: This is the simplest method. Determine the average value or mode value for all the records of an attribute and then use this value to fill in all the missing values. This method depends on the type of problem you are trying to solve. For example, if you have time-series data, this method is not recommended.

> *Fill in the values with an attribute mean belonging to the same bin*: If your data set has an attribute classified into categories—for example, income group as high, low, and average—and another attribute, say, *population*, has several missing values, you can fill in the missing values with a mean value for that particular category. In this example, if the *population* of the high-income group is missing, use the mean population for the high-income group.

The following is another example of how binning can be used to fill in missing values:

1. Data set *income*: 100, 210, 300, 400, 900, 1000, 1100, 2000, 2100, 2500

2. Partition the data into different bins based on the distance between two observations:

    Bin 1: 100, 210, 300, 400

    Bin 2: 900, 1000, 1100

    Bin 3: 2000, 2100, 2500

3. Take the average of the entries in each bin.

   Bin 1 Average: 252.5

   Bin 2 Average: 1,000

   Bin 3 Average: 2,200

4. Use the average bin values to fill in the missing value for a particular bin.

Predict the values based on the most probable value: Based on the other attributes in the data set, you can fill in the value based on the most probable value it can take. You can use some of the statistical techniques such as Bayes' theorem or a decision tree to find the most probable value.

5.4.2.2 Handling Duplicates, Junk, and Null Values

Duplicate, junk, and null characters should be cleaned from the database before the analytics process. The same process discussed for handling empty values can be used. The only challenge is to identify the junk characters, which is sometimes hard and can cause a lot of issues during the analysis.

5.4.3 Data Preprocessing with R

Normally, tools provide an interface for performing data cleaning and data preprocessing before the analysis. This section describes how this can be achieved using R. Multiple solutions are available to perform the same tasks, so this example is just one solution. The data preprocessing methods discussed are as follows:

- Understanding the variable types

- Changing the variable types

- Finding missing and null values

- Cleaning missing values with appropriate methods

All variables in R are represented as vectors. The following are the basic data types in R:

Numeric: Real numbers.

Integer: Whole numbers.

Factor: Categorical data to define various categories. For example, 1 for male, 2 for female. Also, 1 for rank 1, 2 for rank 2.

Character: Data strings of characters defining, for example, the name of a person, animal, or place.

The basic operations in R are performed as vector operations (element-wise) including basic arithmetical operations (such as addition and subtraction), logical operations (such as & and !), comparison operations (such as ==, <, >) and some of the basic math functions (such as sin, cos, and exp). The R example (given below) demonstrates the following:

1. Reading the data set.

2. Checking the variable type.

3. Transforming the variable to a different type.

4. Changing the name of the variable.

5. Finding missing values. We usually see NA and NaN in R. NA is generally interpreted as a missing value. NaN indicates a mathematical error (for example, dividing by 0). However, is. na() returns TRUE for both NA and NaN.

6. Replacing missing values and NAs.

Let's get started with the example by looking at the data set:

```
>
> mydata<-read.csv("Stocks.csv")
> str(mydata)
'data.frame':   960 obs. of  12 variables:
 $ X1      : int  2 3 4 5 6 7 8 9 10 11 ...
 $ X17.219: Factor w/ 415 levels ".","17.438","17.891",..: 3 5 7 2 4 6 7 6 10 9$
 $ X50.5  : Factor w/ 273 levels ".","19.25","20",..: 206 202 207 187 187 190 1$
 $ X18.75 : Factor w/ 96 levels ".","12.75","12.875",..: 57 59 60 60 56 53 54 5$
 $ X43    : Factor w/ 187 levels ".","34.375","34.5",..: 72 71 72 51 55 60 64 6$
 $ X60.875: Factor w/ 374 levels ".","27.75","28",..: 195 194 200 179 178 186 1$
 $ X26.375: Factor w/ 154 levels ".","14.125","14.25",..: 91 100 105 89 95 100 $
 $ X67.75 : Factor w/ 204 levels ".","58","58.375",..: 72 75 82 33 57 53 55 53 $
 $ X19    : Factor w/ 100 levels ".","16.375","16.5",..: 21 14 15 3 7 5 5 7 10 $
 $ X48.75 : num  48.8 49 49.6 47.5 47.8 ...
 $ X34.875: Factor w/ 204 levels ".","34","34.375",..: 12 17 16 11 3 2 5 6 14 1$
 $ High   : Factor w/ 3 levels "High","Low","Medium": 2 3 1 2 2 2 3 2 3 3 ...
> |
```

From these str() details, it is clear that the data set does not have variable names. R has appended an X suffix to the first value in the column. And almost all the variable types are defined as *factors* by default. Further, to view the first few lines of the data, you can use the head() command:

```
>
> head(mydata)
  X1 X17.219  X50.5 X18.75    X43 X60.875 X26.375 X67.75    X19 X48.75 X34.875   High
1  2  17.891 51.375 19.625     44      62  26.125 68.125 19.125 48.750  35.625    Low
2  3  18.438 50.875 19.875 43.875  61.875   27.25   68.5  18.25 49.000  36.375 Medium
3  4  18.672   51.5     20     44  62.625  27.875 69.375 18.375 49.625   36.25   High
4  5  17.438     49     20 41.375   59.75  25.875  63.25   16.5 47.500    35.5    Low
5  6  18.109     49   19.5 41.875  59.625  26.625  66.25 17.125 47.750  34.375    Low
6  7  18.563 49.375 19.125   42.5   60.75   27.25  65.75 16.875 47.875      34    Low
> |
```

■ **Note** str() gives the summary of the object in active memory, and head() enables you to view the first few (six) lines of data.

The next step is to provide a proper variable name to each column. The data set we are using in this example is the Stock Price data set. The first column is the date, and the second column to the tenth column hold stock prices for various stocks. The last column is the rating for the volume of transactions for the day (high, low, or medium).

```
> names(mydata)[1:12]<-c("day","Stock1","Stock2","Stock3","Stock4","Stock5","Stock6","Stock$
> names(mydata)[1:12]
 [1] "day"      "Stock1"   "Stock2"   "Stock3"   "Stock4"   "Stock5"   "Stock6"   "Stock7"
 [9] "Stock8"   "Stock9"   "Stock10"  "Ratings"
> str(mydata)
'data.frame':   960 obs. of  12 variables:
 $ day     : int  2 3 4 5 6 7 8 9 10 11 ...
 $ Stock1  : Factor w/ 415 levels ".","17.438","17.891",...: 3 5 7 2 4 6 7 6 10 9 ...
 $ Stock2  : Factor w/ 273 levels ".","19.25","20",..: 206 202 207 187 187 190 196 193 199 1$
 $ Stock3  : Factor w/ 96 levels ".","12.75","12.875",..: 57 59 60 60 56 53 54 52 53 57 ...
 $ Stock4  : Factor w/ 187 levels ".","34.375","34.5",..: 72 71 72 51 55 60 64 66 71 72 ...
 $ Stock5  : Factor w/ 374 levels ".","27.75","28",..: 195 194 200 179 178 186 193 193 194 1$
 $ Stock6  : Factor w/ 154 levels ".","14.125","14.25",..: 91 100 105 89 95 100 106 114 119 $
 $ Stock7  : Factor w/ 204 levels ".","58","58.375",..: 72 75 82 33 57 53 55 53 62 59 ...
 $ Stock8  : Factor w/ 100 levels ".","16.375","16.5",..: 21 14 15 3 7 5 5 7 10 8 ...
 $ Stock9  : num  48.8 49 49.6 47.5 47.8 ...
 $ Stock10 : Factor w/ 204 levels ".","34","34.375",..: 12 17 16 11 3 2 5 6 14 12 ...
 $ Ratings : Factor w/ 3 levels "High","Low","Medium": 2 3 1 2 2 2 3 2 3 3 ...
> |
```

Looking at this output from str(mydata), all the variables (except day and Stock9) are of type factor(). However, they are integers except the Ratings variable. Let's convert the variables to the appropriate data types:

```
>
> dat $Stock1<-as.numeric(as.character(dat$Stock1))
> dat$Stock2<-as.numeric(as.character(dat$Stock2))
> dat$Stock3<-as.numeric(as.character(dat$Stock3))
> dat$Stock4<-as.numeric(as.character(dat$Stock4))
> dat$Stock5<-as.numeric(as.character(dat$Stock5))
> dat$Stock6<-as.numeric(as.character(dat$Stock6))
> dat$Stock7<-as.numeric(as.character(dat$Stock7))
> dat$Stock8<-as.numeric(as.character(dat$Stock8))
> dat$Stock9<-as.numeric(as.character(dat$Stock9))
> dat$Stock10<-as.numeric(as.character(dat$Stock10))
> str(dat)
'data.frame':   960 obs. of  12 variables:
 $ day     : int  2 3 4 5 6 7 8 9 10 11 ...
 $ Stock1  : num  17.9 18.4 18.7 17.4 18.1 ...
 $ Stock2  : num  51.4 50.9 51.5 49 49 ...
 $ Stock3  : num  19.6 19.9 20 20 19.5 ...
 $ Stock4  : num  44 43.9 44 41.4 41.9 ...
 $ Stock5  : num  62 61.9 62.6 59.8 59.6 ...
 $ Stock6  : num  26.1 27.2 27.9 25.9 26.6 ...
 $ Stock7  : num  68.1 68.5 69.4 63.2 66.2 ...
 $ Stock8  : num  19.1 18.2 18.4 16.5 17.1 ...
 $ Stock9  : num  48.8 49 49.6 47.5 47.8 ...
 $ Stock10 : num  35.6 36.4 36.2 35.5 34.4 ...
 $ Ratings : Factor w/ 3 levels "High","Low","Medium": 2 3 1 2 2 2 3 2 3 3 ...
```

Using the as.numeric() function, the variables Stock1, Stock2, Stock3, and so forth, have been converted to the numeric data type. In this case, we have nested as.numeric() with as.character(). If you convert factors to numeric values, R may not give actual values. Hence, first convert the value to a character and then to a numeric. Similarly, other functions are available to identify and perform the task of converting one data type to another type:

```
is.numeric(), is.character(), is.vector(), is.matrix(), is.data.frame()
are used to identify the data type and as.numeric(), as.character(), as.
vector(), as.matrix(), as.data.frame() are used to convert one data type to
the other
```

Finally, let's identify the missing values, junk characters, and null values and then clean the data set.

Using the is.na() function, this table indicates that there are 95 missing values (NA) in the data set. The table() function provides the tabular output by cross-classifying factors to build a contingency table of the counts at each combination of factor levels:

```
> table(is.na(dat))
FALSE   TRUE
11425     95
```

The function complete.cases() returns a logical vector indicating which cases are complete (TRUE or FALSE). The following example shows how to identify NAs (missing values) in the data set by using the complete.cases() function:

```
> complete.cases(dat)
   [1]  TRUE  TRUE  TRUE  TRUE  TRUE  TRUE  TRUE  TRUE  TRUE  TRUE  TRUE  TRUE
  [15]  TRUE  TRUE  TRUE  TRUE  TRUE  TRUE  TRUE  TRUE  TRUE  TRUE  TRUE  TRUE
  [29]  TRUE  TRUE  TRUE  TRUE  TRUE  TRUE  TRUE  TRUE  TRUE  TRUE  TRUE  TRUE
  [43]  TRUE  TRUE  TRUE  TRUE  TRUE  TRUE  TRUE  TRUE  TRUE  TRUE  TRUE  TRUE
  [57]  TRUE  TRUE  TRUE  TRUE  TRUE  TRUE  TRUE  TRUE  TRUE  TRUE  TRUE  TRUE
  [71]  TRUE  TRUE  TRUE  TRUE  TRUE  TRUE  TRUE  TRUE  TRUE  TRUE  TRUE  TRUE
  [85]  TRUE  TRUE  TRUE  TRUE  TRUE  TRUE  TRUE  TRUE  TRUE  TRUE  TRUE

> dat[!complete.cases(dat),]
        day Stock1 Stock2 Stock3 Stock4 Stock5 Stock6 Stock7 Stock8 Stock9 Stock10
950 951 48.125        48.5 19.375 49.625     NA     NA     NA     NA 40.125      NA
951 952     NA     NA     NA     NA     NA     NA     NA     NA 39.875      NA
952 953     NA     NA     NA     NA     NA     NA     NA     NA 39.875      NA
953 954     NA     NA     NA     NA     NA     NA     NA     NA 38.875      NA
954 955     NA     NA     NA     NA     NA     NA     NA     NA 39.625      NA
955 956     NA     NA     NA     NA     NA     NA     NA     NA 39.500      NA
956 957     NA     NA     NA     NA     NA     NA     NA     NA 39.500      NA
957 958     NA     NA     NA     NA     NA     NA     NA     NA 39.625      NA
958 959     NA     NA     NA     NA     NA     NA     NA     NA 39.000      NA
959 960     NA     NA     NA     NA     NA     NA     NA     NA 38.625      NA
960 961     NA     NA     NA     NA     NA     NA     NA     NA 38.750      NA
>
```

The following example shows how to fill NAs (missing values) with the mean value of that particular column. You can adopt any other method discussed in the previous sections. Depending on the type of data set, you can use other methods and write a function to perform the same.

```
> dat$Stock1[is.na(dat$Stock1)]=mean(dat$Stock1,na.rm=TRUE)
> tail(dat)
    day  Stock1 Stock2 Stock3 Stock4 Stock5 Stock6 Stock7 Stock8 Stock9 Stock10 Ratings
955 956 37.95812     NA     NA     NA     NA     NA     NA     NA 39.500     NA  Medium
956 957 37.95812     NA     NA     NA     NA     NA     NA     NA 39.500     NA  Medium
957 958 37.95812     NA     NA     NA     NA     NA     NA     NA 39.625     NA    High
958 959 37.95812     NA     NA     NA     NA     NA     NA     NA 39.000     NA     Low
959 960 37.95812     NA     NA     NA     NA     NA     NA     NA 38.625     NA  Medium
960 961 37.95812     NA     NA     NA     NA     NA     NA     NA 38.750     NA    High
> |
```

You can repeat the same for other variables by using the same method, or use any apply() method discussed in earlier sections.

5.5   Exploring and Visualizing the Data

Once you have a clean data set, the next step is exploratory data analysis. This is the process of exploring your data, understanding the kind of data you have, and examining the structure and components of your data sets. Also, you need to understand the distribution of the individual variables and the relationships between two or more variables. This exploratory analysis relies heavily on representations using graphs and tables. The information conveyed by this visualization analysis is easily understood and can be quickly absorbed. Therefore, exploring data by using data visualization is the most important part of the overall business analytics process.

Figure 5-2 summarizes the data collection and data preprocessing steps described in the previous sections, before this data exploration and data visualization phase.

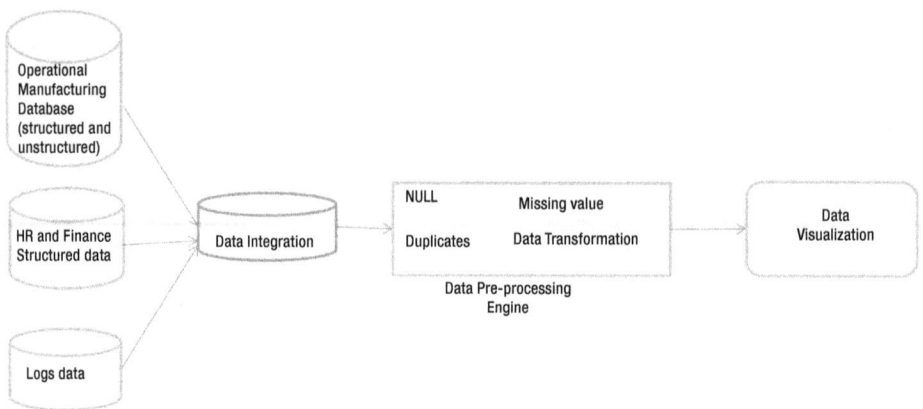

Figure 5-2. *Workflow up to data visualization*

The goal of the exploratory analysis is as follows:

- To determine the distribution and other statistics of the data set
- To determine whether the data set needs normalization

- To determine whether the data set can answer the business problem you are trying to solve
- To come up with a blueprint to solve the business problem

The following sections describe the tables and graphs required for carrying out good data analysis.

5.5.1 Tables

The easiest and most common tool available for looking at data is a table. Tables contain rows and columns. The raw data is displayed as rows of observations and columns of variables. Tables are useful for smaller sets of samples, so it can be difficult to display the whole data set if you have many records. By presenting the data in tables, you can gain insight about the data, including the type of data, variable names, and the way the data is structured. However, it is not possible to identify relationships between variables by looking at tables. In R, we can view data in a table format by using the `View()` command, as shown in Figure 5-3.

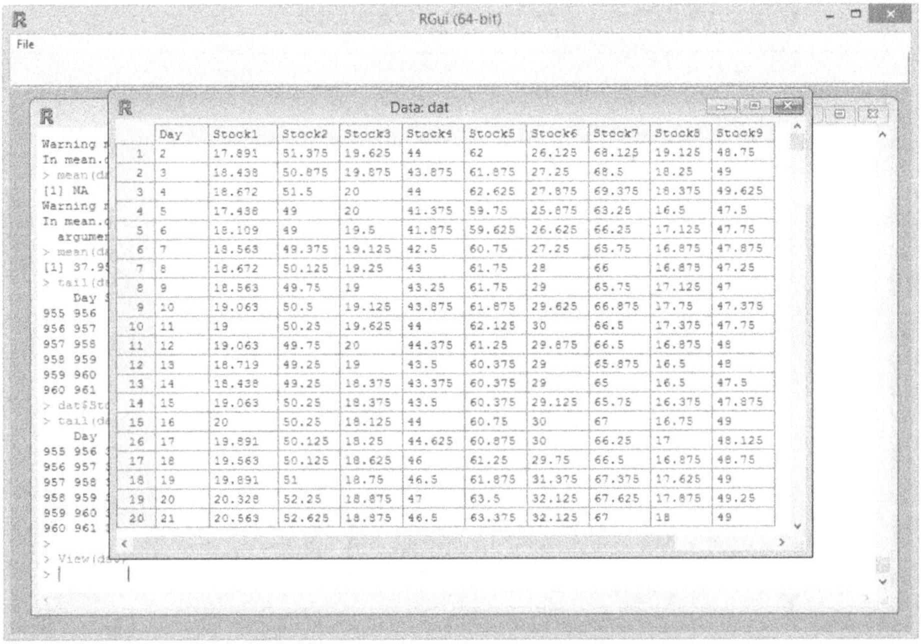

	Day	Stock1	Stock2	Stock3	Stock4	Stock5	Stock6	Stock7	Stock8	Stock9
1	2	17.891	51.375	19.625	44	62	26.125	68.125	19.125	48.75
2	3	18.438	50.875	19.875	43.875	61.875	27.25	68.5	18.25	49
3	4	18.672	51.5	20	44	62.625	27.875	69.375	18.375	49.625
4	5	17.438	49	20	41.375	59.75	25.875	63.25	16.5	47.5
5	6	18.109	49	19.5	41.875	59.625	26.625	66.25	17.125	47.75
6	7	18.563	49.375	19.125	42.5	60.75	27.25	65.75	16.875	47.875
7	8	18.672	50.125	19.25	43	61.75	28	66	16.875	47.25
8	9	18.563	49.75	19	43.25	61.75	29	65.75	17.125	47
9	10	19.063	50.5	19.125	43.875	61.875	29.625	66.875	17.75	47.375
10	11	19	50.25	19.625	44	62.125	30	66.5	17.375	47.75
11	12	19.063	49.75	20	44.375	61.25	29.875	66.5	16.875	48
12	13	18.719	49.25	19	43.5	60.375	29	65.875	16.5	48
13	14	18.438	49.25	18.375	43.375	60.375	29	65	16.5	47.5
14	15	19.063	50.25	18.375	43.5	60.375	29.125	65.75	16.375	47.875
15	16	20	50.25	18.125	44	60.75	30	67	16.75	49
16	17	19.891	50.125	18.25	44.625	60.875	30	66.25	17	48.125
17	18	19.563	50.125	18.625	46	61.25	29.75	66.5	16.875	48.75
18	19	19.891	51	18.75	46.5	61.875	31.375	67.375	17.625	49
19	20	20.328	52.25	18.875	47	63.5	32.125	67.625	17.875	49.25
20	21	20.563	52.625	18.875	46.5	63.375	32.125	67	18	49

Figure 5-3. *Output of View()*

5.5.2   Summary Tables

We already discussed statistics and their significance in Chapter 4. Descriptive statistics provide a common way of understanding data. These statistics can be represented as summary tables. Summary tables show the number of observations in each column and the descriptive statistics for each column. The following statistics are commonly used:

> *Minimum*: The minimum value

> *Maximum*: The maximum value

> *Mean*: The average value

> *Median*: The value at the midpoint

> *Sum*: The sum of all observations in the group

> *Standard deviation*: A standardized measure of the deviation of a variable from the mean

> *First quartile*: Number between the minimum and median value of the data set

> *Third quartile*: Number between the median and the maximum value of the data set

The following output is the descriptive statistics of our Stock Price data set.

```
> summary(dat)
      Day            Stock1           Stock2           Stock3           Stock4           Stock5
 Min.   :   2.0   Min.   :17.44   Min.   :19.25   Min.   :12.75   Min.   :34.38   Min.   :27.75
 1st Qu.:241.8   1st Qu.:27.78   1st Qu.:35.41   1st Qu.:16.12   1st Qu.:41.38   1st Qu.:49.62
 Median :481.5   Median :38.71   Median :49.00   Median :19.38   Median :44.00   Median :61.75
 Mean   :481.5   Mean   :37.96   Mean   :43.95   Mean   :18.71   Mean   :45.36   Mean   :60.86
 3rd Qu.:721.2   3rd Qu.:46.88   3rd Qu.:53.25   3rd Qu.:20.88   3rd Qu.:48.22   3rd Qu.:71.88
 Max.   :961.0   Max.   :61.50   Max.   :60.25   Max.   :25.12   Max.   :60.12   Max.   :94.12
                                 NA's   :10      NA's   :10      NA's   :10      NA's   :11
      Stock6           Stock7           Stock8           Stock9           Stock10          Ratings
 Min.   :14.12   Min.   :58.00   Min.   :31.50   Min.   :31.50   Min.   :34.00   High   :175
 1st Qu.:18.00   1st Qu.:65.62   1st Qu.:21.25   1st Qu.:41.62   1st Qu.:41.38   Low    :436
 Median :25.75   Median :68.62   Median :22.50   Median :44.75   Median :46.75   Medium :349
 Mean   :24.12   Mean   :70.68   Mean   :23.30   Mean   :44.15   Mean   :47.01
 3rd Qu.:28.88   3rd Qu.:76.38   3rd Qu.:26.38   3rd Qu.:47.62   3rd Qu.:52.12
 Max.   :35.25   Max.   :87.25   Max.   :29.25   Max.   :53.00   Max.   :62.00
 NA's   :11      NA's   :11      NA's   :11                      NA's   :11
>
```

Some tools, such as Microsoft Excel PivotTables and Tableau support three-dimensional data analysis. This is beyond the scope of this book.

5.5.3   Graphs

Graphs represent data visually and provide more details about the data, enabling you to identify outliers in the data, distribute data for each column variable, provide a statistical description of the data, and present the relationship between the two or more variables.

Chapter 4 discussed several data visualization graphs used in exploring data. Some types of graphs include bar charts, histograms, box plots, and scatter plots. In addition, looking at the graphs of multiple variables simultaneously can provide more insights into the data.

Univariate analysis analyzes one variable at a time. It is the simplest form of analyzing data. You analyze a single variable, summarize the data, and find the patterns in the data. You can use several visualization graphs to perform univariate data analysis, including bar charts, pie charts, box plots, and histograms. All these plots have already been discussed in the previous chapter.

A *histogram* represents the frequency distribution of the data. Histograms are similar to bar charts but group numbers into ranges. Also, a histogram lets you show the frequency distribution of continuous data. This helps in analyzing the distribution (for example, normal or Gaussian), any outliers present in the data, and skewness. Figure 5-4 describes the first variable of the Stock Price data set in a histogram plot.

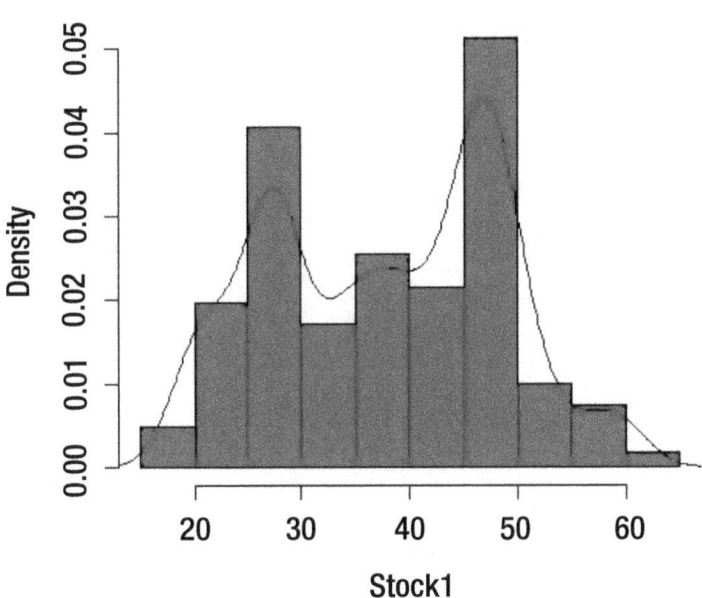

Figure 5-4. *Histogram and density function*

5.5.3.1   Box plots

A box, or whisker plot is also a graphical description of data. Box plots, created by John W. Tukey, show the distribution of a data set based on a five-number summary: minimum, maximum, median, first quartile, and third quartile. Figure 5-5 explains how to interpret a box plot and its components.

The central rectangle spans the first and third quartile (*interquartile* range, or IQR). The line inside the rectangle shows the median. The lines, also called whiskers, that are above and below the rectangle show the maximum and minimum of the data set.

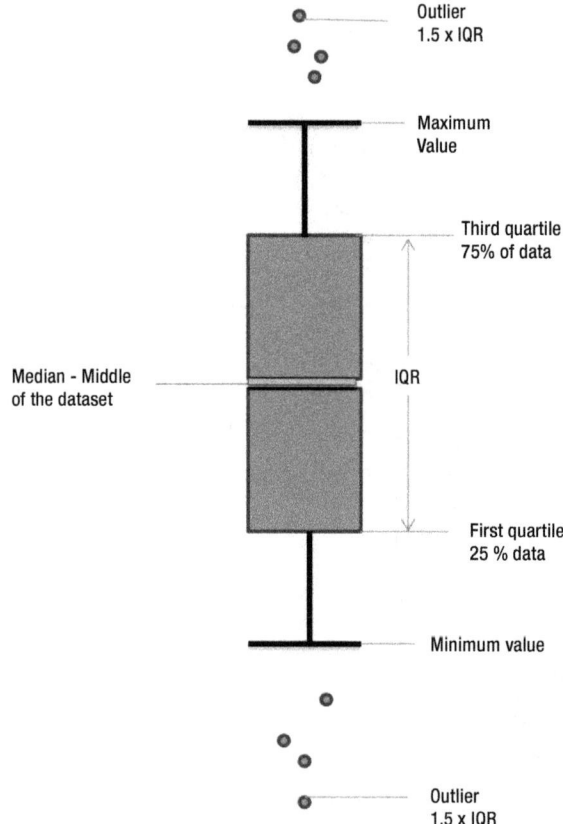

Figure 5-5. *Box plot*

Normal data sets do not have a surprisingly high maximum value or low minimum value. Outliers are generally outside the two whisker lines. Tukey has provided following definitions for outliers:

> *Outliers*—2/3 IQR above the third quartile or 2/3 IQR below the first quartile
>
> *Suspected outliers*—1.5 IQR above the third quartile or 1.5 IQR below the first quartile.

If the data is normally distributed, then

$IQR = 1.35 \, \sigma$, where σ is the population standard deviation

You can plot multiple variables in box plots and compare the data of each variable side by side. Figure 5-6 shows an example.

Box Plot of 4 variables

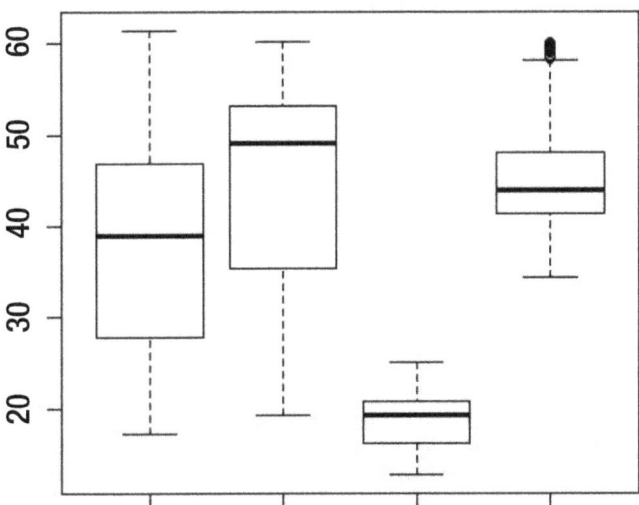

Figure 5-6. *Side-by-side box plot*

Notched plots look like box plots with notches, as shown in Figure 5-7. If two boxes' notches do not overlap, that shows "strong evidence" that their medians differ (Chambers *et al.*, 1983, p. 62).

Notched Plot of 2 variables

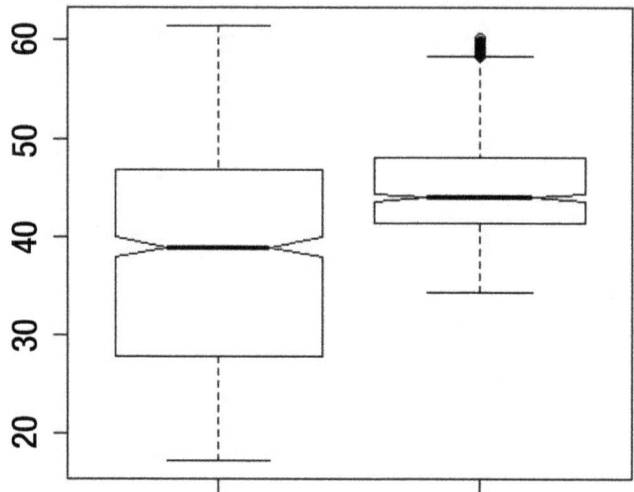

Figure 5-7. *Notched plot*

Bivariate data analysis is used to compare relationships between two variables in the data. The major purpose of bivariate analysis is to explain the correlations of two variables, for comparisons and suspect causal relationships if any contingent on the values of the other variables, and the relationships between independent and dependent variables. If more than one variable is made on each observation, then *multivariate analysis* is applied.

5.5.3.2   Scatter plots

The most common data visualization tool used for bivariate analysis is the *scatter plot*. Scatter plots can be used to identify the relationships between two continuous variables. Each data point on a scatter plot is a single observation. All the observations can be plotted on a single chart.

Figure 5-8 shows a scatter plot of the number of employees vs. revenue (in millions of dollars) of various companies. As you can see, there is a strong relationship between the two variables that is almost linear. However, you cannot draw any causal implications without further statistical analysis.

Scatterplot

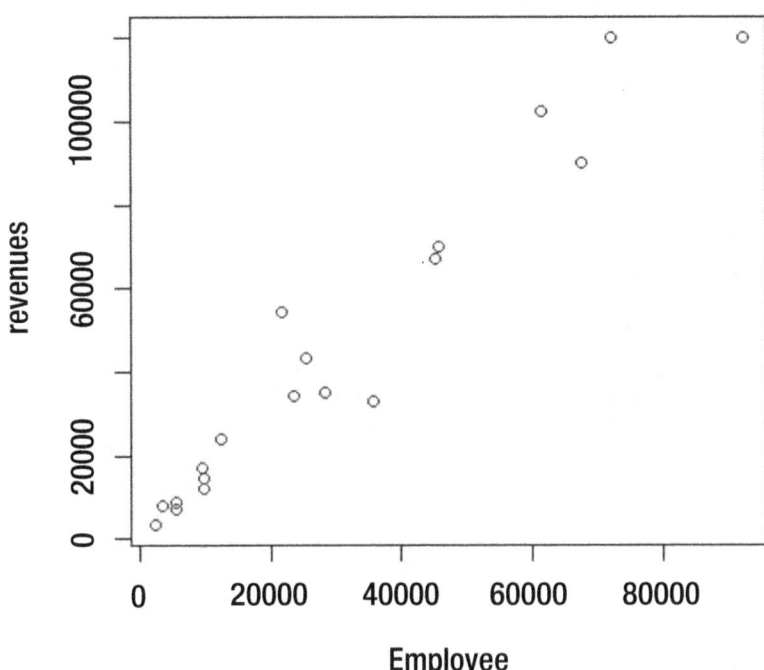

Figure 5-8. *A scatter plot of the number of employees vs. revenue (in millions of dollars)*

Unfortunately, scatter plots are not always useful for finding patterns or relationships. If there are too many data points, the scatter plot does not give much information. For example, Figure 5-9 does not indicate whether any correlation exists between casual bike users and registered bike users.

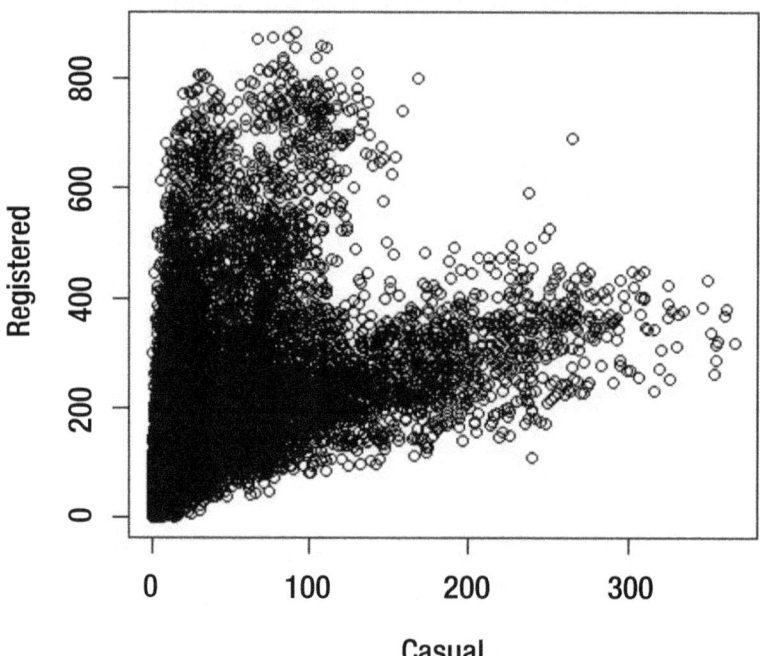

Figure 5-9. *Registered users vs. casual users*

5.5.4   Scatter Plot Matrices

A scatter plot matrix graph plots pairwise scatter plots to look for patterns and relationships in the data set. A scatter plot matrix graph takes two variables pairwise and selects all the variables in the data set plots as a single graph so that you can get a complete picture of your data set and understand the patterns and relationships between pairs of variables. The pairs() command in R should plot a scatter matrix graph.

You can read the data from the file by using the read.table() function first and then use the pairs() function to plot the graph:

```
> hou<-read.table(header=TRUE,sep="\t","housing.data")
```

```
> str(hou)
'data.frame':   506 obs. of  14 variables:
 $ CRIM    : num   18 0.0273 0.0273 0.0324 0.069 ...
 $ ZN      : num   2.31 0 0 0 0 0 12.5 12.5 12.5 12.5 ...
 $ INDUS   : num   0 7.07 7.07 2.18 2.18 2.18 7.87 7.87 7.87 7.87 ...
 $ CHAS    : num   0.538 0 0 0 0 0 0 0 0 ...
 $ NOX     : num   6.575 0.469 0.469 0.458 0.458 ...
 $ RM      : num   65.2 6.42 7.18 7 7.15 ...
 $ AGE     : num   4.09 78.9 61.1 45.8 54.2 58.7 66.6 96.1 100 85.9 ...
 $ DIS     : num   1 4.97 4.97 6.06 6.06 ...
 $ RAD     : int   296 2 2 3 3 3 5 5 5 5 ...
 $ TAX     : num   15.3 242 242 222 222 222 311 311 311 311 ...
 $ PTRATIO : num   396.9 17.8 17.8 18.7 18.7 ...
 $ B       : num   4.98 396.9 392.83 394.63 396.9 ...
 $ LSTAT   : num   24 9.14 4.03 2.94 5.33 ...
 $ MEDV    : num   NA 21.6 34.7 33.4 36.2 28.7 22.9 27.1 16.5 18.9 ...
> pairs(hou)
> |
```

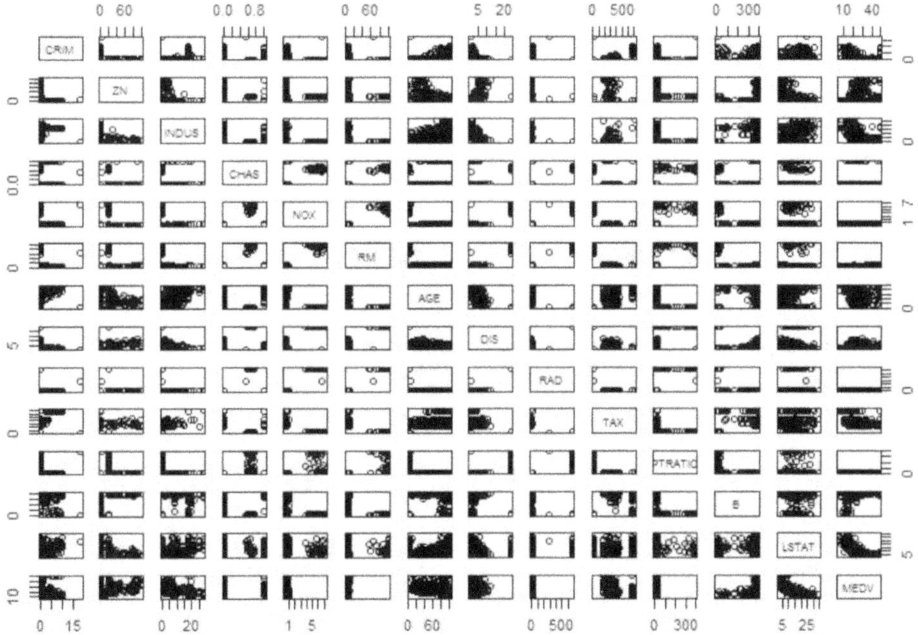

Figure 5-10. *Scatter plot matrix plot*

In this example, the variables are on the diagonal, from top left to bottom right (see Figure 5-10). Each variable is plotted against the other variables. For example, the plot that is to the right of CRM and above ZN represents a plot of ZN on the x axis and CRM on the y axis. Similarly, the plot of Age vs. CRM, plotting Age on the x axis and CRM on the y axis, would be the sixth plot down from CRM and the sixth plot to the left of AGE. In this particular example, we do not see any strong relationships between any two pairs of variables.

5.5.4.1   Trellis Plot

Trellis graphics is a framework for data visualization that lets you examine multiple variable relationships. The following example shows the relationships of variables in the Boston Housing data set. A trellis graph can be produced by any type of graph component such as a histogram or a bar chart. A trellis graph is based on partitioning one or more variables and analyzing that with the others. For categorical variables, a plot is based on different levels of that variable, whereas for numerical values, the data subset is based on the intervals of that variable.

In the Boston Housing data set, the value of a house is analyzed based on its age as a subset of tax. A similar analysis can be performed for other variables. The problem with a simple scatter plot is overplotting, which makes it hard to interpret the structures in the data. A trellis plot creates different depths and intervals to make the interpretation clearer. In this example, the trellis creates the MEDV tax in different intervals: The MEDV value increases from left to right, and as you can see in Figure 5-11, higher taxes are concentrated in lower age groups, and vice versa.

```
>
> library(lattice)
> tax<-cut(houl$TAX,4)
> xyplot(MEDV~AGE|tax,data=houl)
> |
```

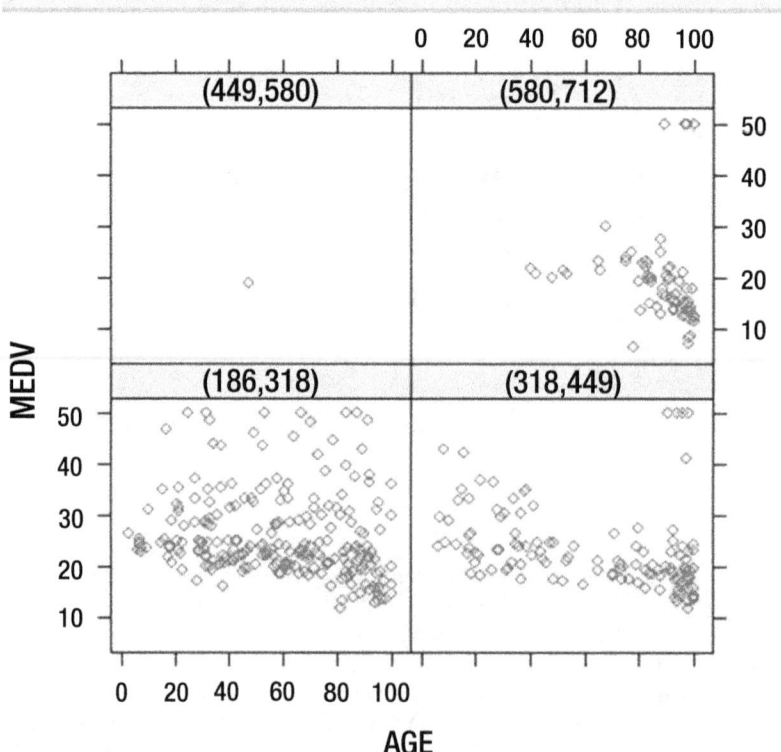

Figure 5-11. *Trellis graph*

5.5.4.2   Correlation plot

Correlation between the two variables can be calculated and plotted by using a *correlation graph*, as shown in Figure 5-12. The pairwise correlation can be plotted in a correlation matrix plot to describe the correlation of two variables:

```
> corrplot(corel,method="circle")
> corel<-cor(stk1[,2:9])
> corrplot(corel,method="circle")
> corel
             Stock1        Stock2        Stock3        Stock4        Stock5        Stock6
Stock1    1.0000000   -0.7405013   -0.6941962    0.22404314   -0.67743812   -0.6892628
Stock2   -0.7405013    1.0000000    0.7277338    0.11507052    0.82781584    0.6658645
Stock3   -0.6941962    0.7277338    1.0000000    0.10310911    0.64034833    0.7547712
Stock4    0.2240431    0.1150705    0.1031091    1.00000000   -0.09176582    0.2933464
Stock5   -0.6774381    0.8278158    0.6403483   -0.09176582    1.00000000    0.5194183
Stock6   -0.6892628    0.6658645    0.7547712    0.29334636    0.51941831    1.0000000
Stock7    0.1594195    0.1696410    0.1770890    0.88253734    0.04719424    0.2942828
Stock8    0.8782477   -0.6385160   -0.4482796    0.47754204   -0.58786308   -0.4267471
             Stock7        Stock8
Stock1   0.15941951    0.8782477
Stock2   0.16964101   -0.6385160
Stock3   0.17708898   -0.4482796
Stock4   0.88253734    0.4775420
Stock5   0.04719424   -0.5878631
Stock6   0.29428277   -0.4267471
Stock7   1.00000000    0.4389946
Stock8   0.43899462    1.0000000
>
```

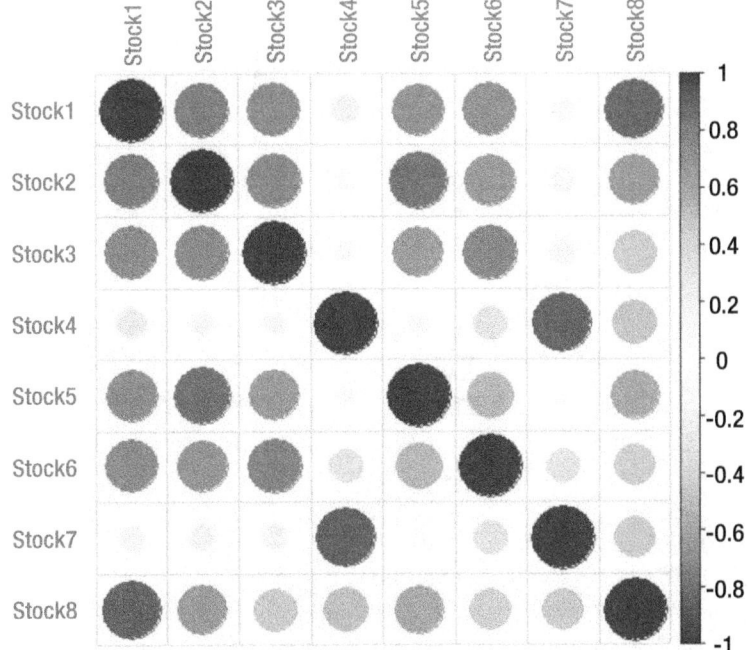

Figure 5-12. *Correlation plot*

In this example, a blue dot represents a positive correlation, and red represents a negative correlation. The larger the dot, the stronger the correlation. The diagonal dots (from top left to bottom right) are perfectly positively correlated, because each dot represents the correlation of each attribute with itself.

5.5.4.3 Density by Class

A density function of each variable can be plotted as a function of the class. Similar to scatter plot matrices, a density plot can help illustrate the separation by class and show how closely they overlap each other.

```
>
> library(caret)
> x<-stk1[,4:9]
> y<-stk1[,12]
> featurePlot(x=x,y=y,plot="density")
>
```

In this example of the Stock Price data set shown in Figure 5-13, some stock prices overlap very closely and are hard to separate.

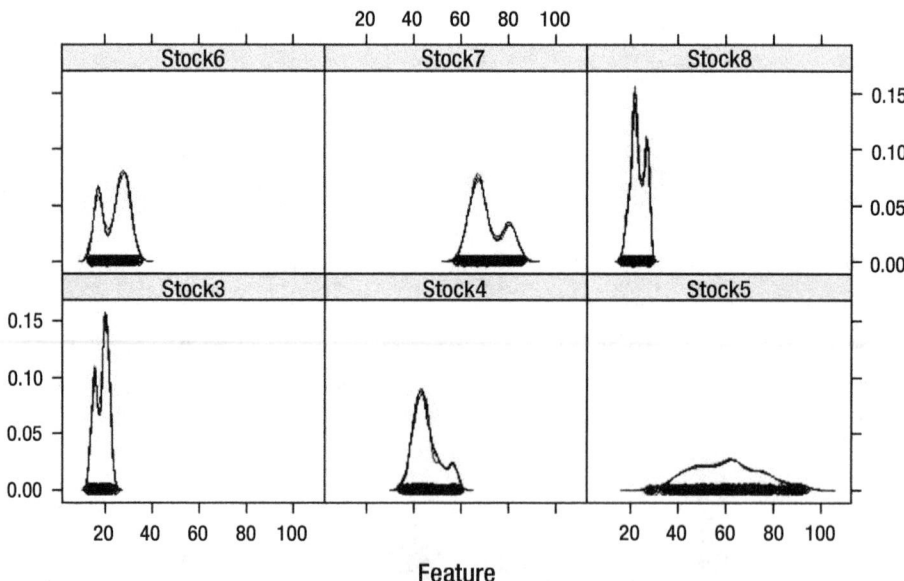

Figure 5-13. *Density plot*

The preceding data visualization methods are some of the most commonly used. Depending on the business problem and the data you are analyzing, you can select a method. No single technique is considered the standard.

5.5.5 Data Transformation

After a preliminary analysis of data, sometimes you may realize that the raw data you have may not provide good results, or doesn't seem to make any sense. For example, data may be skewed, data may not be normally distributed, or measurement scales may be different for different variables. In such cases, data may require transformation. Common transformation techniques include normalization, data aggregation, and smoothing. After the transformation, before presenting the analysis results, the inverse transformation should be applied.

5.5.5.1 Normalization

Certain techniques such as regression assume that the data is normally distributed and that all the variables should be treated equally. Sometimes the data we collect for various predictor variables may differ in their measurement units, which may have an impact on the overall equation. This may cause one variable to have more influence over another variable. In such cases, all the predictor variable data is normalized to one single scale. Some common normalization techniques include the following:

> *Z-score normalization (zero-mean normalization)*: The new value is created based on the mean and standard deviations. The new value A' for a record value A is normalized by computing the following:
>
> $A' = (A - mean_A) / SD_A$
>
> where $mean_A$ is the mean, and SD_A is the standard deviation of attribute A
>
> This type of transformation is useful when we do not know the minimum and maximum value of an attribute or when there is an outlier dominating the results.
>
> *Min-max normalization*: In this transformation, values are transformed within the range of values specified. Min-max normalization performs linear transformations on the original data set. The formula is as follows:
>
> New value $A' = ((A - Min_A) / (Max_A - Min_A))(Range of A') + Min_{A'}$
>
> Range of $A' = Max_{A'} - Min_{A'}$
>
> Min-max transformation maps the value to a new range of values defined by the range $[Max_{A'} - Min_{A'}]$. For example, for the new set of values to be in the range of 0 and 1, the new Max = 1 and the new Min = 0; the old value is 50, with a min value of 12 and a max of 58, then

$A' = ((50 - 12) / (58 - 12))*1 + 0 = 0.82$

Data aggregation: Sometimes a new variable may be required to better understand the data. You can apply mathematical functions such as sum or average to one or more variables to create a new set of variables.

Sometimes, in order to confirm to the normal distribution, it may be necessary to use $\log()$ or exponential functions or use a Box-Cox transformation. The formula for a Box-Cox transformation is as follows:

$A' = (A' - 1) / \lambda$

where λ is a value greater than 1

5.6 Using Modeling Techniques and Algorithms

At this point, you have the data ready to perform further analysis. Based on the business problem you are trying to solve, an appropriate method is selected. Analytics is about explaining the past and predicting the future. It combines knowledge of statistics, machine learning, databases, and artificial intelligence.

5.6.1 Descriptive Analytics

Descriptive analytics explains the patterns hidden in data. These patterns could be the number of market segments, or sales numbers based on regions, or groups of products based on reviews, software bug patterns in a defect database, behavioral patterns in an online gaming user database, and more. These patterns are purely based on historical data. You also can group observations into the same clusters, and this analysis is called *clustering analysis*.

Similarly, *association rules* or *affinity analysis* can be used on a transactional database to find the associations among items purchased in department stores. This analysis is performed based on past data available in the database, to look for associations among various items purchased by customers. This helps businesses extend discounts, launch new products, and manage inventory effectively.

5.6.2 Predictive Analytics

Prediction consists of two methods: classification and regression analysis.

Classification is a basic form of data analysis in which data is classified into classes. For example, a credit card can be approved or denied, flights at a particular airport are on time or delayed, and a potential employee will be hired or not. The class prediction is based on previous behaviors or patterns found in the data. The task of the classification model is to determine the class of data from a new set of data that was not seen before.

Regression is predicting the value of a numerical variable—for example, company revenue numbers or sales numbers. Most books refer to prediction as the prediction of a value of a continuous variable. However, classification can also be considered for prediction, as the classification model predicts the class of new data that is of an unknown class label. One of the techniques used for this is *Logistic Regression*.

5.6.3   Machine Learning

Machine learning is about making computers learn and perform tasks better based on past historical data. Learning is always based on observations from the data available. The emphasis is on making computers build mathematical models based on that learning and perform tasks automatically without the intervention of humans. The system cannot always predict with 100 percent accuracy, because the learning is based on past data that's available, and there is always a possibility of new data arising that was never learned earlier by the machine. Machines build models based on iterative learning to find hidden insights. Because there is always a possibility of new data, this iteration is important because the machines can independently adapt to new changes. Machine learning has been around for a long time, but recent developments in computing, storage, and programming; new complex algorithms; and big data architectures such as Hadoop, have helped it gain momentum. There are two types of machine learning: supervised machine learning and unsupervised machine learning.

5.6.3.1   Supervised Machine Learning

As the name suggests, in supervised machine learning, a machine builds a predictive model under supervision—that is, with the help of a training data set. The training data set is prepared under supervision that's similar to a teacher guiding students. The model is based on an iterative process, and the learning stops when the algorithm achieves an acceptable level of performance. Classification and regression can be grouped under supervised machine learning.

In a *classification* problem, the output variable is typically a category such as Yes or No, or Fraudulent or Not Fraudulent. In a *regression* problem, the output variable is a real value, such as Revenues or Volumes.

Figure 5-14 shows how supervised machine learning works.

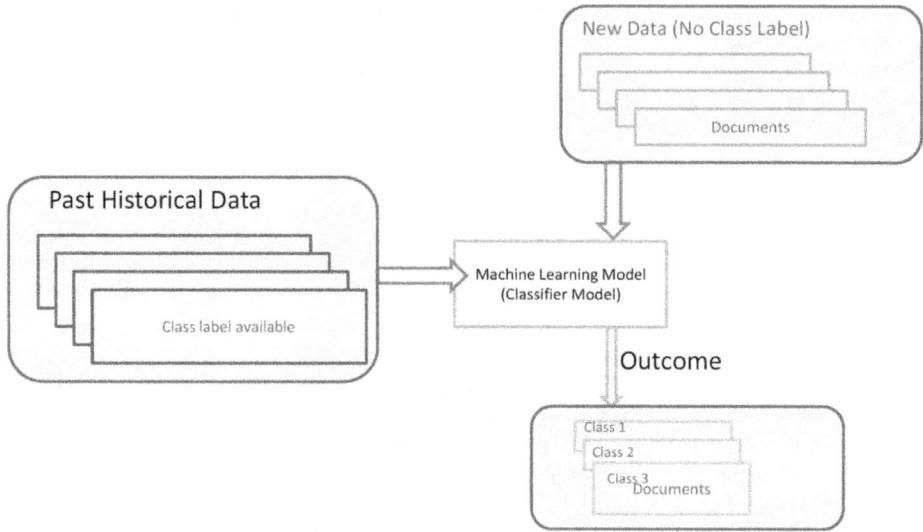

Figure 5-14. *Supervised machine learning*

In this example, the classifier model is developed based on the training data set. This data set has a set of documents (data) that are already categorized and labeled into different classes, manually and under expert supervision. This is called the *training data set*. The classification algorithm (model) learns based on this training data set, which already has class labels. Once the learning is complete, the model is ready for the classification of documents (new data) whose labels are unknown. Common classification supervised-learning algorithms include support vector machines, naïve Bayes, k-nearest neighbor, and decision trees.

5.6.3.2   Unsupervised Machine Learning

In unsupervised machine learning, there is no training data to learn. Hence, there is no target variable to predict. Association rules and clustering are examples of unsupervised learning. In unsupervised learning, all data set observations are put into the learning, and the outcome could be different clusters or associations between two variables. Because there is no outcome class to identify by itself, further analysis is required to properly understand the results of the model.

Figure 5-15 shows the output of an unsupervised machine-learning algorithm. Two clusters are formed based on the words that are similar in the data set. These similarities may be based on meaning or other measures. Hence, further analysis could lead to labeling of the clusters, for example, as +ve words and –ve words.

Unsupervised Learning

A clustering algorithm partitions the adjectives into two subsets

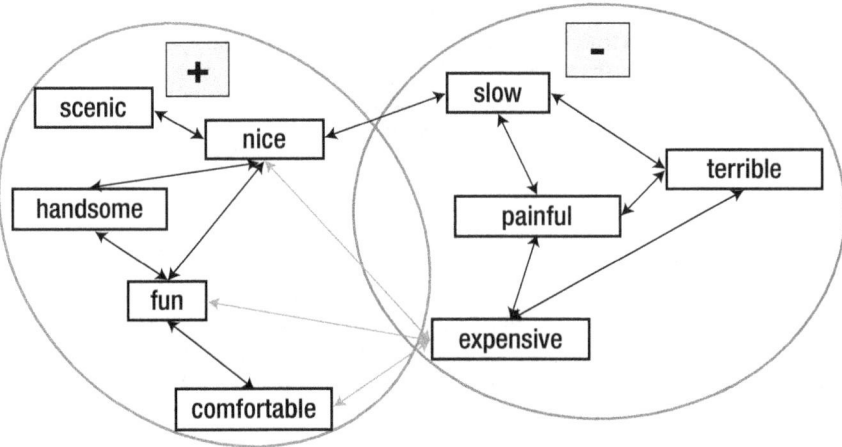

Figure 5-15. *Unsupervised machine learning*

You can solve a business problem by using the available data either via simple analytics such as data visualization or advance techniques such as predictive analytics. The business problem can be solved via supervised machine learning or unsupervised machine learning. It can be a classification problem or a regression problem. Depending on the business problem you are trying to solve, different methods are selected and different algorithms are used to solve the problem. The next chapters discuss various classification, regression, clustering, and association techniques in detail.

The techniques and algorithms used are based on the nature of the data available. Table 5-1 summarizes the variable type and important algorithms that can be used to solve a business problem.

Table 5-1. *Business Analytics Methods Based on Data Types*

	Response Variable Continuous	Response Variable Categorical	No Response Variable
Predictor Variable— Continuous	Linear regression Neural Network K-nearest Neighbor (KNN)	Logistic regression KNN Neural network	Cluster analysis Principal component Analysis
Predictor Variable— Categorical	Linear regression Neural network	Decision/ classification trees Logistic regression Naïve Bayes	Association rule

121

5.7   Evaluating the Model

Evaluating model performance is a key aspect to understanding how good your prediction is when you apply new data. Because many algorithms are used to build a model, you can compare the performance for each algorithm and decide which model should be deployed based on that performance. However, when you use the same set of data to develop a model and assess its performance, you may introduce bias. To address this problem, data is divided into partitions. One partition is used to build the model, and the other partition is used to assess the model. Typically, the data set is divided into three partitions: a training set, a test set, and sometimes an additional validation set.

5.7.1   Training Data Partition

The *training data partition* is used to train the model. The outcome variable details are already known. For a classification problem, the class of the outcome variable is already determined and sometimes created manually with human intervention. For example, let's say we are trying to predict the sentiment of a movie based on a Twitter database. The initial training data set is created manually by labeling each tweet as part of the positive sentiment class or negative sentiment class. The more data in the training set, the better the performance of the model.

5.7.2   Test Data Partition

The *test data partition* is a subset of the data set that is not in the training set. It is used to assess the performance of the model for new data. This partition is sometimes called a *holdout* partition. The model should perform well for both the training set data and test data.

5.7.3   Validation Data Partition

The *validation data partition* is used to fine-tune the model performance and reduce overfitting problems. This partition can be used to assess multiple models and select the best model. This data set is not used to build the model. So the model has never seen this data set before. This helps fine-tune the model performance and reduce overfitting.

For example, let's say you have a total of 1,000 records, and out of these you could use 800 for training the model and the remaining 200 for testing.

The performance of the model depends on the training set (apart from other parameters such as predictor variables, hidden parameters, and algorithms used). The more training data, the better the learning and performance. When a model is deployed with the new unseen data, the model performs poorly because some data is not present in the training set. Hence, before deploying the model to the field, the performance is measured in multiple test partitions, which gives an opportunity to improve the model performance and also avoid overfitting problems. The more we test, the more likely we eliminate noise in the data set and improve performance.

5.7.4   Cross-Validation

To avoid any bias, the data set is partitioned randomly. When you have a limited amount of data, to achieve an unbiased performance estimate, you can use k-fold cross-validation. In *k-fold cross validation*, you divide the data into *k* folds and build the model using *k* – 1 folds, and the last fold is used for testing. You can repeat this process *k* times; every time the test sample is different, each time "leaving out" one subset from the training and using it as test set. If *k* equals the sample size, this is referred as a *leave-one-out* cross-validation method.

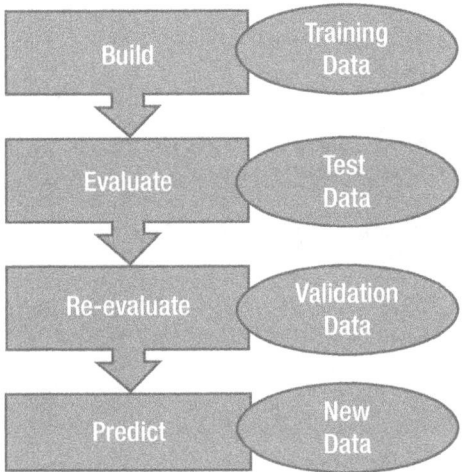

Figure 5-16. *Data partition representation model*

Classification and regression are the two types of predictive models, and each has a different set of criteria for evaluation. Let's briefly look at the various criteria for each model. Details are discussed in subsequent chapters.

5.7.5   Classification Model Evaluation
5.7.5.1   Confusion Matrix

The simplest way of measuring the performance of a classifier is by judging the number of mistakes. We call this a *misclassification error*: the observation belongs to one class, but the model classifies it as a different class. A perfect classifier is one that predicts the class with no errors. In the real world, such classifiers are not able to construct due to "noise" and not having all the information needed to precisely classify the observations.

A classification matrix, referred to as a *confusion matrix*, gives an estimate of the true classification and misclassification rates. A confusion matrix shows the number of correct and incorrect classifications made by the model. Table 5-2 shows simple 2 × 2 confusion matrix for two classes (positive and negative). Some of the common measures include the following:

Accuracy: This is a ratio indicating the number of predictions that were correct.

Precision: The ratio of positive cases that were correctly identified.

Recall (*sensitivity*): The ratio of actual positive cases that are identified correctly.

Table 5-2. *Confusion Matrix*

		Predicted Class		
		Positive (C_0)	Negative (C_1)	
Actual Class	Positive (C_0)	a = number of correctly classified C_0 cases	c = number of C_0 cases incorrectly classified as C_1	Precision = a/(a+c)
	Negative (C_1)	b = number of C_1 cases incorrectly classified as C_0	d = number of correctly classified C_1 cases	
		Sensitivity (Recall) = a/(a+b)	Specificity = d/(c+d)	Accuracy = (a+b)/(a+b+c+d)

Specificity: The ratio of actual negative cases that are identified correctly.

Table 5-3 shows an example confusion matrix.

Table 5-3. *Example of Classification Accuracy Measurement*

		Predicted Class		
		Positive (C_0)	Negative (C_1)	
Actual Class	Positive (C_0)	80	30	Precision = 80/110 = 0.63
	Negative (C_1)	40	90	
		Recall = 80/120 = 0.67	Specificity = 90/120 = 0.75	Accuracy = 80+90/240 = 0.71

5.7.5.2   Lift Chart

Lift charts are commonly used for marketing problems. For example, say you want to determine an effective marketing campaign on the Internet. You have a set of cases where the "probability of responding" to an online ad click is assigned. The lift curve helps determine how effectively the online advertisement campaign can be done by selecting arelatively small group and getting maximum responders. The lift , is a measure of the effectiveness of the model by calculating ratios with or with out the model.
A confusion matrix evaluates the effectiveness of the model as a whole population, whereas the lift chart evaluates a portion of the population.

The graph is constructed with the number of cases on the x axis and the cumulative true-positive cases on the y axis. True positives are those observations that are classified correctly. Table 5-4 shows the true cases actually predicted correctly (true positives) in the first column, second column represents the cumulative average of the true positive class and the third column represents the cumulative average prediction of class.

Table 5-4. *Sample data for Lift chart*

Actual Class	Cumulative of True Positive Class	Cumulative Average of Class
0	0	0.5
1	1	1
1	2	1.5
1	3	2
1	4	2.5
0	4	3
1	5	3.5
1	5	4
1	6	4.5
1	7	5
1	8	5.5
0	8	6
0	8	6.5
1	9	7
1	10	7.5
0	10	8
0	10	8.5
0	10	9
0	10	9.5
0	10	10
0	10	10.5

Lift chart measures the effectiveness of a classification model by comparing the true positives without a model. Also, it provides an indication of how well the model performs if you select the samples randomly from a population. For example, in Figure 5-17, if we select 10 cases randomly, our model has performed with an accuracy of 65% whereas without the model, it would have been just 45%. With the lift chart, you can compare how well different models are performing for a set of random cases.

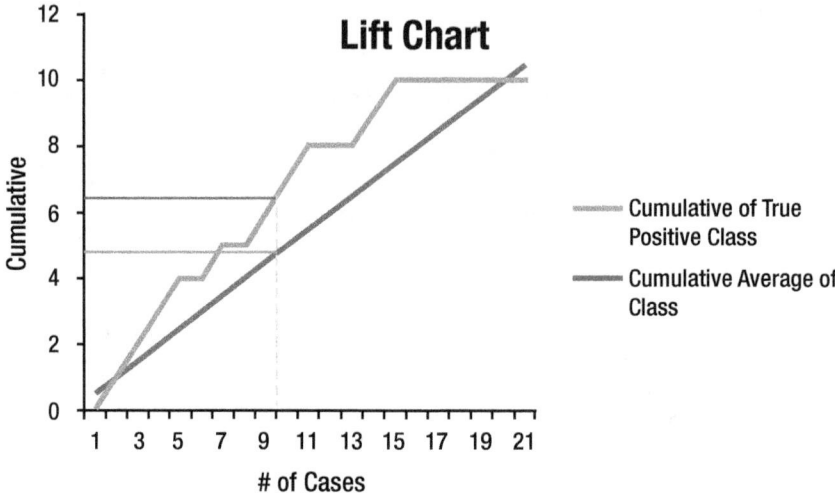

Figure 5-17. Lift chart

The lift will vary with the number of cases we choose. The red line is a reference line. If we have to predict positive cases in case there was no model, then this line provides a benchmark.

5.7.5.3   ROC Chart

A receiver operating characteristic (ROC) chart is similar to a lift chart. It is a plot of the true-positive rate on the y axis and the false-positive rate on the x axis.

ROC graphs are another way of representing the performance of a classifier. In recent years, ROC has become a common method in the machine-learning community due to the fact that simple classification accuracy is not a good measure for performance of a classifier (Provost and Fawcett, 1997; Provost et al., 1998). ROC is plotted as a function of true positive rate (sensitivity) vs. function of false positive rate (specificity) as shown in Figure 5-18.

For a good classifier model, sensitivity rate should be higher and false positive rate should be lower as shown in Figure 5-18. Instead of just looking at the confusion matrix, the Area Under Curve (AUC) for a ROC curve provides a simple pictorial representation of the classifier performance. In the example, we have plotted ROC for three different models and the AUC for the first line (green) is highest. For each classifier, ROC curve is fitted and the results are compared with each of the classifier models over its entire operating range. An AUC less than 0.5 might indicate that the model is not performing well and needs attention. Normally, AUC should fall between 0.5 and 1.0. When separation of the two classes is so perfect and has no overlapping of the distributions, the area under the ROC curve reaches to 1 and ideally that is the goal for any machine learning model.

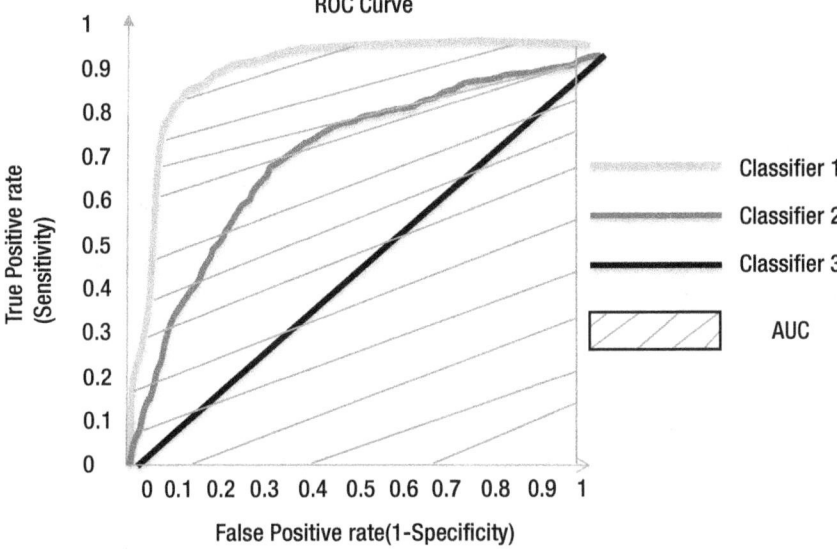

Figure 5-18. *ROC chart*

Research indicates that algorithms that have two classes are most suited for the ROC approach. A neural network is an example of an appropriate classifier, whereas decision-tree classifiers are less suited.

5.7.6   Regression Model Evaluation

A *regression model* has many criteria for measuring its performance. The following are some of the evaluation methods for regression.

5.7.6.1   Root-Mean-Square Error

A regression line predicts the y values for a given x value. Note that the values are around the average. The prediction error (called the *root-mean-square error*, or *RSME*) is given by the following formula:

$$\mathrm{RMSE} = \sqrt{\frac{\sum_{k=0}^{n}(\hat{y}_k - y_k)^2}{n}}$$

5.8 Presenting a Management Report and Review

In this phase, your mathematical model is presented to the business leaders in business terms. It is important to align your model's mathematical output with business objectives and be able to communicate to management and business leaders. Once management is satisfied with the results and model, the model is ready for deployment. If there are any changes to be made, the whole cycle is repeated.

Typically, the following points are addressed during the presentation of the model and its use in solving the business problems.

5.8.1 Problem Description

First, you specify the problem defined by the business and solved by the model. This is important, as it connects the management of the organization back to the objective of the data analysis. In this step, you are revalidating the precise problem intended to be solved.

5.8.2 Data Set Used

Here you specify the data you have used— including the period of the data, source of data, and features/fields of the data used. This important step reconfirms to management that the right data has been used. You also emphasize the assumptions made.

5.8.3 Data Cleaning Carried Out

Here you specify the issues encountered in the data. You note which nonreliable data had to be removed and which had to be substituted. The rationale for such decisions is presented along with the possible downsides, if any.

5.8.4 Method Used to Create the Model

Here you present the method, technique, or algorithm used to create the model and present your reasoning for this choice. Your aim is to convince management that the approach is moving the business in the right direction to solve the problem. Also, you present how the model solves the problem. This includes how the model was evaluated and optimized.

5.8.5 Model Deployment Prerequisites

Here you present the prerequisites for model deployment, including the data requirements and preprocessing requirements. You also present the model deployment hardware and software requirements.

5.8.6   Model Deployment and Usage

Here you present how the model will be deployed for use and how it will be used by end users. You can provide reports and their interpretation, to specify the dos and don'ts related to the model's use. You also emphasize the importance of not losing sight of the problem you are supposed to be solving by using the model.

5.8.7   Issues Handling

Here you present the ideal process for recording the issues observed and the ways they will be reported, analyzed, and addressed. You also emphasize how this step may lead to the optimization of the model over a period of time, as these may indicate the changes happening to the basic assumptions and structure.

5.9   Deploying the Model

This is a challenging phase of the project. The model is now deployed for end users and is in a production environment analyzing the live data. Depending on the deployment scenario and business objective, the model can perform predictive analytics or simple reporting. The model also can behave differently in the production environment, as it may see a totally different set of data from the actual model. In such scenarios, the model is revisited for improvements.

Success of the deployment depends on the following:

- Proper sizing of the hardware, ensuring required performance

- Proper programming to handle the capabilities of the hardware

- Proper data integration and cleaning

- Effective reports, dashboards, views, decisions, and interventions to be used by end users or end-user systems

- Effective training to the users of the model

The following are the typical issues observed during the deployment:

- Hardware capability (for example, memory or CPUs) is not in tune with the requirements of data crunching, or with effective and efficient model usage (for example, the data takes more time to crunch than the time window available or takes so much time that the opportunity for using the generated analysis is reduced). This may also impede the use of real-time data and real-time decision making.

- Programs used are not effective in using the parallelism and hence reduce the possibility of effectively using the results

- Data integration from multiple sources in multiple formats including real-time data

- Data sanitization or cleaning before use

- Not recognizing the changes in data patterns, nullifying or reducing the model's usability or resulting in making wrong decisions

- Not having standby mechanisms (redundancy) to the hardware or network, and not having backup or replication for the data

- Changes to the data sources or data schema, leading to issues with usability of the model

- Lack of effective user training, leading them to use the model in a defective or wrong way, resulting in wrong decisions

- Wrong setups of the systems by the administrators, leading to suboptimal or inefficient use of system resources

5.10   Summary

The chapter focused on the processes involved in business analytics, including identifying and defining a business problem, data preparation, data collection, data modeling, evaluating model performance, and reporting to management on the findings.

You learned about various methods involved in data cleaning, including normalization, transformation of variables, handling missing values, and finding outliers. You also delved into data exploration, which is the most important process in business analytics. You saw various tables, charts, and plots which are used in these regards.

Further, you explored supervised machine learning, unsupervised machine learning, and how to choose different methods based on business requirements. You learned how to partition the data set into a training set, test set, and validation set and saw why each set is important. Finally, you learned about various metrics to measure the performance of different models including predictive models.

CHAPTER 6

Supervised Machine Learning—Classification

Classification and prediction are two important methods of data analysis used to find patterns in data. *Classification* predicts the categorical class (or discrete values), whereas *regression* and other models predict continuous valued functions. However, Logistic Regression addresses categorical class also. For example, a classification model may be built to predict the results of a credit-card application approval process (credit card approved or denied) or to determine the outcome of an insurance claim. Many classification algorithms have been developed by researchers and machine-learning experts. Most classification algorithms are memory intensive. Recent research has developed parallel and distributed processing architecture, such as Hadoop, which is capable of handling large amounts of data.

This chapter focuses on basic classification techniques. It explains some classification methods including naïve Bayes, decision trees, and other algorithms. It also provides examples using R packages available to perform the classification tasks.

6.1 What Is Classification? What Is Prediction?

Imagine that you are applying for a mortgage. You fill out a long application form with all your personal details, including income, age, qualification, location of the house, valuation of the house, and more. You are anxiously waiting for the bank's decision on whether your loan application has been approved. The decision is either Yes or No. How does the bank decide? The bank reviews various parameters provided in your application form, and then—based on similar applications received previously and the experience the bank has had with those customers—the bank decides whether the loan should be approved or denied.

Now imagine that you have to make a decision about launching a new product in the market. You have to make a decision of Launch or No Launch. This depends on various parameters. Your decision will be based on similar experiences you had in the past launching products, based on numerous market parameters.

Next, imagine that you want to predict the opinions expressed by your customers on the products and services your business offers. Those opinions can be either positive or negative and can be predicted based on numerous parameters and past experiences of your customers with similar products and services.

© Dr. Umesh R. Hodeghatta and Umesha Nayak 2017
U. R. Hodeghatta and U. Nayak, *Business Analytics Using R - A Practical Approach*,
DOI 10.1007/978-1-4842-2514-1_6

Finally, imagine that airport authorities have to decide, based on a set of parameters, whether a particular flight of a particular airline at a particular gate is on time or delayed. This decision is based on previous flight details and many other parameters.

Classification is a two-step process. In the first step, a model is constructed by analyzing the database and the set of attributes that define the *class* variable. A classification problem is a supervised machine-learning problem. The training data is a sample from the database, and the class attribute is already known. In a classification problem, the class of Y, a categorical variable, is determined by a set of input variables {x1, x2, x3, ...}. In classification, the variable we would like to predict is typically called class variable C, and it may have different values in the set {c1, c2, c3, ...}. The observed or measured variables X1, X2, ... Xn are the attributes, or input variables, also called explanatory variables. In classification, we want to determine the relationship between the Class variable and the inputs, or explanatory variables. Typically, models represent the classification rules or mathematical formulas. Once these rules are created by the learning model, this model can be used to predict the class of future data for which the class is unknown.

There are various types of classifier models: based on a decision boundary, based on probability theory, and based on discriminant analysis. We begin our discussion with a classifier based on the probabilistic approach. Then we will look at the decision trees and discriminant classifiers.

6.2   Probabilistic Models for Classification

Probabilistic classifiers and, in particular, the naïve Bayes classifier, is the most popular classifier used by the machine-learning community. The *naïve Bayes* classifier is a simple probabilistic classifier based on Bayes' theorem, the most popular theorem in natural-language processing and visual processing. It is one of the most basic classification techniques, with applications such as e-mail spam detection, e-mail sorting, and sentiment analysis. Even though naïve Bayes is a simple technique, it provides good performance in many complex real-world problems.

The study of probabilistic classification is based on the study of approximating joint distribution with an assumption of independence and then decomposing this probability into a product of conditional probability. A conditional probability of event A, given event B—denoted by P(A|B)—represents the chances of event A occurring, given that event B also occurs.

In the context of classification, Bayes theorem provides a formula for calculating the probability of a given record belonging to a class for the given set of record attributes. Suppose you have m classes, $C_1, C_2, C_3, ... C_m$ and you know the probability of classes $P(C_1), P(C_2), ... P(C_m)$. If you know the probability of occurrence of $x_1, x_2, x_3, ...$ attributes within each class, then by using Bayes' theorem, you can calculate the probability that the record belongs to class C_i:

$$P\left(Ci \mid X_1, X_2, X_3, ... X_p\right) = \frac{P\left(X_1, X_2, X_3, ... X_p \mid C_i\right) P\left(C_i\right)}{P\left(X_1, X_2, ... X_p \mid C_1\right) + P\left(X_1, X_2, ... X_p \mid C_2\right) ...... P\left(X_1, X_2, .. X_p \mid C_m\right)}$$

$P(C_i)$ is the prior probability of belonging to class C_i in the absence of any other attributes. $(C_i|X_1)$ is the posterior probability of X_1 belonging to class C_1. In order to classify a record using Bayes' theorem, you compute its chance of belonging to each class C_1. You then classify based on the highest probability score calculated using the preceding formula.

It would be extremely computationally expensive to compute $P(X|C_i)$ for data sets with many attributes. Hence, a naïve assumption is made that presumes that each record is independent of the others, given the class label of the sample. It is reasonable to assume that the predictor attributes are all mutually independent within each class, so we can simplify the equation:

$$P(X|C_i) = \prod_{k=1}^{n} P(X_k|C_i)$$

Assume that each data sample is represented by an n-dimensional vector, $X = \{x_1, x_2, \dots x_n\}$, samples from n attributes of categorical class values $A_1, A_2, \dots A_n$ with m classes C1, C2, ... Cm, then $P(X_k|C_i) = n/N$, where n is the number of training samples of class C_i having value X_k for A_k, and N is the total number of training samples belonging to C_i.

6.2.1 Example

Let's look at one example and see how to predict a class label by using a Bayesian classifier. Table 6-1 presents a training set of data tuples for a bank credit-card approval process.

***Table 6-1.** Sample Training Set*

ID	Purchase Frequency	Credit Rating	Age	Class Label: Yes = Approved No = Denied
1	Medium	OK	< 35	No
2	Medium	Excellent	< 35	No
3	High	Fair	35–40	Yes
4	High	Fair	> 40	Yes
5	Low	Excellent	> 40	Yes
6	Low	OK	> 40	No
7	Low	Excellent	35–40	Yes
8	Medium	Fair	< 35	No
9	Low	Fair	< 35	No
10	Medium	Excellent	> 40	No
11	High	Fair	< 35	Yes
12	Medium	Excellent	35–40	No
13	Medium	Fair	35–40	Yes
14	High	OK	< 35	No

The data samples in this training set have the attributes Age, Purchase Frequency, and Credit Rating. The class label attribute has two distinct classes: Approved or Denied. Let C_1 correspond to the class Approved, and C_2 correspond to class Denied. Using the naïve Bayes classifier, we want to classify an unknown label sample X:

X = (Age >40, Purchase Frequency = Medium, Credit Rating = Excellent)

To classify a record, first compute the chance of a record belonging to each of the classes by computing $P(C_i | X_1, X_2, \dots X_p)$ from the training record. Then classify based on the class with the highest probability.

In this example, there are two classes. We need to compute $P(X|C_i)P(C_i)$. $P(C_i)$ is the prior probability of each class:

P(Application Approval = Yes) = 6/14 = 0.428

P(Application Approval = No) = 8/14 = 0.571

Let's compute $P(X|C_i)$, for i =1, 2, ... conditional probabilities:

P(Age > 40 | Approval = Yes) = 2/6 = 0.333

P(Age > 40 | Approval = No) = 2/8 = 0.25

P(Purchase Frequency = Medium | Approval = Yes) =1/6 = 0.167

P(Purchase Frequency = Medium | Approval = No) = 5/8 = 0.625

P(Credit Rating = Excellent | Approval = Yes) = 2/6 = 0.333

P(Credit Rating = Excellent | Approval = No) = 3/8 = 0.375

Using these probabilities, you can obtain the following:

P(X | Approval = Yes) = 0.333 × 0.167 × 0.333 = 0.0185

P(X | Approval = No) = 0.25 × 0.625 × 0.375 = 0.0586

P(X | Approval = Yes) × P(Approval = Yes) = 0.29 × 0.428 = 0.0079

P(X | Approval = No) × P(Approval = No) = 0.586 × 0.571= 0.03346

The naïve Bayesian classifier predicts Approval = No for the given set of sample X.

6.2.2   Naïve Bayes Classifier Using R

Let's try building the model by using R. We'll use the same example. The data sample sets have the attributes Age, Purchase Frequency, and Credit Rating. The class label attribute has two distinct classes: Approved or Denied. The objective is to predict the class label for the new sample, where Age > 40, Purchase Frequency = Medium, Credit_Rating = Excellent.

The first step is to read the data from the file:

```
> credData
   ID PurchaseFrequency CreditRating   Age Approval
1   1            Medium           OK   <35       No
2   2            Medium    Excellent   <35       No
3   3              High         Fair 35-40      Yes
4   4              High         Fair   >40      Yes
5   5               Low    Excellent   >40      Yes
6   6               Low           OK   >40       No
7   7               Low    Excellent 35-40      Yes
8   8            Medium         Fair   <35       No
9   9               Low         Fair   <35       No
10 10            Medium    Excellent   >40       No
11 11              High         Fair   <35      Yes
12 12            Medium    Excellent 35-40       No
13 13            Medium         Fair 35-40      Yes
14 14              High           OK   <35       No
> |
```

```
> str(credData)
'data.frame':   14 obs. of  5 variables:
 $ ID               : int  1 2 3 4 5 6 7 8 9 10 ...
 $ PurchaseFrequency: Factor w/ 3 levels "High","Low","Medium": 3
3 1 1 2 2 3 2 3 ...
 $ CreditRating     : Factor w/ 3 levels "Excellent","Fair",..: 3
1 2 2 1 3 1 2 2 1 ...
 $ Age              : Factor w/ 3 levels "<35",">40","35-40": 1 1
3 2 2 2 3 1 1 2 ...
 $ Approval         : Factor w/ 2 levels "No","Yes": 1 1 2 2 2 1 2
 1 1 1 ...
>
```

The next step is to build the classifier (naïve Bayes) model by using the mlbench and e1071 packages:

```
> nbmodel

Naive Bayes Classifier for Discrete Predictors

Call:
naiveBayes.default(x = X, y = Y, laplace = laplace)

A-priori probabilities:
Y
       No       Yes
0.5714286 0.4285714

Conditional probabilities:
     CreditRating
Y     Excellent      Fair        OK
  No  0.3750000 0.2500000 0.3750000
  Yes 0.3333333 0.6666667 0.0000000

     PurchaseFrequency
Y          High       Low    Medium
  No  0.1250000 0.2500000 0.6250000
  Yes 0.5000000 0.3333333 0.1666667

     Age
Y          <35       >40     35-40
  No  0.6250000 0.2500000 0.1250000
  Yes 0.1666667 0.3333333 0.5000000
```

```
> ctest
  ID PurchaseFrequency CreditRating Age
1  1            Medium     Exellent >40
>
>
> pred<-predict(nbmodel,ctest)
> pred
[1] No
Levels: No Yes
```

For the new sample data X = (Age > 40, Purchase Frequency = Medium, Credit Rating = Excellent), the naïve Bayes model has predicted Approval = No.

6.2.3   Advantages and Limitations of the Naïve Bayes Classifier

The naïve Bayes classifier is the simplest classifier of all. It is computationally efficient and gives the best performance when the underlying assumption of independence is true. The more records you have, the better the performance of naïve Bayes.

The main problem with the naïve Bayes classifier is that the classification model depends on posterior probability, and when a predictor category is not present in the training data, the model assumes zero probability. This can be a big problem if this attribute value is important. With zero value, the conditional probability values calculated could result in wrong predictions. *When the preceding calculations are done using computers, sometimes it may lead to floating-point errors. It is therefore better to perform computation by adding algorithms of probabilities.* The class with the highest log probability is still the most significant class. If a particular category does not appear in a particular class, its conditional probability equals 0. Then the product becomes 0. If we use the second equation, log (0) is infinity. To avoid this problem, we use add-one or Laplace smoothing by adding 1 to each count. For numeric attributes, normal distribution is assumed. However, if we know the attribute is not a normal distribution and is likely to follow some other distribution, you can use different procedures to calculate estimates—for example, kernel density estimation does not assume any particular distribution. Another possible method is to discretize the data.

Although conditional independence does not hold in real-world situations, naïve Bayes tends to perform well.

6.3   Decision Trees

A *decision tree* builds a classification model by using a tree structure. A decision tree structure consists of a root node, branches, and leaf nodes. Leaf nodes hold the class label, each branch denotes the outcome of the decision-tree test, and the internal nodes denote the decision points.

Figure 6-1 demonstrates a decision tree for the loan-approval model. Each internal node represents a test on an attribute. In this example, the decision node is Purchase Frequency, which has two branches, High and Low. If Purchase Frequency is High, the next decision node would be Age, and if Purchase Frequency is Low, the next decision node is Credit Rating. The leaf node represents the classification decision: Yes or No. This structure is called a tree structure, and the topmost decision node in a tree is called the *root node*. The advantage of using a decision tree is that it can handle both numerical and categorical data.

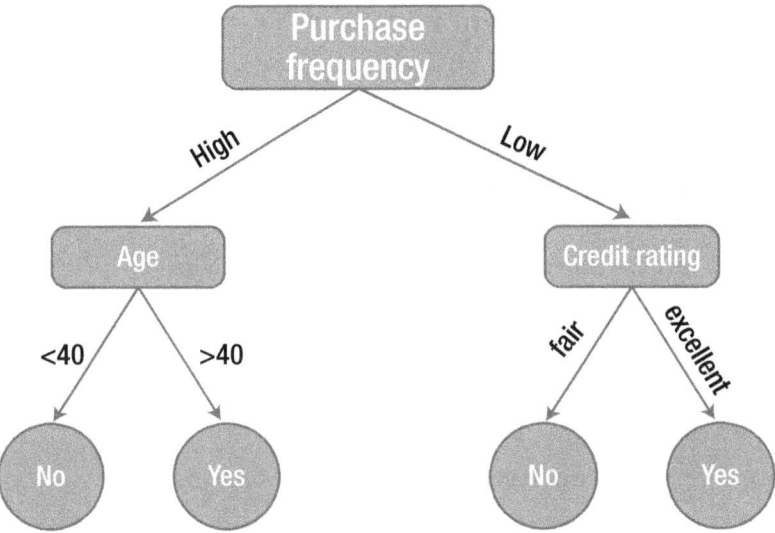

Figure 6-1. *Example of a decision tree*

The decision tree has several benefits. It does not require any domain knowledge, the steps involved in learning and classification are simple and fast, and the model is easy to comprehend. This machine-learning algorithm develops a decision tree based on divide-and-conquer rules. Let x_1, x_2, and x_3 be independent variables; and Y denotes the dependent variable, which is a categorical variable. The X variables can be continuous, binary, or ordinal. A decision tree uses a recursive partitioning algorithm to construct the tree. The first step is selecting one of the variables, x_i, as the root node to split. Depending on the type of the variable and the values, the split can be into two parts or three parts. Then each part is divided again by choosing the next variable. The splitting continues until the decision class is reached. Once the root node variable is selected, the top-level tree is created, and the algorithm proceeds recursively by splitting on each child node. We call the final leaf *homogeneous*, or as pure as possible. *Pure* means the final point contains only one class; however, this may not be always possible. The challenge here is selecting the nodes to split and knowing when to stop the tree or *prune* the tree, when you have lot of variables to split.

6.3.1   Recursive Partitioning Decision-Tree Algorithm

The basic strategy for building a decision tree is a recursive divide-and-conquer approach. The following are the steps involved:

1. The tree starts as a single node from the training set.

2. The node attribute or decision attribute is selected based on the information gain, or entropy measure.

3. A branch is created for each known value of the test attribute.

4. This process continues until all the attributes are considered for decision.

The tree stops when the following occur:

- All the samples belong to the same class.

- No more attributes remain in the samples for further partitioning.

- There are no samples for the attribute branch.

6.3.2   Information Gain

In order to select the decision-tree node and attribute to split the tree, we measure the information provided by that attribute. Such a measure is referred to as a measure of the *goodness of split*. The attribute with the highest information gain is chosen as the test attribute for the node to split. This attribute minimizes the information needed to classify the samples in the recursive partition nodes. This approach of splitting minimizes the number of tests needed to classify an object and guarantees that a simple tree is formed. Many algorithms use entropy to calculate the homogeneity of a sample.

Let N be a set consisting of n data samples. Let the k is the class attribute, with m distinct class labels C_i (for i = 1, 2, 3, ... m).

The Gini impurity index is defined as follows:

$$G(N) = 1 - \sum_{k=1}^{m}(p_k)^2$$

Where p_k is the proportion of observations in set N that belong to class k. G(N) = 0 when all the observations belong to the same class, and G(N) = (m – 1) / m when all classes are equally represented. Figure 6-2 shows that the impurity measure is at its highest when $p_k = 0.5$.

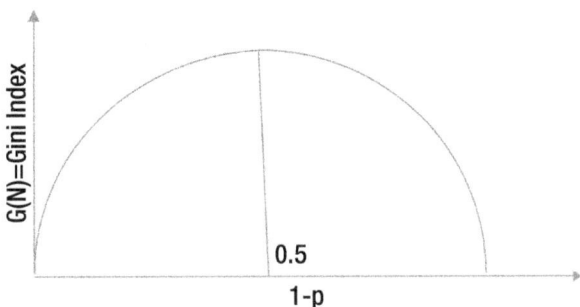

Figure 6-2. Gini index

The second impurity measure is the entropy measure. For the class of n samples having distinct m classes, C_i (for i = 1, ... m) in a sample space of N and class C_i, the expected information needed to classify the sample is represented as follows:

$$I(n_1, n_2, n_3, \ldots n_m) = -\sum_{K=1}^{n} p_k \log_2(p_k) \tag{1}$$

Where p_k is the probability of an arbitrary sample that belongs to class C_i.

This measure ranges between 0 (the most pure—all observations belong to the same class) and $\log_2(m)$ (all classes are equally represented). The entropy measure is maximized at $p_k = 0.5$ for a two-class case.

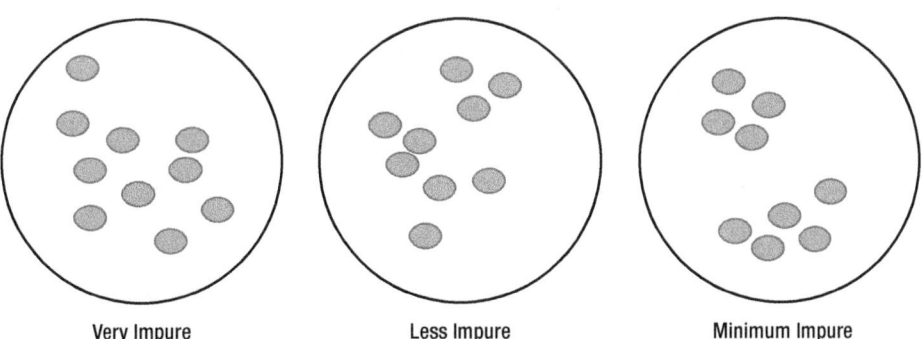

| Very Impure | Less Impure | Minimum Impure |

Figure 6-3. Impurity

Let X be attributes with n distinct records A = {a_1, a_2, a_3, ... a_n}. X attributes can be partitioned into subsets as {S_1, S_2, ... S_v}, where S_k contains the a_j values of A. The tree develops from a root node selected from one of these attributes, based on the information gain provided by each attribute. Subsets would correspond to the branches grown from this node, which is a subset of S. The *entropy*, or *expected information*, of attributes A is given as follows:

$$E(A) = \sum_{j=1}^{n} \frac{S_{1j} + S_{2j} + S_{3j} + ...S_{mj}}{S} = I(S_{1j}, S_{2j}, ...S_{mj}) \qquad (2)$$

The purity of the subset partition depends the value of entropy. The smaller the entropy value, the greater the purity. The information gain of each branch is calculated on X attributes as follows:

$$\text{Gain } (A) = I (s_1, s_2, s_3, ... s_m) - E(A) \qquad (3)$$

Gain (A) is the difference between the entropy of each attribute of X. It is the expected reduction on entropy caused by individual attributes. The attribute with the highest information gain is chosen as the root node for the given set S, and the branches are created for each attribute as per the sampled partition.

6.3.3   Example of a Decision Tree

Let's illustrate the decision tree algorithm with an example. Table 6-2 presents a training set of data tuples for a retail store credit-card loan approval process.

Table 6-2. *Sample Training Set*

ID	Purchase Frequency	Credit Rating	Age	Class Label: Yes = Approved No = Denied
1	Medium	OK	< 35	No
2	Medium	Excellent	< 35	No
3	High	Fair	35–40	Yes
4	High	Fair	> 40	Yes
5	Low	Excellent	> 40	Yes
6	Low	OK	> 40	No
7	Low	Excellent	35–40	Yes
8	Medium	Fair	< 35	No
9	Low	Fair	< 35	No
10	Medium	Excellent	> 40	No
11	High	Fair	< 35	Yes
12	Medium	Excellent	35–40	No
13	Medium	Fair	35–40	Yes
14	High	OK	< 35	No

The data samples in this training set have the attributes Age, Purchase Frequency, and Credit Rating. The Class Label attribute has two distinct classes: Approved or Denied. Let C_1 correspond to the class Approved, and C_2 correspond to the class Denied. Using the decision tree, we want to classify the unknown label sample X:

X = (Age > 40, Income = Medium, Credit Rating = Excellent)

6.3.4 Induction of a Decision Tree

In this example, we have three variables: Age, Purchase Frequency, and Credit Rating. To begin the tree, we have to select one of the variables to split. How to select? Based on the entropy and information gain for each attribute:

Loan Approval	
Yes	No
6	8

In this example, the Class Label attribute representing Loan Approval, has two values (namely, Approved or Denied); therefore, there are two distinct classes ($m = 2$). C_1 represents the class Yes, and class C_2 corresponds to No. There are eight samples of class Yes and six samples of class No. To compute the information gain of each attribute, we use equation 1 to determine the expected information needed to classify a given sample:

$$I\,(\text{Loan Approval}) = I(C_1, C_2) = I(6,8) = -\,6/14\,\log_2(6/14) - 8/14\,\log_2(8/14)$$

$$= -(0.4285 \times -1.2226) - (0.5714 \times -0.8074)$$

$$= 0.5239 + 0.4613 = 0.9852$$

Next, compute the entropy of each attribute—Age, Purchase Frequency, and Credit Rating.

For each attribute, we need to look at the distribution of Yes and No and compute the information for each distribution. Let's start with the Purchase Frequency attribute. The first step is to calculate the entropy of each income category as follows:

For Purchase Frequency=High, $C_{11} = 3$ $C_{21} = 1$. Here, first subscript 1 represents Yes, second subscript 1 represents Purchase Frequency=High, first subscript 2 represents No.

$$I(C_{11}, C_{21}) = I(3,1); I(3,1) = -\,3/4\log_2(3/4) - 1/4\,\log_2(1/4)$$
$$= -(0.75 \times -0.41) + (0.25 \times -2)$$

$$I(C_{11}, C_{21}) = 0.3075 + 0.5 = 0.8075$$

For Purchase Frequency = Medium

$$I(C_{12}, C_{22}) = I\,(1,5) = -1/6\,\log(1/6) - 5/6\,\log(5/6) = -(0.1666 \times -2.58)$$
$$- (0.8333 \times -0.2631) = 0.4298 + 0.2192$$

$$I(C_{12}, C_{22}) = 0.6490$$

For Purchase Frequency = Low

$$I\,(C_{13}, C_{23}) = I\,(2,2) = -(0.5 \times -1) - (0.5 \times -1) = 1$$

Using equation 2:

$$E\,(\text{Purchase Frequency}) = 4/14 \times I(C_{11}, C_{12}) + 6/14 \times I(C_{12}, C_{22}) +$$
$$4/14 \times I(C_{13}, C_{23})$$

$= 0.2857 \times 0.8075 + 0.4286 \times 0.6490 + 0.2857 \times 1$

E(Purchase Frequency) $= 0.2307 + 0.2781 + 0.2857 = 0.7945$

Gain in information for the attribute Purchase Frequency is calculated as follows:

Gain (Purchase Frequency) $=$ I (C_1, C_2) – E(Purchase Frequency)

Gain (Purchase Frequency) $= 0.9852 - 0.7945 = 0.1907$

Similarly, compute the Gain for other attributes, Gain (Age) and Gain (Credit Rating). Whichever has the highest information gain among the attributes, it is selected as the root node for that partitioning. Similarly, branches are grown for each attribute's values for that partitioning. The decision tree continues to grow until all the attributes in the partition are covered.

For Age < 35, I $(C_{11}, C_{12}) = I(1,5) = 0.6498$

For Age > 40, $I(C_{12}, C_{22}) = I (2,2) = 1$

For Age 35 – 40, $I(C_{13}, C_{23}) = I(3,1) = 0.8113$

E (Age) $= 6/14 \times 0.6498 + 4/14 \times 1 + 4/14 \times 0.8113$
$= 0.2785 + 0.2857 + 0.2318 = 0.7960$

Gain (Age) $=$ I (C_1,C_2) – E(Age) $= 0.9852 - 0.7960 = 0.1892$

For Credit Rating Fair, $I(C_{11},C_{12}) = I(4,2) = - 4/6 \log(4/6) - 2/6 \log(2/6)$

$= -(0.6666 \times -0.5851) - (0.3333 \times -1.5851 = 0.3900 + 0.5\ 283$
$= 0.9183$

For Credit Rating OK, $I(C_{21},C_{22}) = I(0,3) = 0$

For Credit Rating Excellent, $I(C_{13},C_{23}) = (2,3)$
$= -2/5 \log(2/5) - 3/5 \log(3/5)$

$= -(0.4 \times -1.3219) - (0.6 \times -0.7370) = 0.5288 + 0.4422 = 0.9710$

E (Credit Rating) $= 6/14 \times 0.9183 + 3/14 \times 0 + 5/14 \times 0.9710$
$= 0.3935 + 0.3467$

E (Credit Rating) $= 0.7402$

Gain (Credit Rating) $=$ I (C_1,C_2) – E (Credit rating)
$= 0.9852 - 0.7402 = 0.245$

In this example, CreditRating has the highest information gain and it is used as a root node and branches are grown for each attribute value. The next tree branch node is based on the remaining two attributes, Age and PurchaseFrequency. Both Age and Purchase Frequency have almost same information gain. Either of these can be used as split node for the branch. We have taken Age as the split node for the branch. The rest of the branches are partitioned with the remaining samples, as shown in Figure 6-4. For Age < 35, the decision is clear. Whereas for the other Age category, PurchaseFrequency parameter has to be looked at before making the loan approval decision. This involves calculating the information gain for the rest of the samples and identifying the next split.

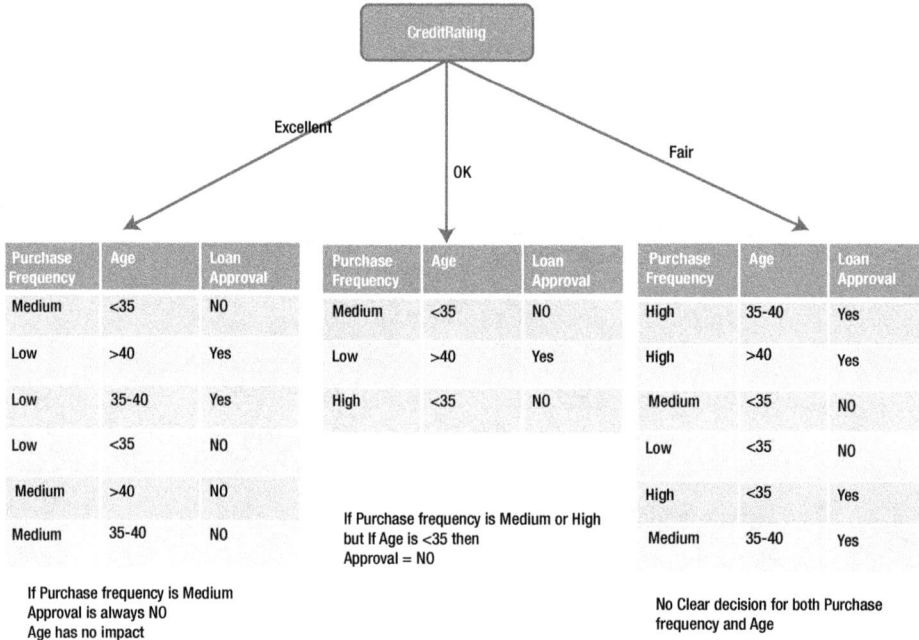

Figure 6-4. *Decision tree for loan approval*

The final decision tree looks like Figure 6-5.

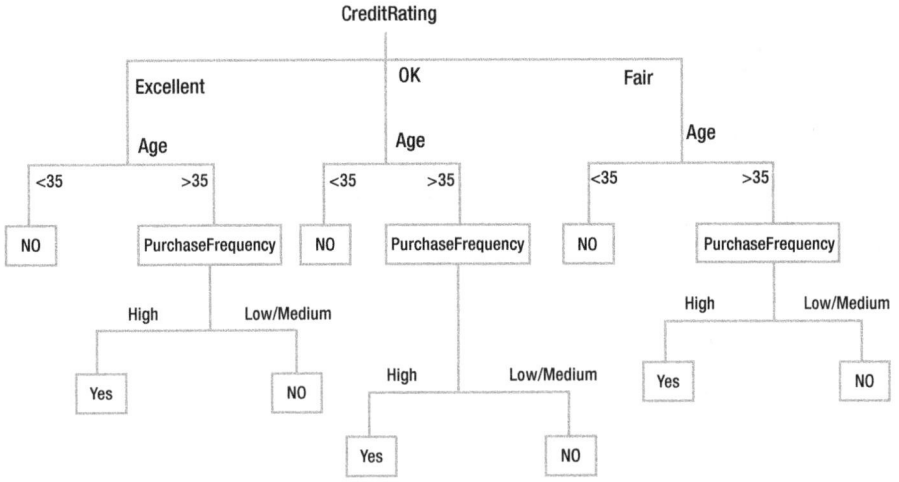

Figure 6-5. *Full-grown decision tree*

6.3.5 Classification Rules from Tree

Decision trees provide easily understandable classification rules. Traversing each tree leaf provides a classification rule. For the preceding example, the best pruned tree gives us following rules:

> *Rule 1*: If Credit Rating is Excellent, Age >35, Purchase Frequency is High then Loan Approval = Yes

> *Rule 2*: If Age < 35, Credit Rating = OK, Purchase Frequency is Low then Loan Approval = No

> *Rule 3*: If Credit Rating is OK or Fair, Purchase Frequency is High then Loan Approval = Yes

> *Rule 4*: If Credit Rating is Excellent, OK or Fair, Purchase Frequency Low or Medium and Age >35 then Loan Approval = No

Using a decision tree, we want to classify an unknown label sample X: X = (Age > 40, Purchase Frequency =Medium, Credit Rating = Excellent). Based on the preceding rules, Loan Approval = No.

6.3.6 Overfitting and Underfitting

In machine learning, a model is defined as a function, and we describe the learning function from the training data as *inductive learning. Generalization* refers to how well the concepts are learned by the model by applying them to data not seen before. The goal of a good machine-learning model is to reduce generalization errors and thus make good predictions on data that the model has never seen.

Overfitting and underfitting are two important factors that could impact the performance of machine-learning models. *Overfitting* occurs when the model performs well with training data and poorly with test data. *Underfitting* occurs when the model is so simple that it performs poorly with both training and test data.

If we have too many features, the model may fit the training data too well, as it captures the noise in the data and then performs poorly on test data. This machine-learning model is too closely fitted to the data and will tend to have a large variance. Hence the number of generalized errors is higher, and consequently we say that overfitting of the data has occurred.

When the model does not capture and fit the data, it results in poor performance. We call this underfitting. Underfitting is the result of a poor model that typically does not perform well for any data.

One of the measures of performance in classification is a contingency table. As an example, let's say your new model is predicting whether your investors will fund your project. The training data gives the results shown in Table 6-3.

Table 6-3. *Contingency Table for Training Sample*

	Actual	
Predicted	1	0
1	80	20
0	15	85

Training Data

The accuracy of the model is quite high. Hence we see the model is a good model. However, when we test this model against the test data, the results are as shown in Table 6-4, and the number of errors is higher.

Table 6-4. *Contingency Table for Test Sample*

	Actual	
Predicted	1	0
1	30	70
0	80	20

Test Data

In this case, the model works well on training data but not on test data. This false confidence, as the model was generated from the training data, will probably cause you to take on far more risk than you otherwise would and leaves you in a vulnerable situation.

The best way to avoid overfitting is to test the model on data that is completely outside the scope of your training data or on unseen data. This gives you confidence that you have a representative sample that is part of the production real-world data. In addition to this, it is always a good practice to revalidate the model periodically to determine whether your model is degrading or needs an improvement, and to make sure it is accomplishing your business objectives.

6.3.7   Bias and Variance

In supervised machine learning, the objective of the model is to learn from the training data and to predict. However, the learning equation itself has hidden factors that have influence over the model. Hence, the prediction model always has an irreducible error factor. Apart from this error, if the model does not learn from the training set, it can lead to other prediction errors. We call these *bias-variance* errors.

Bias occurs normally when the model is underfitted and has failed to learn enough from the training data. It is the difference between the mean of the probability distribution and the actual correct value. Hence, the accuracy of the model is different for different data sets (test and training sets). To reduce the bias error, data scientists repeat the model-building process by resampling the data to obtain better prediction values.

Variance is a prediction error due to different sets of training samples. Ideally, the error should not vary from one training sample to another sample, and the model should be stable enough to handle hidden variations between input and output variables. Normally this occurs with the overfitted model.

If either bias or variance is high, the model can be very far off from reality. In general, there is a trade-off between bias and variance. The goal of any machine-learning algorithm is to achieve low bias and low variance such that it gives good prediction performance.

In reality, because of so many other hidden parameters in the model, it is hard to calculate the real bias and variance error. Nevertheless, the bias and variance provide a measure to understand the behavior of the machine-learning algorithm so that the model model can be adjusted to provide good prediction performance.

Figure 6-6 illustrates an example. The bigger circle in blue is the actual value, and small circles in red are the predicted values. The figure shows a bias-variance illustration of variance cases.

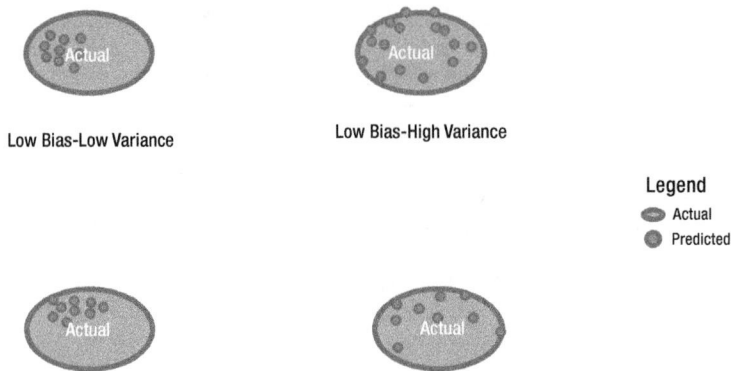

Figure 6-6. Bias-variance

6.3.8 Avoiding Overfitting Errors and Setting the Size of Tree Growth

Using the entire data set for a full-grown tree leads to complete overfitting of the data, as each and every record and variable is considered to fit the tree. Overfitting leads to poor classifier performance for the unseen, new set of data. The number of errors for the training set is expected to decrease as the number of levels grows—whereas for the new data, the errors decrease until a point where all the predictors are considered, and then the model considers the noise in the data set and starts modeling noise; thus the overall errors start increasing, as shown in Figure 6-7.

There are two ways to limit the overfitting error. One way is to set rules to stop the tree growth at the beginning. The other way is to allow the full tree to grow and then prune the tree to a level where it does not overfit. Both solutions are discussed next.

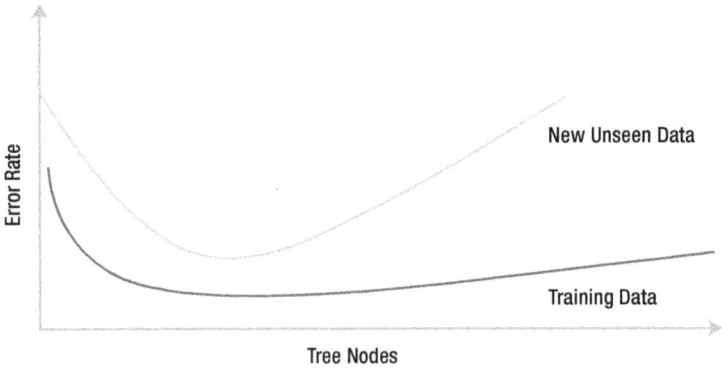

Figure 6-7. *Overfitting error*

6.3.8.1   Limiting Tree Growth

One way to stop tree growth is to set some rules at the beginning, before the model starts overfitting the data. Though you can use several methods (such as identifying a minimum number of records in a node or the minimum impurity, or reducing the number of splits), it is not easy to determine a good point for stopping the tree growth.

One popular method is Chi-Squared Automatic Interaction Detection (CHAID), based on a recursive partitioning method that is based on the famous Classification and Regression Tree (CART) algorithm, which has been widely used for several years by marketing applications and others. CHAID uses the well-known statistical test (chi-squared test for independence) to assess whether splitting a node improves the purity of a node and whether that improvement is statistically significant. At each node split, the variables that have the strongest association with the response variable is selected and the measure is the p-value of a chi-squared test of independence. The tree split is stopped when this test does not show a significant association and this proces is stopped. This method is more suitable for categorical variables, but it can be adopted by transforming continuous variables into categorical bins.

Most tools provide an option to select the size of the split and the method to prune the tree. If you do not remember the chi-squared test, that's okay. However, it is important to know which method to choose and when and why to choose it.

6.3.8.2 Pruning the Tree

The other solution is to allow the tree to grow fully and then prune the tree. The purpose of pruning is to identify the branches that hardly reduce the error rate and remove them. The process of pruning consists of successively selecting a decision node and redesignating it as a leaf node, thus reducing the size of the tree by reducing misclassification errors. The pruning process reduces the misclassification errors and the noise but captures the tree patterns. This is the point where the error curve of the unseen data begins to increase, and this is the point where we have to prune the tree.

This method is implemented in multiple software packages such as SAS based on CART (developed by Leo Breiman et al.) and SPSS based on C4.5 (developed by Ross Quinlan). In C4.5, the training data is used both for growing the tree and for pruning it.

Regression trees, part of the CART method, can also be used to predict continuous variables. The output variable, Y, is a continuous variable. The trees are constructed and the splits are identified similarly to classification trees, measuring impurity at each level. The goal is to create a model for predicting continuous variable values.

6.4 Other Classifier Types

A decision tree is a simple classifier that shows the important predictor variable as a root node of a tree. From the user perspective, a decision tree requires no transformation of variables or selecting variables to split the tree branch that is part of the decision-tree algorithm, and even pruning is taken care of automatically without any user interference. The construction of trees depends on the observation values and not on the actual magnitude values; therefore, trees are intrinsically robust to outliers and missing values. Also, decision trees are easy to understand because of the simple rules they generate.

However, from a computational perspective, building a decision tree can be relatively expensive because of the need to identify splits for multiple variables. Further pruning also adds computational time.

Another disadvantage is that a decision tree requires a large data set to construct a good performance classifier. It also does not depend on any relationships among predictor variables, unlike in other linear classifiers such as discriminant classifiers, and hence may result in lower performance. Recently, Leo Breiman and Adele Cutler introduced *Random Forests*, an extension to classification trees that tackles these issues. This algorithm creates multiple decision trees, a tree forest, from the data set and optimizes the output to obtain a better-performing classifier.

In this section, we briefly introduce other popular classification methods including k-nearest neighbor (K-NN), Random Forests, and neural networks. We will also explore when and under what conditions these classifiers can be used.

6.4.1 K-Nearest Neighbor

The *k-nearest neighbor* (*K-NN*) classifier is based on learning numeric attributes in an n-dimensional space. All of the training samples are stored in an n-dimensional space with a distinguished pattern. When a new sample is given, the K-NN classifier searches for the pattern spaces that are closest to the sample and accordingly labels the class in the k-pattern space (called k-nearest neighbor). The "closeness" is defined in terms of Euclidean distance, where Euclidean distance between two points, $X = (x_1, x_2, x_3, \dots x_n)$ and $Y = (y_1, y_2, y_3, \dots y_n)$ is defined as follows:

$$d(X,Y) = \sum_{i=1}^{n}(x_i - y_i)^2$$

The unknown sample is assigned the nearest class among the k-nearest neighbors pattern. The idea is to look for the records that are similar to, or "near," the record to be classified in the training records that have values close to $X = (x_1, x_2, x_3, \dots)$. These records are grouped into classes based on the "closeness," and the unknown sample will look for the class (defined by k) and identifies itself to that class that is nearest in the k-space.

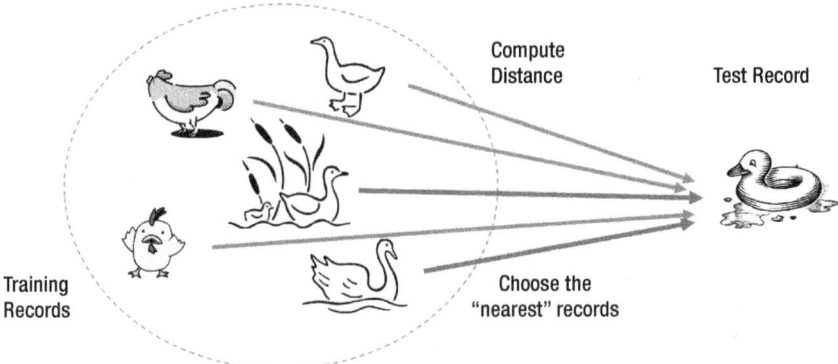

Figure 6-8. *K-NN example*

Figure 6-8 shows a simple example of how K-NN works. If a new record has to be classified, it finds the nearest match to the record and tags to that class. For example, if it walks like a duck and quacks like a duck, then it's probably a duck.

K-nearest neighbor does not assume any relationship among the predictors (X) and class (Y). Instead, it draws the conclusion of class based on the similarity measures between predictors and records in the data set. Though there are many potential measures, K-NN uses Euclidean distance between the records to find the similarities to label the class. Please note that the predictor variables should be standardized to a common scale before computing the Euclidean distances and classifying.

After computing the distances between records, we need a rule to put these records into different classes (k). A higher value of k reduces the risk of overfitting due to noise in the training set. Ideally, we balance the value of k such that the misclassification error is minimized. Ideally, the value of k can be between 2 and 10; for each time, we try to find the misclassification error and find the value of k that gives the minimum error.

6.4.2   Random Forests

A decision tree is based on a set of true/false decision rules, and the prediction is based on the tree rules for each terminal node. This is similar to a tree with a set of nodes (corresponding to true/false questions), each of which has two branches, depending on the answer to the question. A decision tree for a small set of sample training data encounters the overfitting problem. In contrast, the Random Forests model is well suited to handle small sample size problems.

Random Forests creates multiple deep decision trees and averages them out, trained on different parts of the same training set. The objective of the random forest is to overcome overfitting problems of individual trees. In other words, random forests are an ensemble method of learning and building decision trees at training time.

A random forest consists of multiple decision trees (the more trees, the better). Randomness is in selecting the random training subset from the training set. This method is called *bootstrap aggregating* or *bagging,* and this is done to reduce overfitting by stabilizing predictions. This method is used in many other machine-learning algorithms, not just in Random Forests.

The other type of randomness is in selecting variables randomly from the set of variables. This means different trees are based on different sets of variables. For example, in our preceding example, one tree may use only Income and Credit Rating, and the other tree may use all three variables. But in a forest, all the trees would still influence the overall prediction by the random forest.

Random Forests have low bias. By adding more trees, we reduce variance and thus overfitting. This is one of the advantages of Random Forests, and hence it is gaining popularity. Random Forests models are relatively robust to set of input variables and often do not care about preprocessing of data. Research has shown that they are more efficient to build than other models such as SVM.

Table 6-5 lists the various types of classifiers and their advantages and disadvantages.

Table 6-5. *Clasification Algorithms—Advantages and Disadvatages*

SI No	Classification Method	Advantages	Disadvantages
1	Naïve Bayes	Computationally efficient when assumption of independence is true.	Model depends on the posterior probability. When a predictor category is not present in the training data, the model assumes the probability and could result in wrong predictions.

(continued)

Table 6-5. (*continued*)

Sl No	Classification Method	Advantages	Disadvantages
2	Decision tree	Simple rules to understand and easy to comprehend. It does not require any domain knowledge. The steps involved in learning and classification are simple and fast. Decision tree requires no transformation of variables or selecting variables to split the tree branch.	Building a decision tree can be relatively expensive, and further pruning adds computational time. Requires a large data set to construct a good performance classifier.
3	Nearest neighbor	Simple and lack of parametric assumptions. Performs well for large training sets.	Time to find the nearest neighbors. Reduced performance for large number of predictors.
4	Random Forests	Performs well for small and large data sets. Balances bias and variance and provides better performance. More efficient to build than other advanced models, such as nonlinear SVMs.	If a variable is a categorical variable with multiple levels, Random Forests are biased toward the variable having multiple levels.

6.5   Classification Example Using R

This example uses student admission data. Students have been divided into different levels based on various test result criteria and then the students are admitted, accordingly, to the school. The data set has already been labeled with different levels. The objective is to build a model to predict the class. We will demonstrate this example by using R.

Once you understand the business problem, the very first step is to read the data set. Data is stored in CSV format. You will read the data. The next step is to understand the characteristics of the data to see whether it needs any transformation of variable types, handling of missing values, and so forth. After this, the data set is partitioned into a training set and a test set. The training set is used to build the model, and the test set is used to test the model performance. You'll use a decision tree to build the classification model. After the model is successfully developed, the next step is to understand the performance of the model. If the model meets customer requirements, you can deploy the model. Otherwise, you can go back and fine-tune the model. Finally, the results are reported and the model is deployed in the real world.

The data set is in CSV format and stored in the grades.csv file. Load the tree library and read the file as follows:

```
>
>
> library(tree)
> grads<-read.csv("grades.csv")
> View(grads)
>
```

Explore the data to understand the characteristics of the data. The R functions are shown here:

```
Console D:/umesh/ResearchAndPublications/WIP/APRESS-PracticalBusinessAnalytics/Chapters/R-Scripts
> View(grads)
> str(grads)
'data.frame':   239 obs. of  9 variables:
 $ ID           : int  20000001 20000002 20000003 20000004 20000005 2000
0006 20000007 20000008 20000009 20000010 ...
 $ Quiz1        : num  10 8 14 12 13 8 8 9 15 15 ...
 $ Quiz2        : num  10 3 15 16.5 11.5 0 30 15 20 25 ...
 $ Quiz3        : num  27 23.5 28 28 21.5 25 22 21.5 23.5 26.5 ...
 $ Quiz4        : int  95 75 70 100 95 100 80 75 85 100 ...
 $ Quiz5        : int  8 9 8 9 9 9 9 8 8 8 ...
 $ Total        : num  75 62 69.8 82 74.5 ...
 $ X8PointScale : num  6.28 5.2 5.85 6.87 6.24 6.05 5.95 5.35 6.27 7.07
...
 $ Level        : Factor w/ 4 levels "A","B","C","D": 3 2 3 1 3 3 3 2 3
1 ...
> table(grads$Level)

  A   B   C   D
 94  25 117   3
>
```

The next step is to partition the data set into a training set and a test set. There are 240 records. Let's use 70 percent as the training data set and 30 percent as the test data set:

```
> set.seed(2134)
> ind<-sample(2,nrow(grads),replace=TRUE,prob=c(0.7,0.3))
> train_set<-grads[ind==1,]
> test_set<-grads[ind==2,]
>
>
> nrow(train_set)
[1] 168
> nrow(test_set)
[1] 71
>
```

Build the decision-tree model by using the tree() function. An ample number of functions have been contributed to R by various communities. In this example, we use the popular tree() package. You are free to try other functions by referring to appropriate documentation.

```
> ##Build Decision Tree Model using tree() function
> mytree<-tree(Level~Quiz1+Quiz2+Quiz3+Quiz4+Quiz5,data=train_set)
> #Summarize the model
> summary(mytree)

Classification tree:
tree(formula = Level ~ Quiz1 + Quiz2 + Quiz3 + Quiz4 + Quiz5,
    data = train_set)
variables actually used in tree construction:
[1] "Quiz4" "Quiz2" "Quiz3" "Quiz1"
Number of terminal nodes:  15
Residual mean deviance:  0.5621 = 86 / 153
Misclassification error rate: 0.1369 = 23 / 168
>
```

The summary of the model shows that residual deviance is 0.5621, and 13.69 percent is the misclassification error. Now, plot the tree structure, as shown in Figure 6-9.

```
> ##Plot the tree
> plot(mytree)
> text(mytree,pretty=0,cex=0.6)
> #mytree
>
```

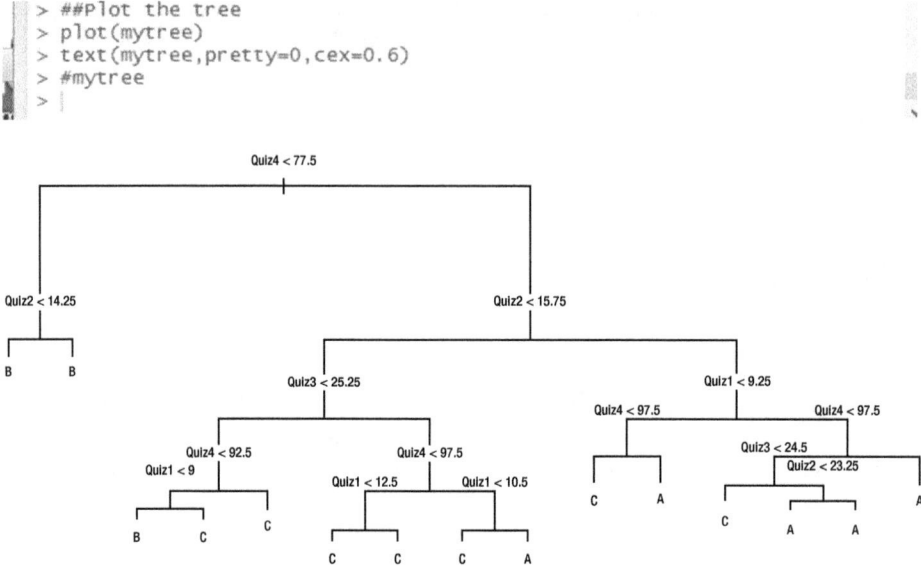

Figure 6-9. *Example plot of the decision-tree structure*

Once the model is ready, test the model with the test data set. We already partitioned the test data set. This test data set was not part of the training set. This will give you an indication of how well the model is performing and also whether it is overfit or underfit.

```
> pred_mytree<-predict(mytree,test_set,type="class")
> pred_mytree
 [1] C B C A A A A A C B B B A A B A A A C A C B C B B C A C C C C C
[33] A A C A C A B C A C B A A C A A A C C C A B C A A C A C C A B C
[65] C C A C C A A
Levels: A B C D
> #Predicted values of CLASS (Grades)
> summary(pred_mytree)
 A  B  C  D
30 12 29  0
> ##compare the predicted with actual
> table(pred_mytree)
pred_mytree
 A  B  C  D
30 12 29  0
> table(test_set[,9])

 A  B  C  D
26  8 35  2
> table(pred_mytree,test_set[,9])

pred_mytree  A  B  C  D
          A 26  0  4  0
          B  0  5  5  2
          C  0  3 26  0
          D  0  0  0  0
> mean(pred_mytree != test_set[,9])
[1] 0.1971831
>
```

As you can see, the misclassification mean error is 19.71 percent. Still, the model seems to be performing well, even with the test data that the model has never seen before. Let's try to improve the model performance by pruning the tree, and then you will work with the training set.

```
Console D:/umesh/ResearchAndPublications/WIP/APRESS-PracticalBusinessAnalytics/Chapters/R-Scripts
> set.seed(2345)
> prune_mytree<-cv.tree(mytree, FUN=prune.misclass)
> prune_mytree
$size
[1] 15  9  7  6  4  3  1

$dev
[1] 42 40 38 39 53 52 88

$k
[1] -Inf  0.0  1.5  3.0  5.5  7.0 19.5

$method
[1] "misclass"

attr(,"class")
[1] "prune"          "tree.sequence"
> plot(prune_mytree$size, prune_mytree$dev, type="b")
> prune_model <- prune.misclass(mytree,best=7)
>
```

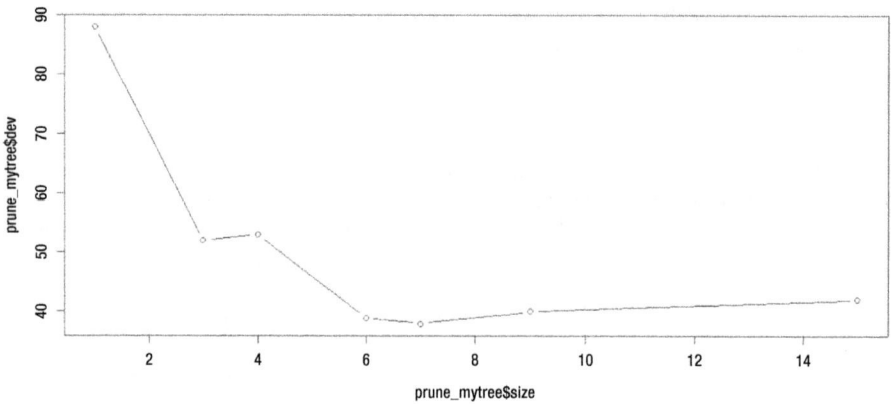

Figure 6-10. *Plotting deviance vs. size*

By plotting the deviance vs. size of the tree plot, the minimum error is at size 7. Let's prune the tree at size 7 and recalculate the prediction performance (see Figure 6-11). You have to repeat all the previous steps.

```
> prune_model <- prune.misclass(mytree,best=7)
> prune_model <- prune.misclass(mytree,best=7)
> summary(prune_model)

classification tree:
snip.tree(tree = mytree, nodes = c(2L, 12L, 26L, 27L, 15L))
variables actually used in tree construction:
[1] "Quiz4" "Quiz2" "Quiz3" "Quiz1"
Number of terminal nodes:  7
Residual mean deviance:  0.8708 = 140.2 / 161
Misclassification error rate: 0.1548 = 26 / 168
>
```

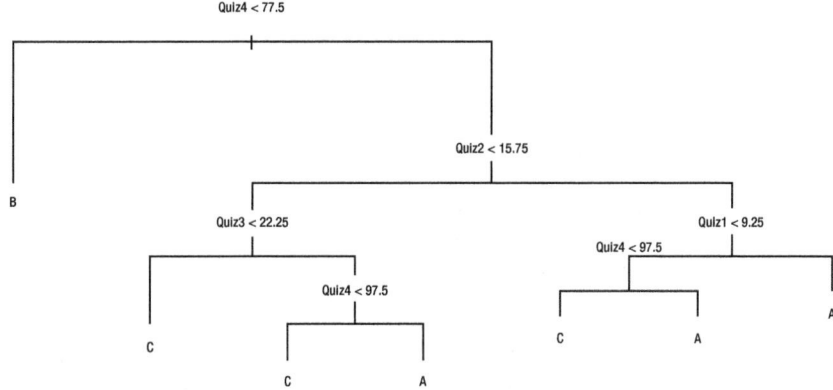

Figure 6-11. *Pruned tree*

```
>
>
> pred_prune<-predict(prune_model,test_set,type="class")
> table(pred_prune,test_set[,9])

pred_prune  A  B  C  D
        A  26  0  7  0
        B   0  5  4  2
        C   0  3 24  0
        D   0  0  0  0
> mean(pred_prune != test_set[,9])
[1] 0.2253521
>
```

For the pruned tree, the misclassification error is 15.48 percent, and the residual mean deviance is 0.8708. The model fits better, but the misclassification error is a little higher than the full tree model. Hence, the pruned tree model did not improve the performance of the model. The next step is to carry out the process called *k-fold validation*. The process is as follows:

1. Split the data set into k folds. The suggested value is k = 10.

2. For each k fold in the data set, build your model on k – 1 folds and test the model to check the effectiveness for the left-out fold.

3. Record the prediction errors.

4. Repeat the steps k times so that each of the k folds are part of the test set.

5. The average of the error recorded in each iteration of k is called the *cross-validation error*, and this will be the performance metric of the model.

6.6 Summary

The chapter explained the fundamental concepts of supervised machine learning and the differences between the classification model and prediction model. You learned why the classification model also falls under prediction.

You learned the fundamentals of the probabilistic classification model using naïve Bayes. You also saw Bayes' theorem used for classification and for predicting classes via an example in R.

This chapter described the decision-tree model, how to build the decision tree, how to select the decision tree root, and how to split the tree. You saw examples of building the decision tree, pruning the tree, and measuring the performance of the classification model.

You also learned about the bias-variance concept with respect to overfitting and underfitting.

Finally, you explored how to create a classification model, understand the measure of performance of the model, and improve the model performance, using R.

CHAPTER 7

Unsupervised Machine Learning

This chapter explores two important concepts of unsupervised machine learning: clustering and association rules. *Clustering* is also part of exploratory analysis, used to understand data and its properties and to identify any outliers that exist. But primarily it is used for identifying hidden groups in a data set. Association rule finds interesting associations or correlations among items in a large transactional data sets in a database. This is heavily used in retail industries to find interesting buying patterns from a transactional database, and can help in cross-marketing, catalog design, product promotions, and other marketing business decisions. In this chapter, you will learn how to perform clustering analysis, the techniques used for performing the clustering, and the concepts of association-rule mining.

7.1   Clustering - Overview

Clustering analysis is performed on data to identify hidden groups or to form different sectors. The objective of the clusters is to enable meaningful analysis in ways that help business. Clustering can uncover previously undetected relationships in a data set. For example, marketing cluster analysis can be used for market segmentation: customers are segmented based on demographics and transaction history so that a marketing strategy can be formulated. Another example is to identify groups who purchase similar products. Similarly, you group people in various clusters based on lifestyle and consumer expenditures so that cluster analysis can be used to estimate the potential demand for products and services and thus help formulate business and marketing strategies.

© Dr. Umesh R. Hodeghatta and Umesha Nayak 2017   161
U. R. Hodeghatta and U. Nayak, *Business Analytics Using R - A Practical Approach*,
DOI 10.1007/978-1-4842-2514-1_7

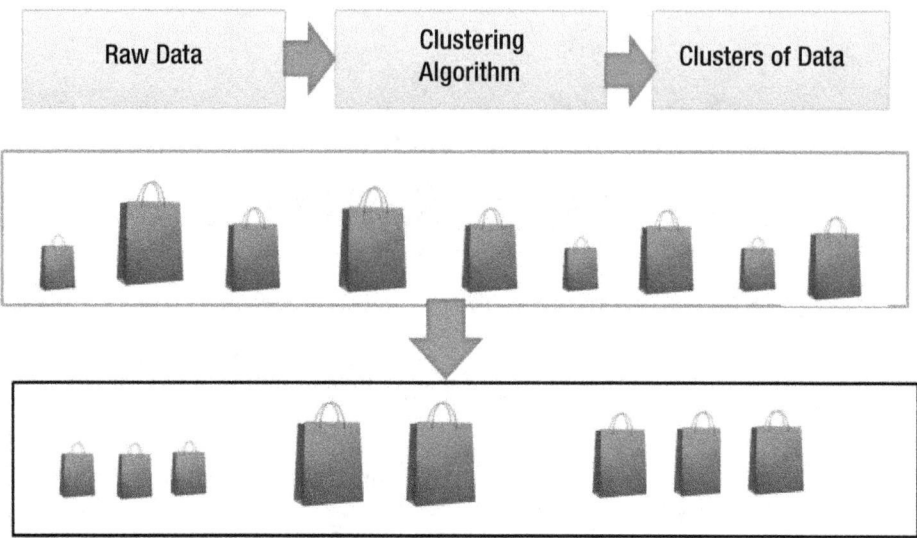

Figure 7-1. *Example of clustering*

Nielsen (and earlier, Claritas) were pioneers in cluster analysis. Through its segmentation solution, Nielsen helped customize demographic data to understand geography based on region, state, zip code, neighborhood, and block. This has helped the company to come up with effective naming and differentiation of groups such as *movers and shakers, fast-track families, football-watching beer aficionados*, and *casual, sweet palate drinkers*. (www.nielsen.com/us/en/solutions/segmentation.html).

In a Human Resources (HR) department, cluster analysis can be used to identify employee skills, performance, and attrition. Furthermore, you can cluster based on interests, demographics, gender, and salary to help a business to act on HR-related issues such as relocating, improving performance, or hiring the properly skilled labor force for forthcoming projects.

In finance, cluster analysis can help create risk-based portfolios based on various characteristics such as returns, volatility, and P/E ratio. Selecting stocks from different clusters can create a balanced portfolio based on risks. Similarly, clusters can be created based on revenues and growth, market capital, products and solutions, and global presence. These clusters can help a business understand how to position in the market.

Similarly, in software life-cycle management, you can group the effectiveness of the software development process based on defects and processes. Similarly, you can group newspaper articles on the Web based on topics such as sports, science, or politics.

The purpose of cluster analysis is to segregate data into groups that help you better understand the overall picture. This idea has been applied in many areas, including archaeology, astronomy, science, education, medicine, psychology, and sociology. In biology, scientists have made extensive use of classes and subclasses to organize various species.

Next, you will look at the methods and techniques involved in cluster analysis as well as its challenges. You'll also learn how to perform cluster analysis on a given data set.

7.2 What Is Clustering?

In statistics, cluster analysis is performed on data to gain insights that help you understand the characteristics and distribution of data. Unlike in classification, clustering does not rely on predefined class labels or training examples. Conventional clustering is based on the similarity measures of geometric distance. There are two general methods of clustering for a data set of *n* records:

> *Hierarchical method*: There are two types of algorithms. The agglomerative algorithm begins with *n* clusters and starts merging sequentially with similar clusters until a single cluster is formed. The divisive is the opposite: the algorithm first starts with one single cluster and then divides into multiple clusters based on dissimilarities.

> *Nonhierarchical method*: In this method, the clusters are formed based on specified numbers initially. The method assigns records to each cluster. Since this method is simple and computationally less expensive, it is the preferred method for very large data sets.

How do we measure closeness or similarities between clusters? Numerous measures can be used. The following section describes some of the measures that are common to both types of clustering algorithms.

7.2.1 Measures Between Two Records

Various methods measure the distance or similarities between two records in a data set. This section covers some of the common methods used.

7.2.1.1 Euclidean Distance and Manhattan Distance

Euclidean distance is the most popular measure. The Euclidean distance, E_{ij} between two records, i and j, is defined as follows:

$$E_{ij} = \sqrt{\left(X_{i1} - X_{j1}\right)^2 + \left(X_{i2} - X_{j2}\right)^2 + \left(X_{i3} - X_{j3}\right)^2 + \ldots\ldots\left(X_{ip} - X_{jp}\right)^2} \tag{1}$$

If you assign weight for each variable, then a weighted Euclidean distance can be calculated as follows:

$$E_{ij} = \sqrt{W_1\left(X_{i1} - X_{j1}\right)^2 + W_2\left(X_{i2} - X_{j2}\right)^2 + W_3\left(X_{i3} - X_{j3}\right)^2 + \ldots\ldots W_p\left(X_{ip} - X_{jp}\right)^2} \tag{2}$$

163

Another well-known measure is *Manhattan (or city block) distance* and is defined as follows:

$$M_{ij} = \left|x_{i1} - x_{j1}\right| + \left|x_{i2} - x_{j2}\right| + \left|x_{i3} - x_{j3}\right| + \ldots + \left|x_{ip} - x_{jp}\right| \tag{3}$$

Both Euclidean distance and Manhattan distance should satisfy the following mathematical requirements of a distance function:

$E_{ij} \geq 0$ and $M_{ij} \geq 0$: The distance is a non-negative number.

$E_{ii} = 0$ and $M_{ii} = 0$: The distance from an object to itself is 0.

$E_{ij} = E_{ji}$ and $M_{ij} = M_{ji}$: The distance is a symmetric function.

7.2.1.2   Pearson Product Correlation (Statistical Measurement)

Sometimes distance is measured in terms of how much the variables differ instead of in terms of physical distance. This dissimilarity is computed by the Pearson coefficient between two variables a and b as follows, where a and b are variables describing objects, and m_a and m_b are mean values of a and b, respectively:

$$R(a,b) = \frac{\sum_{i=1}^{n}(x_{ia} - m_a)(x_{ib} - m_b)}{\sqrt{\sum_{i=1}^{n}(x_{ia} - m_a)^2} \sqrt{\sum_{i=1}^{n}(x_{ib} - m_b)^2}}$$

In addition, x_{ia} is the value of a for the ith object, and x_{ib} is the value of b for the ith object.

Having variables with a high positive correlation means that their dissimilarity coefficient is close to 0, and the variables are very similar. Similarly, a strong negative correlation is assigned a dissimilarity coefficient close to 1, and the variables are very dissimilar.

Minkowski distance represents the generalization of Euclidean and Manhattan distance. It is defined as follows:

$Min(i, j) = -\left(\left|x_{i1} - x_{j1}\right|^q\right) + \left|x_{i2} - x_{j2}\right|^q + \left|x_{i3} - x_{j3}\right|^q \ldots \left|x_{ip} - x_{jp}\right|^q\right)^{1/q}$

It represents the Manhattan distance if $q = 1$ and it represents Euclidean distance if $q = 2$.

7.2.2   Distance Measures for Categorical Variables

A *categorical variable* has two or more states. The distance measure to calculate distance between two categorical variables of simple type 0 and 1 is not the same measure as numerical variables. One approach is to compute the distance using simple contingency table as shown in Table 7-1. In this example, we will compute the distance between two variables with 0 and 1 category (symmetric).

Table 7-1. *Contingency table*

Variable 1

		1	0	Sum
Variable 2	1	x	y	x + y
	0	a	b	a + b
	Sum	x + a	y + b	

Here, x is the total number of records with category 1 for both variables 1 and 2. Similarly b is the total number of records with category 0 for both variables 1 and 2 and vice-verse. Total number of records with all the categories is sum of a, b, x and y and is represented as p = a + b + x + y.

The well known measure to calculate the distance between the two variables is the simple matching coefficient, which is defined below:

$$d(i,j) = (a + y) / (a + b + x + y)$$

7.2.3 Distance Measures for Mixed Data Types

Usually, data sets have a combination of categorical and continuous variables. To measure the similarity between these variables, we can use a similarity measure proposed by Ducker and others (1965), and extended by Kaufman and Rousseeus (1990). This measure combines the variables into a dissimilarity matrix, bringing them into a common scale. It is defined as follows:

$$d_{(i,j)} = \frac{\sum_{m=1}^{m=p} W_{ijm}\, d_{ijm}}{\sum_{m=1}^{p} W_{ijm}}$$

The contribution of variable f to the dissimilarity between i and j is computed dependent on its type:

1. If m is binary or nominal, $d_{(i,j)}^{(m)} = 0$ if $x_{im} = x_{jm}$; otherwise, $d_{(i,j)}^{(m)} = 1$.

2. If m is interval-based:

$$d_{(i,j)}^{m} \frac{\left|x_{im} - x_{jm}\right|}{\max\left(x_{hm}\right) - \min\left(x_{hm}\right)}$$

Where h runs over on all nonmissing objects for variable m.

3. For continuous measurements, d (ijm) =

$$1 - \frac{\left|x_{im} - x_{jm}\right|}{\max\left(x_{m}\right) - \min\left(x_{m}\right)}$$

7.2.4 Distance Between Two Clusters

Various measures can be used to find the distance between two clusters. The most commonly used measures are single linkage, complete linkage, centroid, and average linkage. Say cluster C includes m records C_1, C_2, C_3 ... C_m, and cluster B includes n records B_1, B_2, B_3 ... B_m. The following metrics are widely used to find the distance between the C and B clusters.

7.2.4.1 Single Linkage (Minimum Distance)

The shortest distance between the two pairs of records in C_i and B_j is mathematically represented as follows:

Min(distance(C_i, B_j)) for i = 1, 2, 3, 4 ... m; j = 1, 2, 3 ... n

Figure 7-2 demonstrates the single-linkage approach.

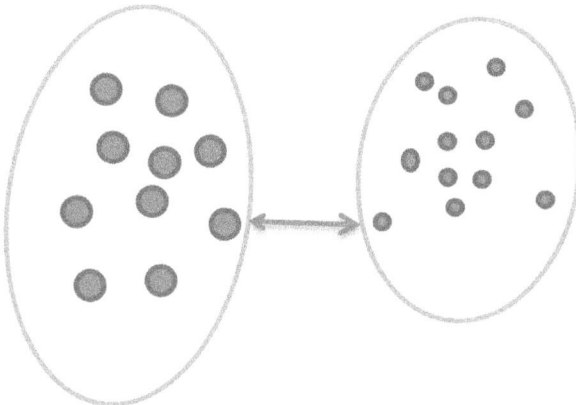

Figure 7-2. *Single linkage*

7.2.4.2   Complete Linkage (Maximum Distance)

The distance between two clusters is defined as the *longest* distance between one point each from each cluster (see Figure 7-3). The farthest distance between a record in each cluster in two clusters C_i and B_j is mathematically represented as follows:

Max (distance (C_i, B_j)) for $I = 1, 2, \dots m; j = 1, 2, 3 \dots n$

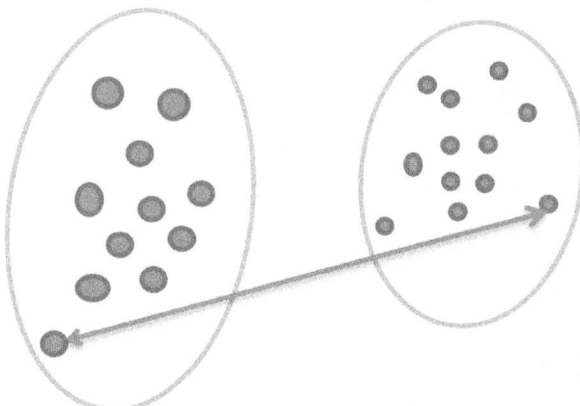

Figure 7-3. *Complete linkage*

7.2.4.3   Average Linkage (Average Distance)

This measure indicates the average of distance between each point in one cluster to every point in the other cluster (see Figure 7-4). The average distance between records in one cluster and records in the other cluster is calculated as follows:

Average (distance (C_i, B_j)) for $I = 1, 2, 3 \dots m; j = 1, 2, 3 \dots n$

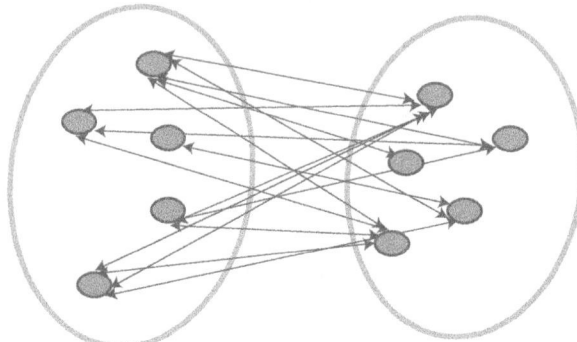

Figure 7-4. *Average linkage*

7.2.4.4   Centroid Distance

The *centroid* is the measurement of averages across all the records in that cluster. For example, in cluster C, the centroid $\bar{X}_a$ =

$$\left(\frac{1}{m}\sum_{i=1}^{m}X_{1i}\ldots\ldots\ldots\frac{1}{m}\sum_{i=1}^{m}X_{pi}\ldots\ldots\ldots\right)$$

The centroid between two clusters C and B is $\left|\bar{X}_a\ \bar{X}_b\right|$

7.3   Hierarchical Clustering

Hierarchical clusters have a predetermined ordering from top to bottom. For example, an organizational chart or all the files and folders on the hard disk in your computer are organized in a hierarchy.

Hierarchical clustering starts with every single object in a single data set as separate cluster. Then in each iteration, a cluster agglomerates (merges) with the closest cluster, based on distance and similarity criteria, until all the data forms into one cluster. The hierarchical agglomerative clustering algorithm is as follows:

1.   Start with *n* clusters. Each record in the data set can be a cluster by itself.

2.   The two closest case observations are merged together as single cluster. The *closeness* is the similarity measure.

3.   Step 2 repeats until a single cluster is formed. At every step, the two clusters with the smallest distance measure are merged together until all records and clusters are combined to form a single cluster. A hierarchy of clusters is created.

7.3.1 Dendrograms

A *dendrogram* demonstrates how clusters are merged in a hierarchy. A dendrogram is a tree-like structure that summarizes the process of clustering and shows the hierarchy pictorially. Similar records are joined by lines whose vertical line reflects the distance measure between two records. Figure 7-5 shows an example of a dendrogram.

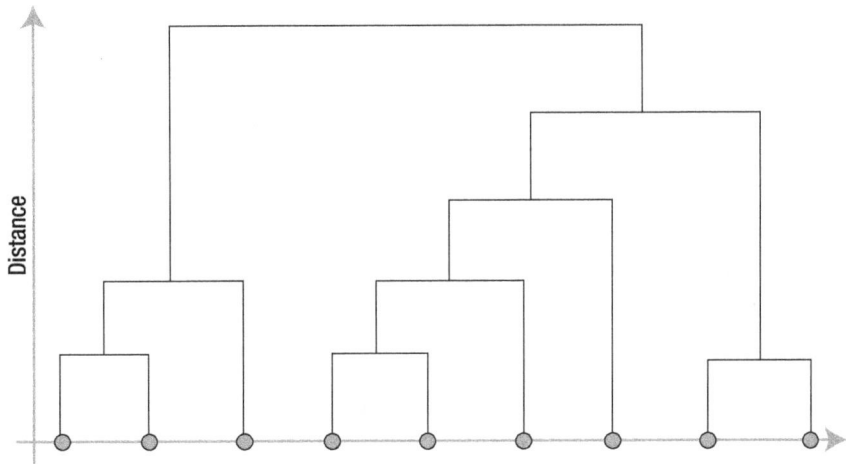

Figure 7-5. *A dendrogram shows how clusters are merged in a hierarchy*

7.3.2 Limitations of Hierarchical Clustering

Hierarchical clustering is simple to understand and interpret. It does not require you to specify the number of clusters to form. However, it has the following limitations:

- For very large data sets, computing and storing the $n \times n$ matrix may be expensive and slow.

- It is sensitive to outliers and missing data.

- It has low stability. Reordering data or dropping a few records can result in a different solution.

- When the metric is changed from one measure to another, results may vary.

7.4 Nonhierarchical Clustering

In nonhierarchical clustering, a desired number of clusters is prespecified, k_1, and you assign each case to one of the clusters so as to minimize the dispersion within the clusters. The goal is to divide the sample into a number of predetermined k clusters so that the clusters are as homogeneous as possible with respect to the metrics used. The algorithm intends to partition n objects into k clusters with the nearest mean. The end result is to produce k different clusters with clear distinctions. This is again an unsupervised machine-learning, numerical, and iterative method. And you always have at least one item in each cluster. The objective of this *k-means* clustering is to minimize total intracluster variance, or, the squared error function:

$$E = \sum_{i=1}^{n}\sum_{i=1}^{k}|(x_i \quad m_j)|^2$$

Where x is the point in space representing the given object$_i$ and m$_i$ is the mean of cluster C. The algorithm works well when the records are well separated from one another.

7.4.1   K-Means Algorithm

The k-means algorithm for clustering is as follows:

1. Select k. It can be 1 or 2 or 3 or anything.

2. Select k points at random as cluster centroids.

3. Start assigning objects to their closest cluster based on Euclidean measurement.

4. Calculate the centroid of all objects in each cluster.

5. Check the distance of the data point to the centroid of its own cluster. If it is closest, then leave it as is. If not, move it to the next closest cluster.

6. Repeat the preceding steps until all the data points are covered and no data point is moving from one cluster to another (the cluster is stable).

The following example demonstrates the k-means algorithm.

Suppose we want to group the visitors to a website using just their age (a one-dimensional space) as follows:

15,15,16,19,19,20,20,21,22,28,35,40,41,42,43,44,60,61,65

Initial clusters:

Centroid (C1) = 16 [16]   Randomly choose 2 points, 16 and 22
Centroid (C2) = 22 [22]

Iteration **1**:   Run algorithm. Find points closer to the
                                    cluster and find centroid
C1 = 15.33 [15,15,16]
C2 = 36.25 [19,19,20,20,21,22,28,35,40,41,42,43,44,60,61,65]

Iteration **2**:

C1 = 18.56 [15,15,16,19,19,20,20,21,22]
C2 = 45.90 [28,35,40,41,42,43,44,60,61,65]

Iteration **3**:

C1 = 19.50 [15,15,16,19,19,20,20,21,22,28]
C2 = 47.89 [35,40,41,42,43,44,60,61,65]

Iteration **4**:

C1 = 19.50 [15,15,16,19,19,20,20,21,22,28]
C2 = 47.89 [35,40,41,42,43,44,60,61,65]

There is no change between iterations 3 and 4, so the algorithm is stopped at this stage. By using clustering, two groups have been identified: 15–28 and 35–65. The initial random selection of cluster centroids can affect the output clusters, so the algorithm is run multiple times with different starting conditions in order to get a fair view of what the clusters should be.

7.4.2 Limitations of K-Means Clustering

K-means is a simple and relatively easy and efficient method. However, you need to specify k at the beginning. A different k can vary the results and cluster formation. A practical approach is to compare the outcomes of multiple runs with different k values and choose the best one based on a predefined criterion. A large k probably decreases the error but may result in overfitting.

Selecting the initial k is driven by external factors such as previous knowledge, practical constraints, or requirements. If we do not have any of these influences, the selection is random; you can try a few different values and compare the resulting clusters. In many cases, no such prior information or knowledge is available, and you can run the algorithm with various k values and then compare the results to reduce the producing of poor clusters. The goal, when comparing the clusters with different k values, is to make sure that the sum of distances reduces with increasing values of k.

7.5 Clustering Case Study

In this section, we present an example of clustering that uses a data set with details about apartments. The data includes rent of the apartments as well as other corresponding variable data such as Distance_from_Airport, Distance_to_Downtown, and Distance_to_University.

Here is the test data set:

Apartment	Rent	Distance from Airport	Distance to Downtown	Distance to University
1	1000	20	10	25
2	1200	18	12	17
3	1200	22	13	15
4	1200	21	11	17
5	1000	17	12	19
6	1800	12	21	8
7	1600	15	15	16
8	1800	12	18	13
9	1000	21	15	21
10	1200	17	12	15
11	2000	11	17	8
12	2200	10	16	9
13	2000	11	19	12
14	1200	21	22	17
15	1100	16	21	18
16	1000	21	13	19
17	2000	8	22	12
18	1900	9	19	11
19	2000	10	21	8
20	1400	19	15	17

```
>
> rent_data <- read.csv("Rent_Data.txt", header = TRUE, sep = ",")
> summary(rent_data)
    Apartment          Rent      Distance_from_Airport Distance_to_Downtown Distance_to_University
 Min.   : 1.00   Min.   :1000   Min.   : 8.00         Min.   :10.00        Min.   : 8.00
 1st Qu.: 5.75   1st Qu.:1175   1st Qu.:11.00         1st Qu.:12.75        1st Qu.:11.75
 Median :10.50   Median :1300   Median :16.50         Median :15.50        Median :15.50
 Mean   :10.50   Mean   :1490   Mean   :15.55         Mean   :16.20        Mean   :14.85
 3rd Qu.:15.25   3rd Qu.:1925   3rd Qu.:20.25         3rd Qu.:19.50        3rd Qu.:17.25
 Max.   :20.00   Max.   :2200   Max.   :22.00         Max.   :22.00        Max.   :25.00
>
> rent_data <- rent_data[-1]
> summary(rent_data)
      Rent       Distance_from_Airport Distance_to_Downtown Distance_to_University
 Min.   :1000   Min.   : 8.00         Min.   :10.00        Min.   : 8.00
 1st Qu.:1175   1st Qu.:11.00         1st Qu.:12.75        1st Qu.:11.75
 Median :1300   Median :16.50         Median :15.50        Median :15.50
 Mean   :1490   Mean   :15.55         Mean   :16.20        Mean   :14.85
 3rd Qu.:1925   3rd Qu.:20.25         3rd Qu.:19.50        3rd Qu.:17.25
 Max.   :2200   Max.   :22.00         Max.   :22.00        Max.   :25.00
>
```

7.5.1   Retain Only Relevant Variables in the Data Set

As you can see in the preceding code, we have removed the apartment number, which has no value to our grouping/clustering activity. Now we have only the parameters, or variables, relevant to the rent in the data set. Otherwise, your starting point would be to remove the irrelevant data variables from the data set. In this example, we want to see how the rents are different or similar based on the distances from various important places such as the airport, downtown, and the university.

7.5.2   Remove Any Outliers from the Data Set

Because outliers have significant impacts on some algorithms, we suggest removing the outliers before proceeding with the clustering process. For this, you can install the package outliers and then use it. One of the functions you can use for various tests for outliers is scores() from this package. In the following code, we use the scores() function and the Interquartile Range (IQR) method for finding the outlier. We use lim = "iqr" to obtain a logical output that suggests whether the data points are outliers. TRUE is returned for an outlier.

```
> scores(rent_data, type = "iqr", prob = NA, lim = "iqr")
   Rent Distance_from_Airport Distance_to_Downtown Distance_to_University
1  FALSE                FALSE                FALSE                  FALSE
2  FALSE                FALSE                FALSE                  FALSE
3  FALSE                FALSE                FALSE                  FALSE
4  FALSE                FALSE                FALSE                  FALSE
5  FALSE                FALSE                FALSE                  FALSE
6  FALSE                FALSE                FALSE                  FALSE
7  FALSE                FALSE                FALSE                  FALSE
8  FALSE                FALSE                FALSE                  FALSE
9  FALSE                FALSE                FALSE                  FALSE
10 FALSE                FALSE                FALSE                  FALSE
11 FALSE                FALSE                FALSE                  FALSE
12 FALSE                FALSE                FALSE                  FALSE
13 FALSE                FALSE                FALSE                  FALSE
14 FALSE                FALSE                FALSE                  FALSE
15 FALSE                FALSE                FALSE                  FALSE
16 FALSE                FALSE                FALSE                  FALSE
17 FALSE                FALSE                FALSE                  FALSE
18 FALSE                FALSE                FALSE                  FALSE
19 FALSE                FALSE                FALSE                  FALSE
20 FALSE                FALSE                FALSE                  FALSE
```

As you can see, there are no outliers in our data as suggested by the IQR method.

7.5.3 Standardize the Data

Because different variables may be of different magnitudes, the range of the variables also may significantly differ from each other. If all the variables have data in a similar range, there is no issue and we can proceed as it is. However, if the range of, say, one of the variables is significantly large compared to the other or others, then we have to scale the data. For this, we can use scale() to convert the data into standardized values. Without scaling the data, the variable with the highest range would influence the clustering more than the other variables. This is not good from the perspective of finding the right pattern.

Let's now standardize our data, as shown here:

```
>
> scaled_rent_data <- scale(rent_data)
> summary(scaled_rent_data)
     Rent          Distance_from_Airport Distance_to_Downtown Distance_to_University
 Min.   :-1.1486   Min.   :-1.5853       Min.   :-1.5624      Min.   :-1.4665
 1st Qu.:-0.7384   1st Qu.:-0.9554       1st Qu.:-0.8694      1st Qu.:-0.6637
 Median :-0.4454   Median : 0.1995       Median :-0.1764      Median : 0.1392
 Mean   : 0.0000   Mean   : 0.0000       Mean   : 0.0000      Mean   : 0.0000
 3rd Qu.: 1.0197   3rd Qu.: 0.9869       3rd Qu.: 0.8316      3rd Qu.: 0.5138
 Max.   : 1.6643   Max.   : 1.3543       Max.   : 1.4616      Max.   : 2.1730
>
```

7.5.4   Calculate the Distance Between the Data Points

Clustering works on the basis of calculating distances between data points (observations). Mathematics and statistics provide various methods to calculate these distances, including Canberra, Manhattan, Euclidean, and Hamming metrics. Euclidean distance, named after the famous mathematician Euclid, is one of the methods suggested in mathematics. We use the dist() function to calculate the distance.

Let's do the same with our data set. The way to do this in R is shown here, followed by the first five observations in the data set:

```
>
> dist_among_observ <- dist(scaled_rent_data, method = "euclidean")
>
```

```
> head(table(dist_among_observ), 5)
dist_among_observ
 0.47688569332196 0.526433710186056 0.610904547152077 0.610904547152078 0.629392393721958
                1                 1                 1                 1                 1
>
```

Please note that the dist() function takes the data set (for scaled data, the scaled data set is used) and method = "euclidean" as arguments. However, euclidean is the default method, so we can omit method = "euclidean" in the preceding code. We would use the method = "manhattan" option for a Manhattan distance calculation, and method = "binary" for Hamming distance.

7.5.4.1   Use the Selected Approaches to Carry Out the Clustering

As we have mentioned, we use a hierarchical clustering approach when the data is small, and we definitely use partition clustering when the data set is huge. The hierarchical clustering approach is also useful when we cannot approximate the possible number of clusters. But we need to provide the number of clusters required as input for the partition clustering approach. Hierarchical clustering is also used for nested clusters.

Let's now use both approaches on our data.

7.5.4.2   Hierarchical Clustering Approach

Let's start with a hierarchical partitioning approach. Here we have the option to use different methods. These are based on the way distances are calculated between the clusters. Typically, five methods are available: single linkage, average linkage, complete linkage, centroid, and ward. The average and the centroid methods are the most popular, as these have fewer disadvantages compared to the other methods.

We use the hclust() function for hierarchical clustering. This takes distance_among_observ we calculated from our data set and the method used. The typical format of this function is cluster_fit <- hclust(distance_matrix, method = "xxx"), where cluster_fit is the name of the output variable used to hold the clusters fitted and xxx is average, centroid, complete, single, or ward.

Let's now try out both the average and centroid methods:

```
> cluster_fit_average <- hclust(dist_among_observ, "average")
> #as you can see above you may omit the word method
> #In the above we use the "average" method
> cluster_fit_centroid <- hclust(dist_among_observ, method = "centroid")
>
```

We have to evaluate the cluster_fit we have obtained by using the preceding methods. For this, we need evaluating indices. We have these indices built into the NbClust package. If you have not already installed this package, you need to install it by using install.packages(NbClust) and then load it by using the library(NbClust) command in R:

```
> library(NbClust)
> #We have to give minimum clusters and maximum clusters as
> #inputs for this analysis along with the dataset i.e. in our
> #case scaled data set as we have scaled the original data set
> number_of_clusters <- NbClust(scaled_rent_data, distance = "euclidean", min.nc=2, max.nc=5, method = "average")
*** : The Hubert index is a graphical method of determining the number of clusters.
                In the plot of Hubert index, we seek a significant knee that corresponds to a
                significant increase of the value of the measure i.e the significant peak in Hubert
                index second differences plot.

*** : The D index is a graphical method of determining the number of clusters.
                In the plot of D index, we seek a significant knee (the significant peak in Dindex
                second differences plot) that corresponds to a significant increase of the value of
                the measure.

*******************************************************************
* Among all indices:
* 9 proposed 2 as the best number of clusters
* 10 proposed 3 as the best number of clusters
* 2 proposed 4 as the best number of clusters
* 2 proposed 5 as the best number of clusters

                 ***** Conclusion *****

* According to the majority rule, the best number of clusters is  3

*******************************************************************
```

This R code shows that ten criteria from the NbClust package suggest that the best number of clusters is three. We have assumed five maximum clusters, as we do not want a single or only two data points in each cluster.

The preceding NbClust() command also produces the corresponding plots shown in Figure 7-6.

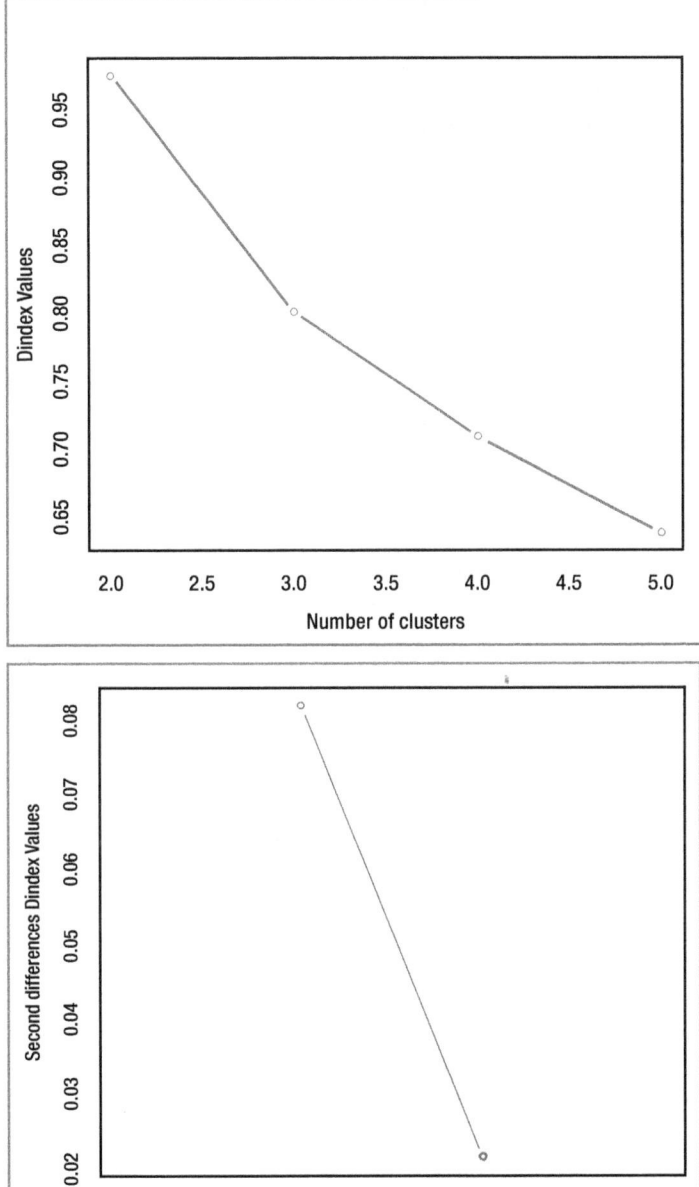

Figure 7-6. *Plots generated by the NbClust() command from the NbClust package, depicting the best number of clusters*

As you can see, the first plot shows a steep drop in Dindex values, from two to three clusters; beyond that, the Dindex values decrease slowly as the number of clusters increase. This suggests three clusters as the best option. The second plot clearly shows three clusters as the best option, as the second differences Dindex value is highest in this case.

We can now generate a dendrogram by using the plot() function as follows:

```
>
> plot(cluster_fit_centroid, rent_data$Rent)
>
```

Figure 7-7 shows the resulting dendrogram.

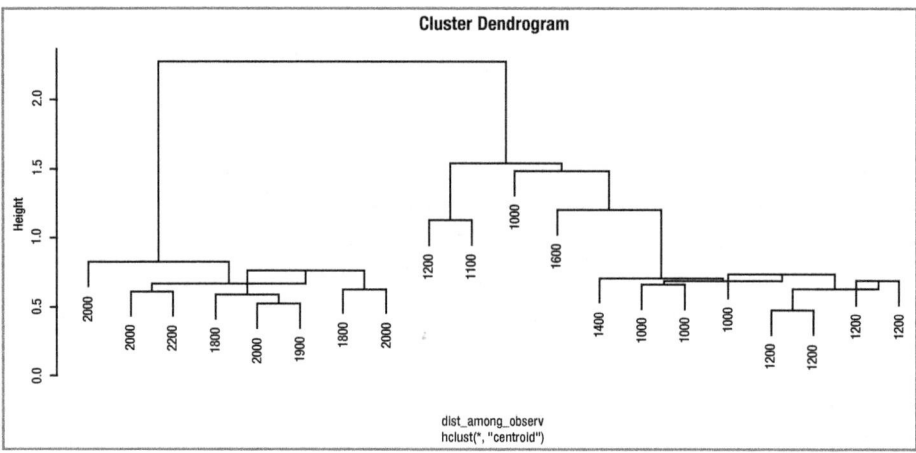

Figure 7-7. *Cluster dendrogram generated using the plot command*

This dendrogram also shows three clusters. Now let's superimpose rectangles on the plot generated by using the rect.hclust() function:

```
>
> rect.hclust(cluster_fit_centroid, k = 3)
>
```

Figure 7-8 shows the resulting dendrogram.

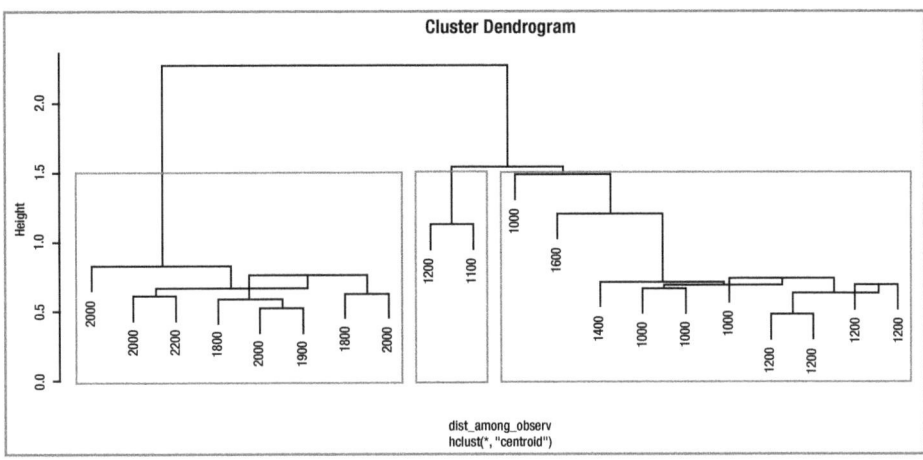

Figure 7-8. *Rectangles superimposed on the three clusters to easily differentiate among them*

Now, based on the best number of clusters determined in the preceding code, we get these clusters with the corresponding data as follows:

```
>
> final_clusters <- cutree(cluster_fit_average, k = 3)
> #Here we are taking the cluster fit got using the Hierarchical
> #Clustering using the method = average
> final_clusters
 [1] 1 1 1 1 1 2 1 2 1 1 2 2 2 3 3 1 2 2 2 1
>
> final_clusters_1 <- cutree(cluster_fit_centroid, k = 3)
> #Here we are taking the cluster fit got using the Hierarchical
> #Clustering using the method = centroid
> final_clusters_1
 [1] 1 1 1 1 1 2 1 2 1 1 2 2 2 3 3 1 2 2 2 1
>
```

The cutree() function cuts the observations into the number of clusters based on the cluster_fit we arrived previously. The numbers are the cluster numbers. As you can see in the preceding code, the same observations are classified into each cluster when using both the average and centroid methods. But, this isn't always the case. We can also see that there are ten data observations in cluster number 1, eight data observations in cluster number 2, and two data observations in cluster number 3. The 1st, 2nd, 3rd, 4th, 5th, 7th, 9th, 10th, 16th, and 20th data observations belong to cluster 1. The 6th, 8th, 11th, 12th, 13th, 17th, 18th, and 19th data observations fall in cluster 2. The 14th and 15th data observations fall in cluster 3.

Let's now interpret and validate the clusters by manually visiting our base data:

```
> rent_data
   Rent Distance_from_Airport Distance_to_Downtown Distance_to_University
1  1000                    20                   10                     25
2  1200                    18                   12                     17
3  1200                    22                   13                     15
4  1200                    21                   11                     17
5  1000                    17                   12                     19
6  1800                    12                   21                      8
7  1600                    15                   15                     16
8  1800                    12                   18                     13
9  1000                    21                   15                     21
10 1200                    17                   12                     15
11 2000                    11                   17                      8
12 2200                    10                   16                      9
13 2000                    11                   19                     12
14 1200                    21                   22                     17
15 1100                    16                   21                     18
16 1000                    21                   13                     19
17 2000                     8                   22                     12
18 1900                     9                   19                     11
19 2000                    10                   21                      8
20 1400                    19                   15                     17
>
```

As you can see, this data suggests that the high rent (cluster 2—$1,800 and above) is expected when the distance to the airport, and distance to the university are very short (less than 12 km from the airport and less than 13 from the university) and distance to downtown is greater (16 km and more). In contrast, very low rents (cluster 1) show long distances from both the airport and university but are <= 15 km from downtown. The third cluster shows lower rent when the distances are far from both the airport and the university along with a greater distance from downtown. From this, we can find that there is appropriate clustering of the data:

```
>
> aggregate(rent_data, by=list(cluster=final_clusters), median)
  cluster Rent Distance_from_Airport Distance_to_Downtown Distance_to_University
1       1 1200                   19.5                 12.5                   17.0
2       2 2000                   10.5                 19.0                   10.0
3       3 1150                   18.5                 21.5                   17.5
>
```

We use the aggregate() function to determine the median value of each cluster. The preceding code clearly supports the analysis we made previously. We use this median as it makes more sense than the mean because of the rounded values of rent.

Now let's group (or cluster) our data by using the partition cluster approach.

7.5.4.3 Partition Clustering Approach

k-means clustering is one of partition clustering methods. Here, we need to provide the number of clusters as inputs, and then the data is continuously rearranged until we get clusters with similar data grouped together. One of the limitations of k-means clustering is that it can work with only continuous data. It cannot work with factor data.

In order to find out the optimal clusters or the best number of clusters, we can use the same NbClust() function, but with the method kmeans. Here you can see how to use this function in R and the resulting output:

```
>
> optimal_clusters <- NbClust(scaled_rent_data, min.nc=2, max.nc=5, method = "kmeans")
*** : The Hubert index is a graphical method of determining the number of clusters.
            In the plot of Hubert index, we seek a significant knee that corresponds to a
            significant increase of the value of the measure i.e the significant peak in Hubert
            index second differences plot.

*** : The D index is a graphical method of determining the number of clusters.
            In the plot of D index, we seek a significant knee (the significant peak in Dindex
            second differences plot) that corresponds to a significant increase of the value of
            the measure.

*******************************************************************
* Among all indices:
* 13 proposed 2 as the best number of clusters
* 2 proposed 3 as the best number of clusters
* 6 proposed 4 as the best number of clusters
* 2 proposed 5 as the best number of clusters

                       ***** Conclusion *****

* According to the majority rule, the best number of clusters is  2

*******************************************************************
```

This output shows that 13 indices support two clusters.

Let's look at how these clusters are organized. If we compare this to our earlier hierarchical clustering, the first cluster under partition clustering is the same as the second cluster under hierarchical clustering. However, the first and third cluster under hierarchical clustering are grouped into the second cluster under partition clustering. If we look at the base data again, we find that this makes sense because the second cluster is now completely comprising the low-rent group with distance from the airport and distance from the university being relatively high, regardless of the distance from downtown, whereas the high-rent group has less distance from the airport and the university. Here, it seems that the distance from downtown does not have any significant impact on the rent.

Alternatively, instead of the NbClust() function from the NbClust package, we can use the kmeansruns() function from the fpc package to determine the optimal clusters.

Now let's use the best option for the clusters we have to regroup the observations:

```
>
> final_clusters_kmeans <- kmeans(scaled_rent_data, 2, nstart = 20)
> final_clusters_kmeans$size
[1] 12  8
```

As we see in practice, the `nstart` value from 20 to 30 works well in most cases. This is nothing but the initial configurations the algorithm will try before suggesting the best configuration.

We will now use the `aggregate()` function with the median to determine the median value of each cluster. The resultant output from R is shown here:

```
>
> cluster1 <- final_clusters_kmeans$cluster
> aggregate(rent_data, by = list(cluster1), median)
  Group.1 Rent Distance_from_Airport Distance_to_Downtown Distance_to_University
1       1 1200                  19.5                   13                      17
2       2 2000                  10.5                   19                      10
>
```

As we mentioned earlier, during the discussion on hierarchical clustering, it makes more sense here also to use the median rather than the mean because of the data profile (even though, technically, R allows us to use the mean instead of the median).

7.6 Association Rule

Another important unsupervised machine-learning concept is *association-rule* analysis, also called *affinity analysis* or *market-basket analysis* (MBA). This type of analysis is often used to find out "what item goes with what item," and is predominantly used in the study of customer transaction databases. Association rules provide a simple analysis in dicating that when an event occurs, an other event occurs with a certain probability. Discovering relationships among a huge number of transactional database records can help in better marketing, inventory management, product promotions, launching new products, and other business decision processes. Association rules indicate relationships by using simple if-then rule structures computed from the data that are probabilistic in nature.

The classic example is in retail marketing. If a retail department wants to find out which items are frequently purchased together, it can use association-rule analysis. This helps the store manage inventory, offer promotions, and introduce new products. This market-basket analysis also helps retailers plan ahead for sales and know which items to promote with a reduced price. For example, this type of analysis can indicate whether customers who purchase a mobile phone also purchase a screen guard or phone cover, or whether a customer buys milk and bread together (see Figure 7-9). Then those stores can promote the phone cover or can offer a new bakery bread at a promotional price for the purchase of milk. These offers might encourage customers to buy a new product at a reduced price.

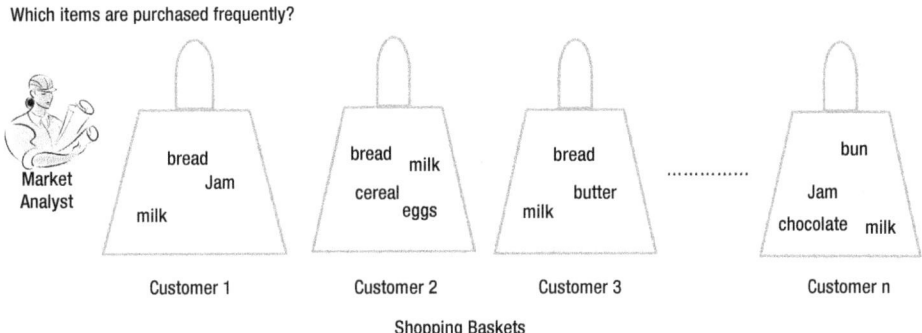

Figure 7-9. *Market basket analysis*

Several algorithms can generate the if-then association rules, but the classic one is the Apriori algorithm of Agrawal and Srikant (1993). The algorithm is simple. It begins by generating frequent-item sets with just one item (a one-item set) and then generates a two-item set with two items frequently purchased together, and then moves on to three-item sets with three items frequently purchased together, and so on, until all the frequent-item sets are generated. Once the list of all frequent-item sets is generated, you can find out how many of those frequent-item sets are in the database. For example, how many two-item sets, how many three-item sets, and so forth. In general, generating n-item sets uses the frequent n – 1 item sets and requires a complete run through the database once. Therefore, the Apriori algorithm is faster, even for a large database with many unique items. The key idea is to begin generating frequent-item sets with just one item (a one-item set) and then recursively generate two-item sets, then three-item sets, and so on, until we have generated frequent-item sets of all sizes.

7.6.1   Choosing Rules

Once we generate the rules, the goal is to find the rules that indicate a strong association between the items, and indicate dependencies between the antecedent (previous item) and the consequent (next item) in the set. Three measures are used: support, confidence, and lift ratios.

7.6.1.1   Support and Confidence

Item set I is defined as a set of all items in a store, $I = \{ i_1, i_2, i_3, ...i_m\}$, from a set of all transactional databases, T. Each t_i is a set of items t such that $t \varepsilon I$. For each transaction t_i, a transaction ID is assigned.

The *support* is simply the number of transactions that include both the antecedent and consequent item sets. It is expressed as a percentage of the total number of records in the database.

B --> A, (B follows A), where A and B are item sets. For example:

{Milk, Jam} ➤ {chocolate}

Support (S) is the fraction of transactions that contain both A and B (antecedent and consequent).

For example, support for the two-item set {bread, jam} in the data set is 5 out of a total of 10 records, which is $(5/10) = 50$ percent. You can define the *support* number and ignore the other item sets from your analysis. If *support* is very low, it is not worth examining.

Confidence (A --> B) is a ratio of *support for* A & B (i.e. antecedents and consequents together), to the *support for* A. It is expressed as a ratio of the number of transactions that contain A & B together to the number of transactions that contain A:

$$conf(A \rightarrow B) = \frac{\dfrac{numTrans(A \cup B)}{|D|}}{\dfrac{numTrans(A)}{|D|}} = \frac{p(A \cap B)}{p(A)} = p(B|A)$$

A high value of confidence suggests a strong association rule. But when B is independent of A—that is, $p(B) = p(B|A)$—and $p(B)$ is high, then we'll have a rule with high confidence. For example, if $p(\text{"buy jam"}) = 85$ percent and is independent of "buy bread," the rule "buy bread" $\Rightarrow$ "*buy jam*" will have a confidence of 85 percent. If nearly all customers buy bread and nearly all customers buy jam, then the confidence level will be high regardless of whether there is an association between the items.

7.6.1.2   Lift

Though support and confidence are good measure to show the strength of the association rule, but sometimes it can be deceptive. For example, if the antecedent or the consequent have a high support, we can have a high confidence even though both are independent. A better measure is to compare the strength of an association rule with the confidence where we can assume that the occurrence of the consequent item in a transaction is independent of the occurrence of the antecedent rules.

$$lift(A \rightarrow B) = \frac{conf(A \rightarrow B)}{p(B)} = \frac{\dfrac{p(A \cap B)}{p(A)}}{p(B)} = \frac{p(A \cap B)}{p(A)p(B)}$$

In other words,

Lift(A --> B) = Support(A & B) / [Support(A) x Support(B)]

Following example, Figure 7-10, demonstrates the three values viz. Support, Confidence and Lift. For the following item sets, we calculate support, confidence and lift ratios:

Transaction 1: shirt, pant, tie, belt

Transaction 2: shirt, belt, tie, shoe

Transaction 3: socks, tie, shirt, jacket

Transaction 4: pant, tie, belt, blazer

Transaction 5: pant, tie, hat, sweater

Let's calculate support, confidence and lift for the above example using the definition. For A --> B,

Support(A & B) = Freq(A & B) / N (where N is the total number of transactions in database)

Confidence(A -->B) = Support(A & B) / Support(A) = Freq(A & B) / Freq(A)

Lift(A -->B) = Support(A & B) / [Support(A) x Support (B)]

Rule	Support(A&B)	Confidence(A→B)	Lift(A→B)
shirt → tie	3/5 = 0.6	3/3 = 1	(3/5)/[(3/5)*(5/5)]=1
socks → shirt	1/5 = 0.2	1/1 = 1	(1/5)/[(1/5)*(3/5)]=5/3= 1.67
pant & tie → belt	2/5 = 0.4	2/3 = 0.67	(2/5)/[(3/5)*(3/5)]=1.11

Figure 7-10. *Association rule example*

Note that, Association rules do not necessarily represent causality or correlation between the two items. A --> B does not mean B causes A or, no Causality and A --> B can be different from B --> A, unlike correlation.

7.6.2 Example of Generating Association Rules

The example in Figure 7-11 demonstrates how to generate frequent-item sets. The algorithm is as follows:

For *k* products,

1. The user sets a minimum support criterion.

2. Generate a list of one-item sets that meets the support criterion.

3. Use the list of one-item sets to generate a list of two-item sets that meets the support criterion.

4. Use the two-item list to generate a three item-list, and so on.

5. Continue the process through *k*-item sets.

6. Decide the final rule based on support, confidence, and lift.

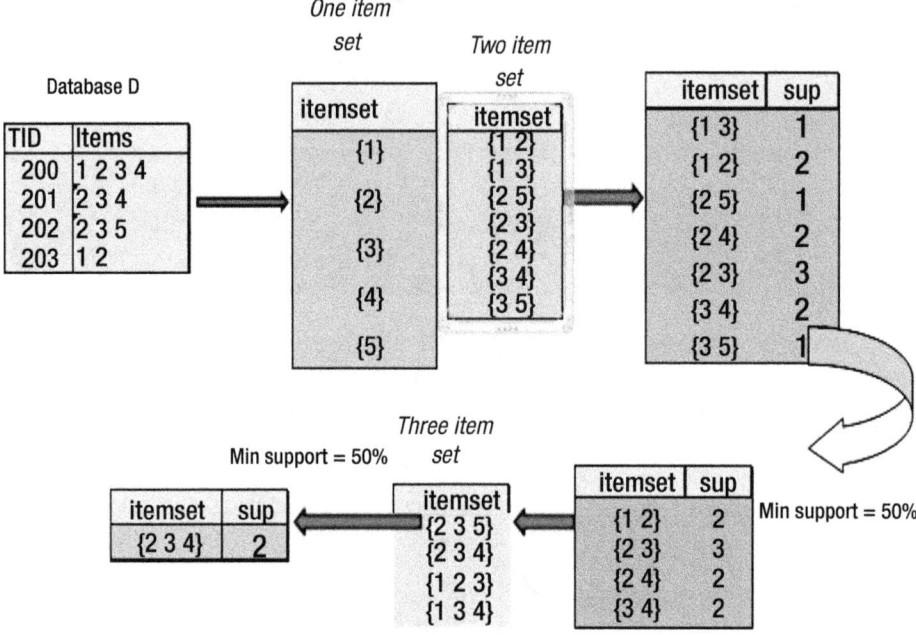

Figure 7-11. *Example of generating a frequent-item set*

7.6.3   Interpreting Results

Once you generate the frequent-item sets, it is useful to look at different measures such as support, confidence, and lift ratios. The support gives you an indication of overall transactions and how they affect the item sets. If you have only a small number of transactions with minimum support, the rule may be ignored. The lift ratio provides the strength of the consequent in a random selection. But the confidence gives the rate at which a consequent can be found in the database. A low confidence indicates a low consequent rate, and deciding whether promoting the consequent is a worthwhile exercise. The more records, the better the conclusion. Finally, the more distinct the rules that are considered, the better the interpretation and outcome. We recommend looking at the rules from a top-down approach that can be reviewed by humans rather than automating the decision by searching thousands of rules.

7.7   Summary

In this chapter, you saw that clustering is an unsupervised technique used to perform data analysis. It is also part of exploratory analysis, for understanding data and its properties. It can be used to identify any outliers in the data. However, primarily it is used for identifying hidden groups in the data set.

Association rules find interesting associations among large transactional item sets in the database. You learned how to perform clustering analysis, techniques used for performing the clustering, and the concepts of association-rule mining.

CHAPTER 8

Simple Linear Regression

8.1 Introduction

Imagine you are a business investor and want to invest in startup ventures which are likely to be highly profitable. What are all the factors you look for in the company you want to invest in? Maybe the innovativeness of the products of the startups, maybe the past success records of the promoters. In this case, we say the profitability of the venture is dependent on or associated with innovativeness of the products and past success records of the promoters. The innovativeness of the product itself may be associated with various aspects or factors like usefulness of the product, competition in the market, and so on. These factors may be a little difficult to gauge, but the past success record of the promoters can be easily found from the available market data. If the promoter had started ten ventures and eight were successful, we can say that 80% is the success rate of the promoter.

Imagine you want to increase the sales of the products of your organization. You may want to get more sales personnel, you may have to have a presence in or the capability to service more territories or markets, you may require more marketing efforts in these markets, and so on. All these aspects or factors are associated with the quantum of sales or impact the quantum of sales. Imagine the attrition of the employees at any company or industry. There are various factors like work environment of the organization, compensation and benefits structure of the organization, how well known the company is in the industry or market, and so forth. Work environment may be how conducive the internal environment is for people to use their thinking, how much guidance or help the seniors in the organization provide, and the current technological or product landscape of the organization (e.g., whether or not you are working on the latest technology). It may be even overall satisfaction level of the employees. Compensation and benefits structure may include salary structure—that is, how good salaries are compared to those in other similar organizations or other organizations in the industry, are there bonus or additional incentives for higher performance or are there additional perquisites, etc. To drive home the point, there may be multiple factors that influence a particular outcome or impact a particular outcome or that are associated with a particular outcome. Again, each one of these may in turn be associated with or influenced by other factors. For example, salary structure may influence the work environment or satisfaction levels of the employees.

© Dr. Umesh R. Hodeghatta and Umesha Nayak 2017
U. R. Hodeghatta and U. Nayak, *Business Analytics Using R - A Practical Approach*,
DOI 10.1007/978-1-4842-2514-1_8

Imagine you are a developer of the properties as well as a builder. You are planning to build a huge shopping mall. The prices of various inputs required like cement, steel, sand, pipes, and so on vary a lot on a day-to-day basis. If you have to decide on the sale price of the shopping mall or rent you need to charge for the individual shops you need to understand the likely cost of building. For this you may have to take into consideration how over a period of time the costs of these inputs (cement, steel, sand, etc.) have varied and what factors influence the price of each of these in the market.

You may want to estimate the profitability of the company, arrive at the best possible cost of manufacturing of a product, estimate the quantum of increase in sales, estimate the attrition of the company so that you can plan well for recruitment, decide on the likely cost of the shopping mall you are building, or decide on the rent you need to charge for a square feet or a square meter. In all these cases you need to understand the association or relationship of these with the ones that influence, decide, or impact them. The relationship between two factors is normally explained in statistics through correlation or, to be precise, coefficient of correlation (i.e., R) or coefficient of determination (i.e., R^2).

Regression equation depicts the relationship between a response variable or dependent variable and the corresponding independent variables. This means that the value of the dependent variable can be predicted based on the values of the independent variables. Where there is a single independent variable, then the regression is called simple regression. When there are multiple independent variables, then the regression is called multiple regression. Again, the regressions can be of two types based on the relationship between the response variable and the independent variables (i.e., linear regression or non-linear regression). In the case of linear regression the relationship between the response variable and the independent variables is explained through a straight line and in the case of non-linear relationship the relationship between the response variable and independent variables is non-linear (polynomial like quadratic, cubic, etc.).

Normally we may find a linear relationship between the price of the house and the area of the house. We may also see a linear relationship between salary and experience. However, if we take the relationship between rain and the production of grains, the production of the grains may increase with moderate to good rain but then decrease if the rain is more than good rain and becomes extreme rain. In this case, the relationship between quantum of rain and the food grains production is normally non-linear; initially food grain production increases and then reduces.

Regression is a supervised method as we know both the exact values of the response (i.e., dependent) variable and the corresponding values of the independent variables. This is the basis for the establishment of the model. This basis or model is then used for predicting the values of the response variable where we know the values of the independent variable and want to understand the likely value of the response variable.

8.2   Correlation

As described in earlier chapters, correlation explains the relationship between two variables. This may be a cause-and-effect relationship or otherwise, but it need not be always a cause-and-effect relationship. However, variation in one variable can be explained with the help of the other parameter when we know the relationship between two variables over a range of values (i.e., when we know the correlation between two variables). Typically the relationship between two variables is depicted through a scatter plot as explained in earlier chapters.

Attrition is related to the employee satisfaction index. This means that "attrition" is correlated with "employee satisfaction index." Normally, the lower the employee satisfaction, the higher the attrition. This means that attrition is inversely correlated with employee satisfaction. In other words, attrition has a negative correlation with employee satisfaction or is negatively associated with employee satisfaction.

Normally the profitability of an organization is likely to grow up with the sales quantum. This means the higher the sales, the higher the profits. The lower the sales, the lower the profits. Here, the relationship is that of positive correlation as profitability increases with the increase in sales quantum and decreases with the decrease in sales quantum. Here, we can say that the profitability is positively associated with the sales quantum.

Normally, the lesser the defects in a product or the higher the speed of response related to issues, the higher will be the customer satisfaction of any company. Here, customer satisfaction is inversely related to defects in the product or negatively correlated with the defects in the product. However, the same customer satisfaction is directly related to or positively correlated with the speed of response.

Correlation explains the extent of change in one of the variables given the unit change in the value of another variable. Correlation assumes a very significant role in statistics and hence in the field of business analytics as any business cannot make any decision without understanding the relationship between various forces acting in favor of or against it.

Strong association or correlation between two variables enables us to better predict the value of the response variable from the value of the independent variable. However, the weak association or low correlation between two variables does not help us to predict the value of the response variable from the value of the independent variable.

8.2.1   Correlation Coefficient

Correlation coefficient is an important statistical parameter of interest which gives us numerical indication of the relationship between two variables. This will be useful only in the case of linear association between the variables. This will not be useful in the case of non-linear associations between the variables.

It is very easy to compute the correlation coefficient. In order to compute the same we require the following:

- Average of all the values of the independent variable

- Average of all the values of the dependent variable

- Standard deviation of all the values of the independent variable

- Standard deviation of all the values of the dependent variable

Once we have the foregoing, we need to convert each value of each variable into standard units. This is done as follows:

- (Each value minus the average of the variable) / (Standard Deviation of the variable) (i.e., [variable value – mean(variable)] / sd(variable)). For example, if a particular value among the values of the independent variable is 18 and the mean of this independent variable is 15 and the standard deviation of this independent variable is 3, then the value of this independent variable converted into standard units will be = (18 – 15)/3 = 1. This is also known as z-score of the variable.

Once we have converted each value of each variable into standard units, the correlation coefficient (normally depicted as 'r' or 'R') is calculated as follows:

- Average of [(independent variable in standard units) x (dependent variable in standard units)] (i.e., mean[Σ(z-score of x) * (z-score of y)])

The correlation coefficient can be also found out using the following formula:

R = [covariance(independent variable, dependent variable) / [(Standard Deviation of the independent variable) x (Standard Deviation of the dependent variable)]

In the above, covariance is = [sum (the value of each independent variable minus average of the independent variable values)*(the value of each dependent variable minus the average of the dependent variable values)] divided by [n minus 1]

In R Programming Language the calculation of the correlation coefficient is very simple. The calculation of correlation coefficient in R is shown in Figure 8-1A and the corresponding scatter plot is shown in Figure 8-1B:

```
>
>
> #the following is an example of "attrition" vs. "employee satisfaction"
> #the following is the attrition data in terms of the percentages of attrition
>  attrition = c(4, 5, 6, 8, 10, 12, 15, 18, 21, 25)
> #the following is the employee satisfaction index data a month prior to the attrition figures
> empsat = c(10, 9, 8, 7, 6, 5, 4, 3, 2, 1)
> #the above data is for each quarter viz. employee satisfaction index is calculated every quarter
> #and the attrition data is calculated as an average for the next 3 months
> #cor is the function used for calculating the correlation coefficient (r or R) in R programming
> #language
> correl_attri_empsat = cor(attrition, empsat)
> correl_attri_empsat
[1] -0.9830268
> #The above shows the near perfect negative correlation between attrition and employee
> #satisfaction index as it is near to the value of -1
>
```

Figure 8-1A. *Calculating correlation coefficient in R*

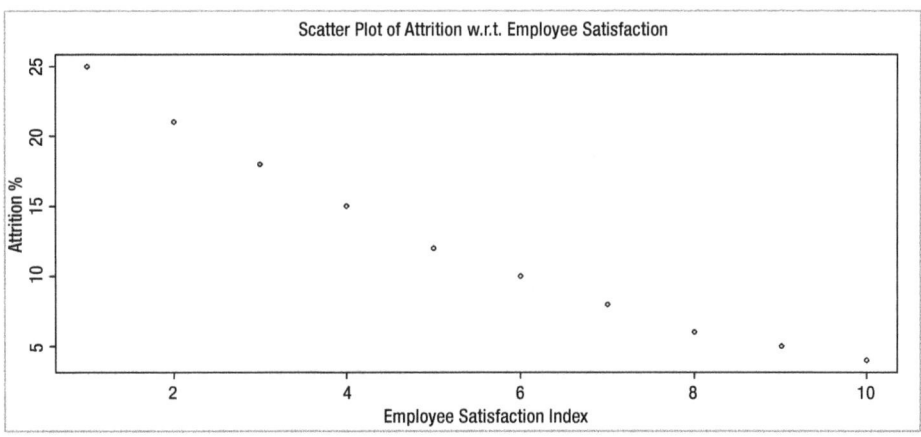

Figure 8-1B. *Scatter plot between Employee Satisfaction Index and Attrition*

As can be seen from the scatter plot in Figure 8-1B, even though the relationship is not linear it is near linear. The same is shown by the correlation coefficient of -0.983. As you can see, the negative sign indicates the inverse association or negative association between attrition percentage and employee satisfaction index. The above plot shows that the deterioration in the employee satisfaction leads to an increased rate of attrition.

Further, the test shown in Figure 8-2 confirms that there is an excellent statistically significant correlation between attrition and the employee satisfaction index:

```
>
> attrition <- c(4, 5, 6, 8, 10, 12, 15, 18, 21, 25)
> empsat <- c(10, 9, 8, 7, 6, 5, 4, 3, 2, 1)
> cor.test(attrition, empsat, method = "spearman")

        Spearman's rank correlation rho

data:  attrition and empsat
S = 330, p-value < 2.2e-16
alternative hypothesis: true rho is not equal to 0
sample estimates:
rho
 -1

> #In the above as the p-value is <0.05 we can conclude
> #that the correlation is significant
> #If p-value is >0.05 we can conclude that that the correlation
> #is not significant
```

Figure 8-2. *Test to find out the significance of correlation in R*

Please note, the previous data is illustrative only and may not be representative of a real scenario. It is used for the purpose of illustrating the correlation. Further, in the case of extreme values (outliers) and associations like non-linear associations, the correlation coefficient may be very low and may depict no relationship or association. However, there may be real and good association among the variables.

8.3   Hypothesis Testing

At this point in time it is apt for us to briefly touch upon hypothesis testing. This is one of the important aspects in statistics. In hypothesis testing we start with an assertion or claim or status quo about a particular population parameter of one or more populations. This assertion or claim or status quo is known as "null hypothesis" or H_0. An example of the null hypothesis may be a statement like the following: the population mean of population 1 is equal to population mean of population 2. There is also another statement known as the alternate hypothesis, or H_1, which is opposite to the null hypothesis. In our example the alternate hypothesis specifies that there is significant difference between population mean of population 1 and the population mean of population 2. Level of significance or Type I error of normally 0.05 is specified. This is nothing but the possibility that the null hypothesis is rejected when actually it is true. This is represented by the symbol α. The smaller the value of α, the smaller the risk of Type I error.

Then we decide the sample size required to reduce the errors.

We use test statistics to either reject the null hypothesis or not to reject the null hypothesis. When we reject the null hypothesis it means that the alternate hypothesis is true. However, we could not reject the null hypothesis does not mean that the alternate hypothesis is true. It only shows that we do not have sufficient evidence to reject the null hypothesis. Normally t-value is the test statistic used.

Then we use the data and arrive at the sample value of the test statistic. We then calculate p-value on the basis of the test statistic. p-value is nothing but the probability that the test statistic is equal to or more than the sample value of the test statistic when the null hypothesis is true. We then compare the p-value with the level of significance (i.e., α). If the p-value is less than the level of significance then the null hypothesis is rejected. This also means that the alternate hypothesis is accepted. If the p-value is greater than or equal to the level of significance then we cannot reject the null hypothesis.

The p-value is used (among many other uses in the field of statistics) to validate the significance of the parameters to the model in the case of regression analysis. If the p-value of any parameter in the regression model is less than the level of significance (typically 0.05), then we reject the null hypothesis that there is no significant contribution of the parameter to the model and we accept the alternate hypothesis that there is significant contribution of the parameter to the model. If p-value of a parameter is greater than or equal to the level of significance then we cannot reject the null hypothesis that there is no significant contribution of the parameter to the model. We include in the final model only those parameters that have significance to the model.

8.4   Simple Linear Regression

As we mentioned in the introduction to this chapter, simple linear regression depicts the linear relationship between two associated variables—a response (i.e., dependent) variable and an independent variable, which can be depicted through a regression equation. This regression equation can be used for the prediction of the unknown response variable when we know the value of the dependent variable. This is so, as the regression describes how one variable (i.e., response variable) depends upon another variable (i.e., independent variable).

It is to be noted that the regression equation guarantees predicting the values of the response variable correctly when the independent variable for which the response variable is required to be predicted is within the range of the data of the independent variable used to create the regression equation. In other cases, the regression equation predicted value may not be reliable. This is so because we do not know whether the regression equation holds well beyond the values of the independent variable we had in hand and used to create the regression equation. However, each predicted value may have some residue. Also, the regression equation may have a small amount of residue.

8.4.1   Assumptions of Regression

There are four assumptions of regression. These need to be fulfilled if we need to rely upon any regression equation. They are

- Linear association between the dependent variable and the independent variable

- Independence of the errors around the regression line between the actual and predicted values of the response variable

- Normality of the distribution of errors

- Equal variance of the distribution of the response variable for each level of the independent variable. This is also known as homoscedasticity.

8.4.2   Simple Linear Regression Equation

The regression line is a smoothed graph of averages. It is basically smoothing of the averages of the response variable for each value of the independent variable. The regression line is drawn in such a way that it minimizes the error of the fitted values with respect to the actual values. This method is known as the least squares method and it minimizes the sum of the squared differences between the actual values of the response variable and the predicted values of the response variable. The Lasso Regression method and Ridge Regression method are a few of the variants of the least squares method. As an alternative to the least squares method, we can use methods like quantile regression or least absolute deviation. The simple linear regression equation takes the following form:

$$Y_1 = \beta_0 + \beta_1 x_1$$

In the foregoing equation, β_0 is known the intercept and the β_1 is known as the slope of the regression line. Intercept is the value of the response variable when the value of the independent variable (i.e., x) is zero. This depicts the point at which the regression line touches the y-axis when x is zero. The slope can be calculated easily using the following formula: (R x Standard Deviation of the response variable) / (Standard Deviation of the independent variable).

From the foregoing you can see that when the value of the independent variable increases by one standard deviation, the value of the response variable increases by R x one standard deviation of the response variable, where R is the coefficient of correlation.

8.4.3   Creating Simple Regression Equation in R

It is very easy to create the regression equation in R. We need to use the following function:

- lm(response variable ~ independent variable, data = dataframe name)

Let us take a simple example to understand the usage of the previous command. Assuming the competence or capability of sales personnel is equal, keeping the sale restricted to one single product, we have a set of data which contains the number of hours of efforts expended by each salesperson and the corresponding number of sales made.

```
> cust_df <- read.table("cust1.txt", header = TRUE, sep = ",")
> cust_df
   Sales_Effort Product_Sales
1           100            10
2            82             8
3            71             7
4           111            11
5           112            11
6            61             6
7            62             6
8           113            11
9           101            10
10           99            10
11           79             8
12           81             8
13           51             5
14           50             5
15           49             5
16           30             3
17           31             3
18           29             3
19           20             2
20           41             4
21           39             4
> summary(cust_df)
  Sales_Effort      Product_Sales
 Min.   : 20.00    Min.   : 2.000
 1st Qu.: 41.00    1st Qu.: 4.000
 Median : 62.00    Median : 6.000
 Mean   : 67.24    Mean   : 6.667
 3rd Qu.: 99.00    3rd Qu.:10.000
 Max.   :113.00    Max.   :11.000
```

Figure 8-3. *Creating a data frame from a text file (data for the examples)*

In Figure 8-3, we have imported a table of data containing 21 records with the **Sales_ Effort** and the **Product_Sales** from a file by name **cust1.txt** into a data frame by name **cust_df**. The **Sales_Effort** is in the number of hours of effort put in by the salesperson during the first two weeks of a month and the **Product_Sales** is the number of sales closed by the salesperson during the same period. The summary of the data is also shown in the above figure.

In this data we can treat **Product_Sales** as the response variable and **Sales_Effort** as the independent variable as the product sales depend upon the sales effort put in place by the salespersons.

We will now run the simple linear regression to model the relationship between **Product_Sales** and **Sales_Effort** using the **lm(response variable ~ independent variable, data = dataframe name)** command of R:

```
> mod_simp_reg <- lm(Product_Sales ~ Sales_Effort, data = cust_df)
> summary(mod_simp_reg)

Call:
lm(formula = Product_Sales ~ Sales_Effort, data = cust_df)

Residuals:
     Min       1Q   Median       3Q      Max
-0.16988 -0.07148 -0.01818  0.09617  0.20779

Coefficients:
              Estimate Std. Error t value Pr(>|t|)
(Intercept)  0.0500779  0.0585019   0.856    0.403
Sales_Effort 0.0984054  0.0007955 123.703   <2e-16 ***
---
Signif. codes:  0 '***' 0.001 '**' 0.01 '*' 0.05 '.' 0.1 ' ' 1

Residual standard error: 0.1086 on 19 degrees of freedom
Multiple R-squared:  0.9988,    Adjusted R-squared:  0.9987
F-statistic: 1.53e+04 on 1 and 19 DF,  p-value: < 2.2e-16

>
```

Figure 8-4. *Generating a simple linear regression model in R*

Figure 8-4 provides the command run in R to generate the simple linear regression model as well as the summary of the model. The model arrived at is named **mod_simp_ reg** and the **summary** command throws up the details of the simple linear regression model arrived at.

The initial part shows which element of the data frame is regressed against which other element and the name of the data frame which contained the data, to arrive at the model.

Residuals depict the difference between the actual value of the response variable and the value of the response variable predicted using the regression equation. Maximum residual is shown as 0.20779. Spread of residuals is provided here by specifying the values of min, max, median, Q1, and Q3 of the residuals. In this case the spread is from -0.16988 to +0.20779. As the principle behind the regression line and regression equation is to reduce the error or this difference, the expectation is that the median value should be very near to 0. As you can see here the median value is -0.01818 which is almost equal to 0. The prediction error can go up—to the maximum value of the residual. As this value (i.e., 0.20779) is very small, we can accept this residual.

The next section specifies the coefficient details. Here β_0 is given by the intercept estimate (i.e., 0.0500779) and β_1 is given by Sales_Effort estimate (0.0984054). Hence, the simple linear regression equation is as follows:

Product_Sales$_1$ = 0.0500779 + 0.0984054 Sales_Effort$_1$

The value next to the coefficient estimate is the ***standard error*** of the estimate. This specifies the uncertainty of the estimate. Then comes the ***"t" value*** of the ***standard error***. This specifies as to how large the coefficient estimate is with respect to the uncertainty. The next value is the probability that absolute(t) value is greater than the one specified which is due to a chance error. Ideally "Pr" or Probability value, or popularly known as ***"p-value,"*** should be very small (like 0.001, 0.005, 0.01, or 0.05) for the relationship between the response variable and the independent variable to be significant. ***p-value*** is also known as the ***value of significance***. As here the probability of the error of the coefficient of Sales_Effort is very less (i.e., almost near 0) (i.e. <2e-16), we reject the null hypothesis that there is no significance of the parameter to the model and accept the alternate hypothesis that there is significance of the parameter to the model. Hence, we conclude that there is significant relationship between the response variable Product_Sales and the independent variable Sales_Effort. Number of asterisks (*s) next to the p-value of each parameter specifies the level of significance. Please refer to "Signif. codes" in the model summary as given in Figure 8-4.

The next section shows the overall model quality-related statistics. Among these,

- The ***degrees of freedom*** specified here is nothing but the number of rows of data minus the number of coefficients. In our case it is 21 – 2 = 19. This is the residual degrees of freedom. Ideally, the number of degrees of freedom should be large compared to the number of coefficients for avoiding the overfitting of the data to the model. We have dealt with overfitting and underfitting of the data to the model in one the chapters. Let us remember for the time being that the overfitting is not good. Normally, by thumb rule 30 rows of data for each variable is considered good for the training sample. Further, we cannot use the ordinary least squares method if the number of rows of data is less than the number of independent variables.

- ***Residual standard error*** shows the sum of the squares of the residuals as divided by the degrees of freedom (in our case 19) as specified in the summary. This is 0.1086 and is very low, as required by us.

- ***Multiple R-squared*** value shown here is nothing but the square of the ***correlation coefficient*** (i.e., R). ***Multiple R-squared*** is also known as the ***coefficient of determination***. However, ***adjusted R-squared value*** is the one which is the adjusted value of R-squared adjusted to avoid overfitting. Here again, we rely more on adjusted R-squared value than on multiple R-squared. The value of adjusted R-squared is 0.9987, which is very high and shows the excellent relationship between the response variable ***Product_Sales*** and the independent variable ***Sales_Effort***.

- Finally, the **F-statistic** is based on **F-test**. As in the case of coefficients here also we want the **p-value** to be very small (like 0.001, 0.005, 0.01, 0.05) for the model to be significant. As you can see in our case it is < 0.001 (i.e. <2.2e-16). Hence, the model is significant. In case of current example there is only one independent variable and hence this p-value is same as that for the independent variable.

As seen above, it seems that there is an excellent association between the response variable Product_Sales and the independent variable Sales_Effort.

8.4.4 Testing the Assumptions of Regression:

Before accepting the model as usable, it is essential to validate that the regression assumptions are true in respect to the fitted model.

8.4.4.1 Test of Linearity

In order to test the linearity, we plot the residuals against the corresponding values of the independent variable. Figure 8-5 depicts this.

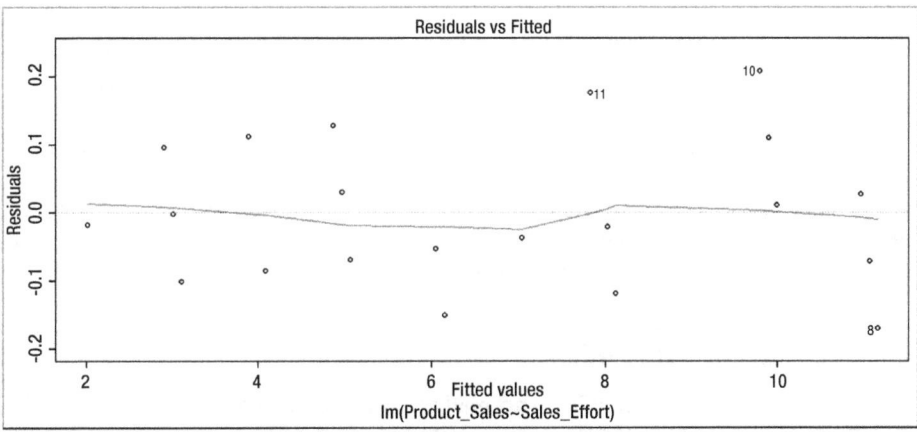

Figure 8-5. *Residuals vs. fitted plot to test the linearity*

For the model to pass the test of linearity we should not have any pattern in the distribution of the residuals and they should be randomly placed around the 0.0 residual line. That is, the residuals will be randomly varying around the mean of the value of the response variable. In our case, as we can see there are no patterns in the distribution of the residuals. Hence, it passes the condition of linearity.

8.4.4.2   Test of Independence of Errors Around the Regression Line

This test is not required to be conducted when the data is collected over the same period of time. In our case, the data is collected over the same two-week period and hence this test is not required. This test is primarily conducted to check the autocorrelation which is introduced when the data is collected over different periods. Further, as seen in the earlier diagram (used in the case of test of linearity) the residuals are distributed randomly around the mean value of the response variable. If we need to test for the autocorrelation, we can use the Durbin-Watson test as shown in Figure 8-6.

```
>
> library(lmtest)
> dwtest(mod_simp_reg)

        Durbin-Watson test

data:  mod_simp_reg
DW = 1.5074, p-value = 0.08608
alternative hypothesis: true autocorrelation is greater than 0

> #if the p value is <0.05 then the residuals are significantly correlated
> #in our case p value is >0.05 which means that there is no evidence of correlation
> |
```

Figure 8-6. *Durbin-Watson test in R to check autocorrelation*

In the case of Durbin-Watson test the null hypothesis (i.e., $H_{0)}$ is that there is no autocorrelation and the alternative hypothesis (i.e., $H_{1)}$ is that there is autocorrelation. If p-value is < 0.05 then we reject the null hypothesis—that is, we conclude that there is autocorrelation. In the foregoing case the p-value is greater than 0.05 and it means that there is no evidence to reject the null hypothesis that there is no autocorrelation. Hence, the test of independence of errors around the regression line passes. Alternatively for this test you can use ***durbinWatsonTest()*** function from library(car).

8.4.4.3   Test of Normality

As per this test the residuals should be normally distributed. In order to check on this we will look at the Normal Q-Q plot (created using the ***plot(model name)*** command):

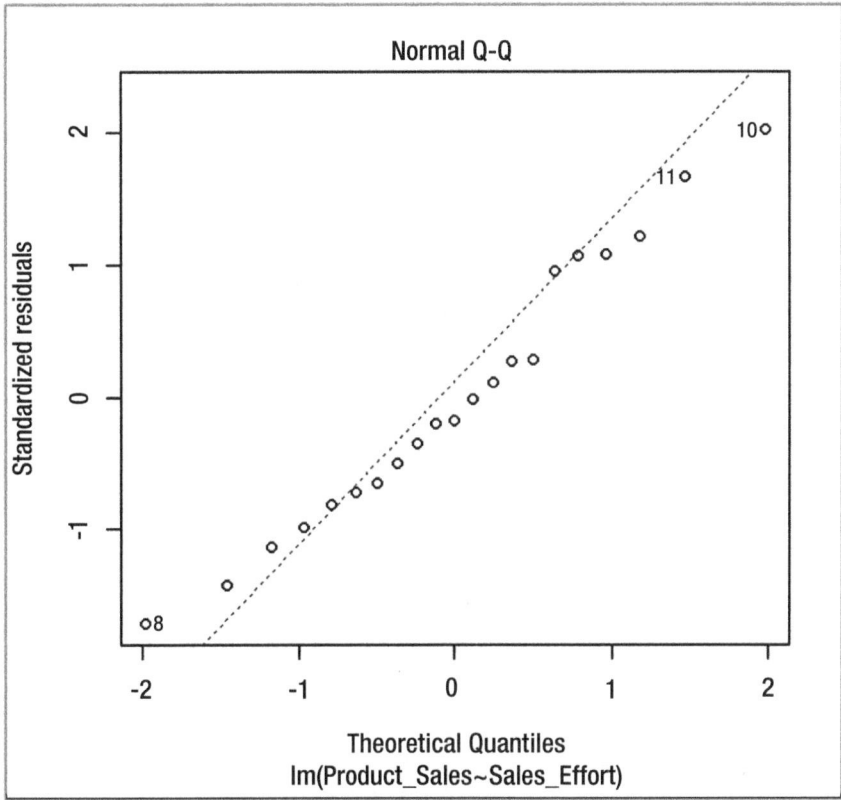

Figure 8-7. *Test for assumption of "normality" using normal Q-Q plot*

Figure 8-7 shows that the residuals are almost on the straight line in the foregoing Normal Q-Q plot. This shows that the residuals are normally distributed. Hence, the normality test of the residuals is passed.

8.4.4.4 Equal variance of the distribution of the response variable

We can use the same plot of the residuals we used for testing the linearity. As we can see from the plot (above in case of test of linearity), there is there no significant difference in the variation of the residuals for different levels of the independent variable's values. Hence, we consider this test as passed.

8.4.4.5   Other ways of validating the assumptions to be fulfilled by a Regression model

There are many other ways of validating whether the assumptions of the regression are fulfilled by the regression model. These are in addition to the ones mentioned earlier.

8.4.4.5.1   Using gvlma library

The other easy way to validate whether a regression model has fulfilled the assumptions of the regression model is by using the *library(gvlma)* which performs the validation of the regression model related assumptions as well as evaluation of other related aspects like skewness, kurtosis, link function, and heteroscedasticity.

Figure 8-8 shows how to use this library and also the output from R.

```
> library(gvlma)
Warning message:
package 'gvlma' was built under R version 3.1.3
> gv_model <- gvlma(mod_simp_reg)
> summary(gv_model)

Call:
lm(formula = Product_Sales ~ Sales_Effort, data = cust_df)

Residuals:
     Min       1Q    Median       3Q       Max
-0.16988 -0.07148 -0.01818  0.09617   0.20779

Coefficients:
               Estimate Std. Error t value Pr(>|t|)
(Intercept)   0.0500779  0.0585019   0.856    0.403
Sales_Effort  0.0984054  0.0007955 123.703   <2e-16 ***
---
Signif. codes:  0 '***' 0.001 '**' 0.01 '*' 0.05 '.' 0.1 ' ' 1

Residual standard error: 0.1086 on 19 degrees of freedom
Multiple R-squared:  0.9988,    Adjusted R-squared:  0.9987
F-statistic: 1.53e+04 on 1 and 19 DF,  p-value: < 2.2e-16


ASSESSMENT OF THE LINEAR MODEL ASSUMPTIONS
USING THE GLOBAL TEST ON 4 DEGREES-OF-FREEDOM:
Level of Significance =  0.05

Call:
 gvlma(x = mod_simp_reg)

                   Value p-value                Decision
Global Stat      1.11278  0.8922 Assumptions acceptable.
Skewness         0.37552  0.5400 Assumptions acceptable.
Kurtosis         0.56546  0.4521 Assumptions acceptable.
Link Function    0.07056  0.7905 Assumptions acceptable.
Heteroscedasticity 0.10124  0.7503 Assumptions acceptable.
```

Figure 8-8. *Using gvlma() function to validate the model assumptions*

In Figure 8-8 we have given the output of *gvlma()* function from R on our model. The Global Stat line clearly shows that the assumptions related to this regression model are acceptable. Here, we need to check for whether the p-value is greater than 0.05. If the p-value is greater than 0.05 then we can safely conclude as shown above that the assumptions are validated. If we have p-value less than 0.05 then we need to revisit the regression model.

8.4.4.5.2   Using the Scale-Location Plot

The Scale-Location graph is the one of the graphs generated using the command *plot(regression model name).* In our case this is *plot(mod_simp_reg).* Figure 8-9 shows this graph.

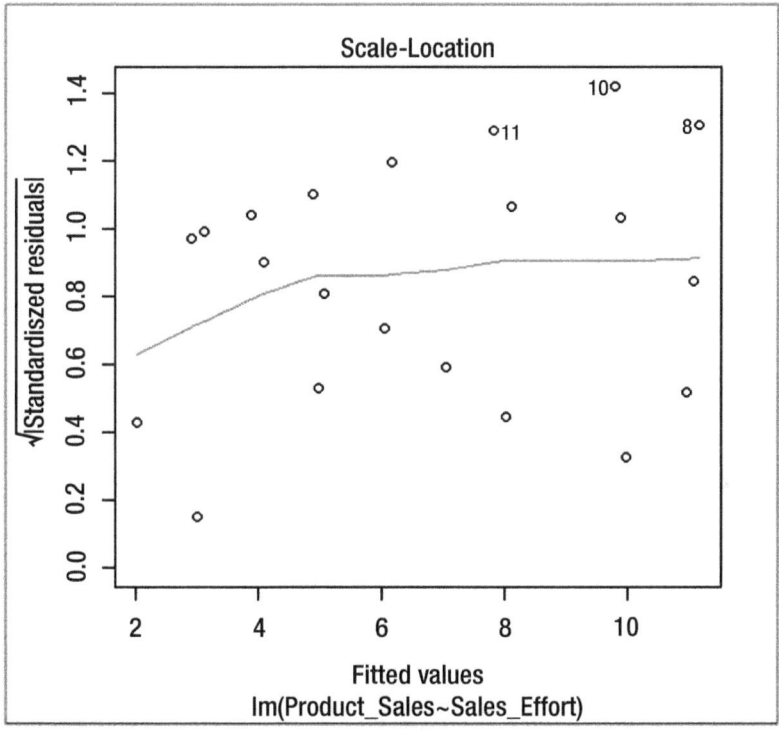

Figure 8-9. *Scale-Location plot generated in R to validate homoscedasticity*

In Figure 8-9 as the points are spread in a random fashion around the near horizontal line, this assures us of that the assumption of constant variance (or homoscedasticity).

8.4.4.5.3 Using crPlots(model name) function from library(car)

We can use ***crPlots(mod_simp_reg)*** command to understand the linearity of the relationship represented by the model. Non-linearity requires us to re-explore the model. The graph in Figure 8-10 shows that the model we created as above (i.e., ***mod_simp_reg***) is linear.

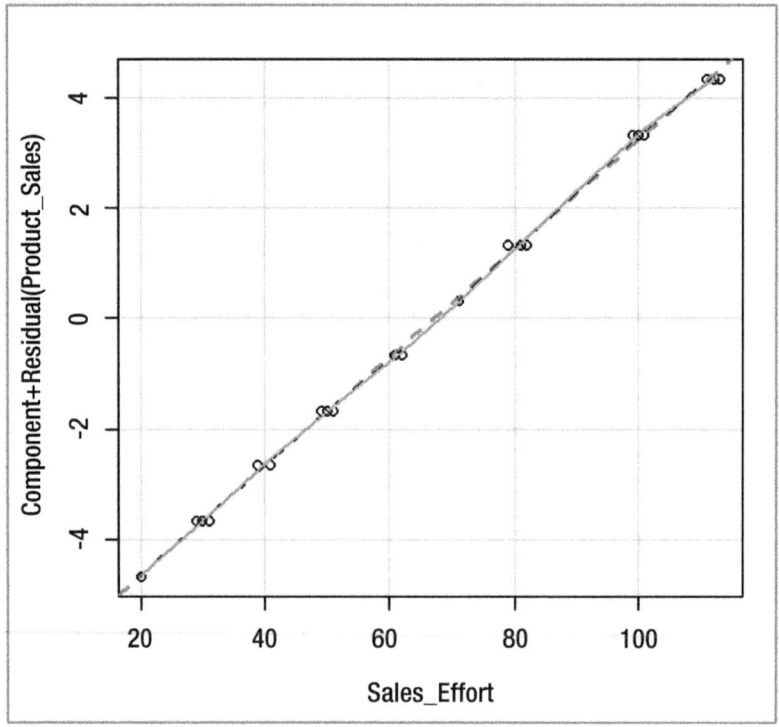

Figure 8-10. *Plot using crPlots() function to validate the linearity assumption*

8.4.5   Conclusion

As seen above, the simple linear regression model fitted using the R function *lm(response variable ~ independent variable, data = dataframe name)* representing the simple linear regression equation, namely, **Product_Sales$_i$ = 0.0500779 + 0.0984054 Sales_ Effort$_i$** is a good model as it passes the tests to validate the assumptions of the regression too. A note of caution here is that there are various ways the regression equation may be created and validated.

8.4.6   Predicting the Response Variable

The fitted model not only explains the relationship between the two variables, viz. response variable and the independent variable, but also provides a mechanism to predict the value of the response variable from the value of the new independent variable. This is done as shown in Figure 8-11.

```
>
> predictor <- data.frame(Sales_Effort = 31)
> predicted <- predict(mod_simp_reg, newdata = predictor)
> predicted
       1
3.100644
>
```

Figure 8-11. *Prediction using the model on the new data set*

This is done using the function ***predict(model name, newdata)*** where model name is the name of the model arrived at from the input data and newdata contains the independent variable data for which the response variable has to be predicted.

A prediction interval which specifies the range of the distribution of the prediction can be arrived at as shown in Figure 8-12, with the additional parameter **interval = "prediction"** on the ***predict()*** function. This uses by default the confidence interval as 0.95.

```
>
> predicted <- predict(mod_simp_reg, newdata = predictor, interval = "prediction")
> predicted
       fit      lwr      upr
1 3.100644 2.860316 3.340972
>
> #the above gives the range of the distribution of the prediction
>
```

Figure 8-12. *Calculating prediction interval using the predict() function*

8.4.7   Additional Notes

It may be observed from the model fitted above that the intercept is not zero but it is 0.0500779 whereas actually when there is no sales efforts ideally there should not be any sales. But, it may not be so; there may be some walk in sales possible because of the other means like advertisements, web sites, etc. Similarly, there cannot be partial product sales like 3.1. However, sales efforts put in would have moved the salesperson toward the next potential sale partially. If we are interested in arriving at the model without intercept (i.e., no product sales when there is no sales effort) then we can do so as shown in Figure 8-13 by forcing the intercept to zero value.

```
> mod_simp_reg_wo_intercept <- lm(cust_df$Product_Sales ~ cust_df$Sales_Effort + 0)
> summary(mod_simp_reg_wo_intercept)

Call:
lm(formula = cust_df$Product_Sales ~ cust_df$Sales_Effort + 0)

Residuals:
      Min        1Q    Median        3Q       Max
-0.190158 -0.060146 -0.001823  0.097205  0.196233

Coefficients:
                       Estimate Std. Error t value Pr(>|t|)
cust_df$Sales_Effort 0.0990279  0.0003201   309.4   <2e-16 ***
---
Signif. codes:  0 '***' 0.001 '**' 0.01 '*' 0.05 '.' 0.1 ' ' 1

Residual standard error: 0.1079 on 20 degrees of freedom
Multiple R-squared:  0.9998,    Adjusted R-squared:  0.9998
F-statistic: 9.573e+04 on 1 and 20 DF,  p-value: < 2.2e-16
```

Figure 8-13.   *Generating simple linear regression model without intercept*

However, if we have to believe this model and use this model we have to validate the fulfillment of the other assumptions of the regression.

8.5   Chapter Summary

- You went through some examples as to how the relationship between various aspects/factors influence or decide or impact other aspects/factors. Understanding these relationships helps us not only to understand what can happen to the other associated factors but also to predict the value of others. You understood how the regression model or regression equation explains the relationship between a response variable and the independent variable(s). You also understood about the linear or non-linear relationship as well as simple regression and multiple regression.

- You explored the concept of correlation with examples. You explored the uses of correlation, strong correlation, positive correlation, negative correlation, and so on. You also understood how to calculate the correlation coefficient (R).

- You understood simple linear regression by highlighting that it is a smoothed line of averages. You also explored the four important assumptions of regression like linearity, equivalence of errors, normality, and homoscedasticity. You understood the simple linear regression, what intercept and slope are, and how to calculate them.

- You explored with examples how, using R, you can arrive at the best-fit simple linear regression model and the simple linear regression equation. You understood through examples as well using various methods how to validate that the best-fit model and equation you arrived at is validated for the fulfillment of the regression assumptions.

- You explored how the simple linear regression model arrived at can be used to predict the value of the response variable when it is not known but when the related independent variable value is known.

- You looked at how, using R, you can arrive at the simple linear regression model without intercept and the usage of the same.

CHAPTER 9

▓ ▓ ▓

Multiple Linear Regression

In Chapter 8, you explored simple linear regression, which depicts the relationship between the response variable and one predictor. You saw that the expectation is that the response variable is a continuous variable that is normally distributed. If the response variable is a discrete variable, you use a different regression method. If the response variable can take values such as yes/no or multiple discrete variables (for example, views such as *strongly agree, agree, partially agree,* and *do not agree*), you use logistic regression. You will explore logistic regression in the next chapter. When you have more than one predictor—say, two predictors or three predictors or *n* predictors (with *n* not equal to 1)—the regression between the response variable and the predictors is known as *multiple regression,* and the linear relationship between them is expressed as *multiple linear regression* or a *multiple linear regression equation.* In this chapter, you will see examples of situations in which many factors affect one response, outcome, or dependent variable.

Imagine that you want to construct a building. Your main cost components are the cost of labor and the cost of materials including cement and steel. Your profitability is positively impacted if the costs of cement, steel, and other materials decrease while keeping the cost of labor constant. Instead, if the costs of materials increase, your profitability is negatively impacted while keeping the cost of labor constant. Your profitability will further decrease if the cost of labor also increases.

Although it is possible in the market for one price to go up or down or all the prices to move in the same direction. Suppose the real estate industry is very hot, and there are lots of takers for the houses, apartments, or business buildings. Then, if there is more demand for the materials and the supply decreases, the prices of these materials are likely to increase. If the demand decreases for the houses, apartments, or business buildings, the prices of these materials are likely to decrease as well (because of the demand being less than the supply).

Now let's presume that the selling prices are quite fixed because of the competition, and hence the profitability is decided and driven primarily by the cost or cost control. We can now collect data related to the cost of cement, steel, and other materials, as well as the cost of labor as predictors or independent variables, and profitability (in percent) as the response variable. Such a relationship can be expressed through a multiple linear regression model or multiple linear regression equation.

In this example, suppose we find that the relationship of the cost of other materials (one of the predictors) to the response variable is dependent on the cost of the cement. Then we say that there is a *significant interaction* between the cost of other materials and the cost of the cement. We include the interaction term *cost of other materials:cost*

© Dr. Umesh R. Hodeghatta and Umesha Nayak 2017
U. R. Hodeghatta and U. Nayak, *Business Analytics Using R - A Practical Approach,*
DOI 10.1007/978-1-4842-2514-1_9

of cement in the formula for generating the multiple linear regression model while also including all the predictors. Thus our multiple linear regression model is built using the predictors *cost of cement, cost of steel, cost of other materials,* and the interaction term, *cost of other materials: cost of cement* vs. the *profitability* as the response variable.

Now imagine that you are a Human Resources (HR) manager or head. You know that the compensation to be paid to an employee depends on her qualifications, experience, and skill level, as well as the availability of other people with that particular skill set vs. the demand. In this case, compensation is the response variable, and the other parameters are the independent variables, or the predictor variables. Typically, the higher the experience and higher the skill levels, the lower the availability of people as compared to the demand, and the higher the compensation should be. The skill levels and the availability of those particular skills in the market may significantly impact the compensation, whereas the qualifications may not impact compensation as much as the skill levels and the availability of those particular skills in the market.

In this case, there may be a possible relationship between experience and skill level; ideally, more experience means a higher skill level. However, a candidate could have a low skill level in a particular skill while having an overall high level of experience—in which case, experience might not have a strong relationship with skill level. This feature of having a high correlation between two or more predictors themselves is known as *multicollinearity* and needs to be considered when arriving at the multiple linear regression model and the multiple linear regression equation.

Understanding the *interactions between the predictors* as well as *multicollinearity* is very important in ensuring that we get a correct and useful multiple regression model. When we have the model generated, it is necessary to validate it on all *four assumptions of regression*:

- Linearity between the response variable and the predictors (also known as independent variables)

- Independence of residuals

- Normality of the distribution of the residuals

- Homoscedasticity, an assumption of equal variance of the errors

The starting point for building any multiple linear regression model is to get our data in a data-frame format, as this is the requirement of the lm( ) function. The expectation when using the lm( ) function is that the response variable data is distributed normally. However, independent variables are not required to be normally distributed. Predictors can contain factors.

Multiple regression modeling may be used to model the relationship between a response variable and two or more predictor variables to *n* number of predictor variables (say, 100 or more variables). The more features that have a relationship with the response variable, the more complicated the modeling will be. For example, a person's health, if quantified through a health index, might be affected by the quality of that person's environment (pollution, stress, relationships, and water quality), the quality of that person's lifestyle (smoking, drinking, eating, and sleeping habits), and genetics (history of the health of the parents). These factors may have to be taken into consideration to understand the health index of the person.

9.1   Using Multiple Linear Regression

Now, we start the discussion as to how to arrive at multiple linear regression.

9.1.1   The Data

To demonstrate multiple linear regression, we have created data with three variables: Annual Salary, Experience in Years, and Skill Level. These are Indian salaries, but for the sake of convenience, we have converted them into US dollars and rounded them into thousands. Further, we have not restricted users to assessing and assigning skill levels in decimal points. Hence, in the context of this data even Skill Level is represented as continuous data. This makes sense, as in an organization with hundreds of employees, it is not fair to categorize all of them, say, into five buckets, but better to differentiate them with skill levels such as 4.5, 3.5, 2.5, 0.5, and 1.5. In this data set, all the variables are continuous variables.

Here, we import the data from the CSV file sal1.txt to the data frame sal_data_1:

```
> sal_data_1 <- read.csv("sal1.txt", header = TRUE, sep = ",")
```

If you use the head() and tail() functions on the data, you will get an idea of what the data looks like, as shown here:

```
> head(sal_data_1)
  Annu_Salary Expe_Yrs Skill_lev
1        4000      0.0       0.5
2        6000      1.0       1.0
3        8000      2.0       1.5
4       10000      3.0       2.0
5       12000      4.0       2.5
6       14000      4.5       3.5
> tail(sal_data_1)
   Annu_Salary Expe_Yrs Skill_lev
43       15000     5.50       3.0
44       15000     5.00       3.5
45       19000     6.50       4.0
46       19000     6.30       4.2
47        5000     0.50       0.5
48        6000     0.75       1.0
```

Please note that we have not shown all the data, as the data set has 48 records. In addition, this data is illustrative only and may not be representative of a real scenario. The data is collected at a certain point in time.

9.1.2 Correlation

We explained correlation in Chapter 8. *Correlation* specifies the way that one variable relates to another variable. This is easily done in R by using the cor() function.

The correlation between these three variables (Annual Salary, Experience in Years, Skill Level) is shown here:

```
> cor(sal_data_1)
            Annu_Salary  Expe_Yrs  Skill_lev
Annu_Salary   1.0000000 0.9888955 0.9414029
Expe_Yrs      0.9888955 1.0000000 0.8923255
Skill_lev     0.9414029 0.8923255 1.0000000
```

As you can see, there is a very high correlation of about 0.9888 between Annual Salary and Experience in Years. Similarly, there is a very high correlation of about 0.9414 between Annual Salary and Skill Level. Also, there is a very high correlation of about 0.8923 between Experience in Years and Skill Level. Each variable is highly correlated to the other variable.

The relationship between two pairs of variables is generated visually by using the R command, as shown here:

```
> library(caret)
> featurePlot(x=sal_data_1[,c("Expe_Yrs","Skill_lev")], y=sal_data_1$Annu_Salary, plot = "pairs")
```

Here, we use the caret package and the featurePlot() function. The response variable is plotted as y, and the predictor variables are plotted as x.

The visual realization of the relationship between the variables generated through this command is shown in Figure 9-1.

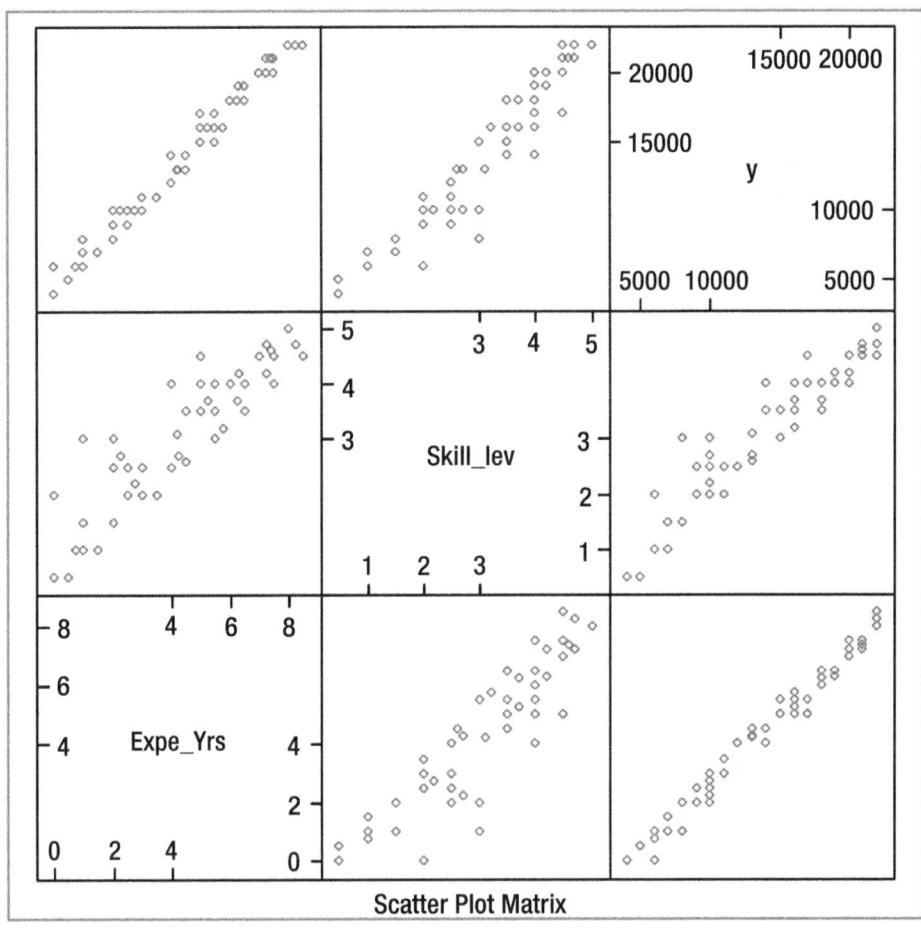

Figure 9-1. *Generated scatter-plot matrix*

9.1.3 Arriving at the Model

Now, let's create the multiple linear regression model by using the lm() function of R. To start, let's generate the model by using all the parameters, as they are highly correlated with Annual Salary as the response (or dependent) variable and we want to use this model to predict, or set, the salary later in tune with this model. The other variables, Experience in Years and Skill Level, will be predictor (or independent) variables. The command in R to generate the multiple linear regression model is shown here:

```
> sal_model_1 <- lm(Annu_Salary ~ Expe_Yrs + Skill_lev, data = sal_data_1)
```

The model created using the lm() function is shown here along with the summary—generated using summary(model name):

```
> summary(sal_model_1)

Call:
lm(formula = Annu_Salary ~ Expe_Yrs + Skill_lev, data = sal_data_1)

Residuals:
    Min      1Q  Median      3Q     Max
 -605.6  -318.5   -23.8   354.3   666.0

Coefficients:
             Estimate Std. Error t value Pr(>|t|)
(Intercept)  3011.66     162.58   18.52  < 2e-16 ***
Expe_Yrs     1589.68      50.86   31.26  < 2e-16 ***
Skill_lev    1263.65     102.03   12.38 4.25e-16 ***
---
Signif. codes:  0 '***' 0.001 '**' 0.01 '*' 0.05 '.' 0.1 ' ' 1

Residual standard error: 377.5 on 45 degrees of freedom
Multiple R-squared:  0.995,     Adjusted R-squared:  0.9948
F-statistic:  4469 on 2 and 45 DF,  p-value: < 2.2e-16
```

You can see in this summary of the multiple regression model that both independent variables are significant to the model, as the p-value for both is less than 0.05. Further, the overall model p-value is also less than 0.05. Further, as you can see, the adjusted R-squared value of 99.48 percent indicates that the model explains 99.48 percent of the variance in the response variable. Further, the residuals are spread around the median value of –23.8, very close to 0.

You can explore the individual aspects of this model by using specific R commands. You can use fitted(model name) to understand the values fitted using the model. You can use residuals(model name) to understand the residuals for each value of Annual Salary fitted vs. the actual Annual Salary as per the data used. You can use coefficients(model name) to get the details of the coefficients (which is part of the summary data of the model shown previously). The following shows the use of these commands in R:

```
> fitted(sal_model_1)
       1        2        3        4        5        6        7        8        9       10       11       12       13       14       15       16
 3643.481  5864.962  5086.484 10307.985 12529.487 14587.975 16014.636 16424.959 17604.314 19825.815 22047.316  9981.956  9980.132  9513.147  8592.279 10939.809
      17       18       19       20       21       22       23       24       25       26       27       28       29       30       31       32
13179.636  6496.806  6659.821 11102.624 13450.690 16646.460 16809.475 20620.654 20475.964 15545.827 15382.812  5535.953 20588.051 13605.611 22065.641 22210.332
      33       34       35       36       37       38       39       40       41       42       43       44       45       46       47       48
16032.961 16177.661 16195.976 17622.658 17767.328 19968.830 19844.140 10244.971 10263.295 10000.281 15545.827 15382.812 18399.152 18339.946  4436.320  5467.563
> residuals(sal_model_1)
       1          2          3          4          5          6          7          8          9         10         11         12
 356.5190663  135.0176519  -86.4637644 -307.9851807 -529.4865971 -587.9734921  -14.6361826 -424.9588508  395.6864857  174.1850693  -47.3165470   15.0439819
      13         14         15         16         17         18         19         20         21         22         23         24
-350.1319385 -513.1465149 -392.2756864   60.1907347 -179.6385638  503.1935674  340.1759861 -102.8238466 -450.6900799  353.5397329  190.5251516  379.3464035
      25         26         27         28         29         30         31         32         33         34         35         36
 524.0361026 -545.8266793 -382.8120950  461.0468146  411.9493197 -605.6109649  -65.6412292 -210.3309283  -32.9610647 -177.6507639 -195.9756461  377.3616033
      37         38         39         40         41         42         43         44         45         46         47         48
 232.6719044   11.1704880  155.8601872 -144.9708994 -163.2954816   -0.2809203 -545.8266793 -382.8120980  600.5478158  666.0536523  561.6804024  532.4369849
> coefficients(sal_model_1)
(Intercept)    Expe_Yrs    Skill_lev
   3011.657    1589.677    1263.648
```

9.1.4   Validation of the Assumptions of Regression

You can use plot(model name) to explore the model further. This command generates diagnostic plots to evaluate the fit of the model. The plots generated are shown in Figures 9-2 to 9-5.

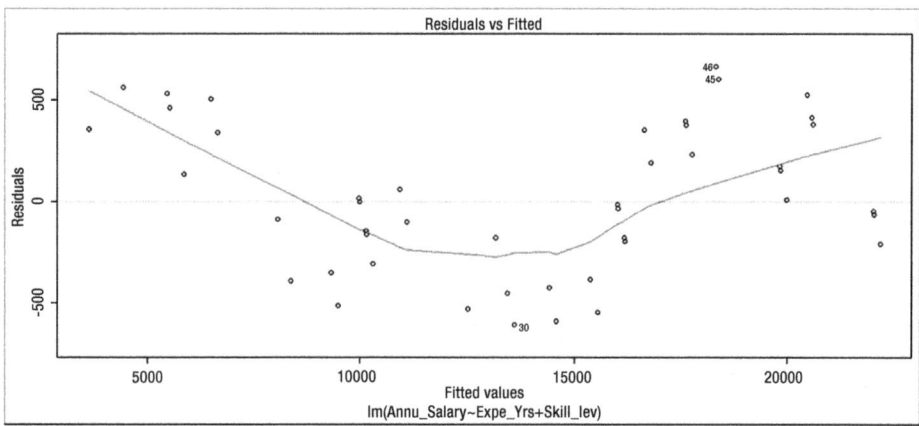

Figure 9-2. *Residuals vs. fitted*

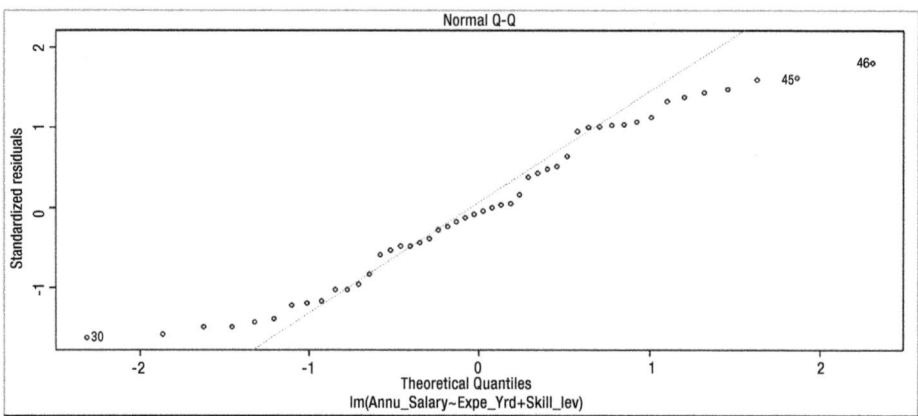

Figure 9-3. *Normal Q-Q plot*

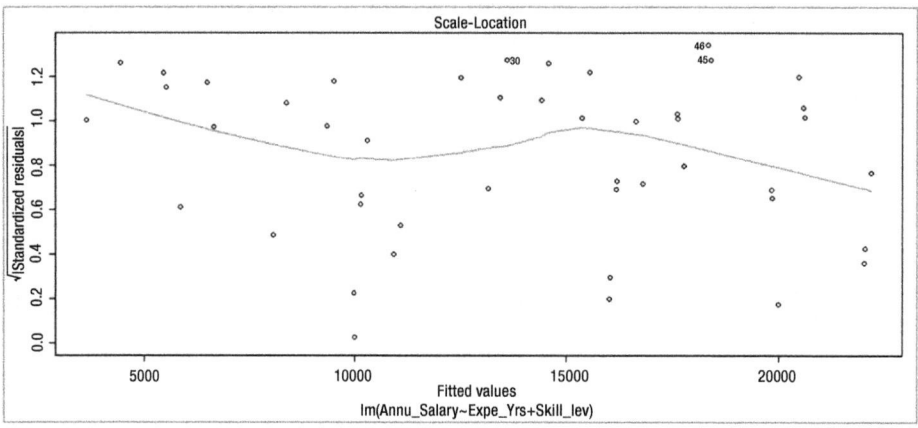

Figure 9-4. *Scale-Location plot*

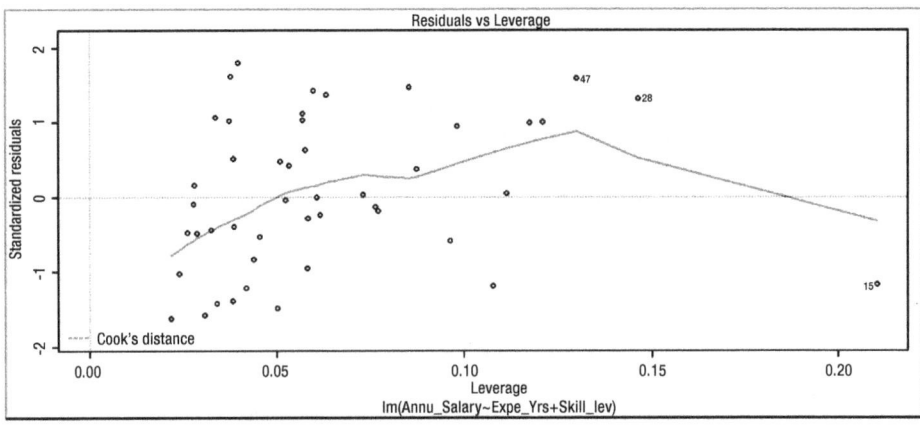

Figure 9-5. *Residuals vs. leverage plot*

Here the residuals vs. fitted plot seems to show that the residuals are spread randomly around the dashed line at 0. If the response variable is linearly related to the predictor variables, there should be no relationship between the fitted values and the residuals. The residuals should be randomly distributed. Even though there seems to be a pattern, in this case we know clearly from the data that there is a linear relationship between the response variable and the predictors. This is also shown through high correlation between the response variable and each predictor variable. Hence, we cannot conclude that the linearity assumption is violated. The linear relationship between the response variable and predictors can be tested through the crPlots(model name) function, as shown in Figure 9-6.

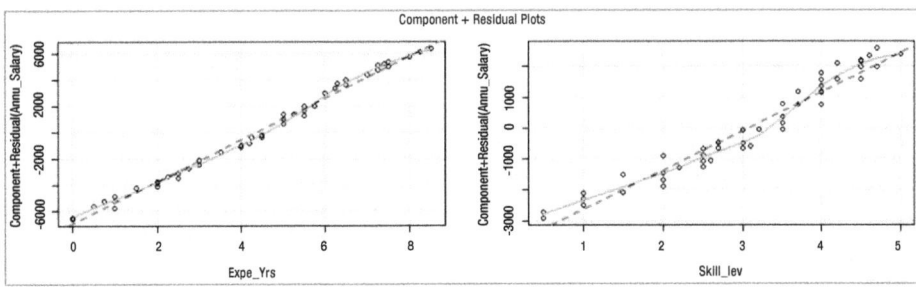

Figure 9-6. *crPlots(model name) plot showing the linearity*

As both the graphs show near linearity, we can accept that the model sal_model_1 fulfills the test of linearity.

Further, the scale-location plot shows the points distributed randomly around a near-horizontal line. Thus, the assumption of constant variance of the errors is fulfilled. We validate this understanding with ncvTest(model name) from the car library. Here, the null hypothesis is that there is constant error variance and the alternative hypothesis is that the error variance changes with the level of fitted values of the response variable or linear combination of predictors. As p-value is >0.05 we cannot reject the null hypothesis that there is constant error variance.

```
> ncvTest(sal_model_1)
Non-constant Variance Score Test
Variance formula: ~ fitted.values
Chisquare = 0.1810408     Df = 1     p = 0.6704803
> #As the p-value is > 0.05 and is not significant, we
> #conclude that the assumption of constant variance
> #is met.
```

The Normal Q-Q plot seems to show that the residuals are not normally distributed. However, the visual test may not always be appropriate. We need to ensure normality only if it matters to our analysis and is really important, because in reality, data may not always be normal. Hence, we need to apply our judgment in such cases. Further, typically, as per the central limit theorem and by rule of thumb, we do not require validating the normality for huge amounts of data, because it has to be normal. Furthermore, if the data is very small, most of the statistical tests may not yield proper results. However, we can validate the normality of the model (that is, of the residuals) through the Shapiro-Wilk normality test by using the shapiro.test(residuals(model name)) command. The resultant output is as follows:

```
> shapiro.test(residuals(sal_model_1))

        Shapiro-Wilk normality test

data:  residuals(sal_model_1)
W = 0.9551, p-value = 0.06401
```

Here, the null hypothesis is that the normality assumption holds good. We reject the null hypothesis if p-value is <0.05. As the p-value is > 0.05, we cannot reject the null hypothesis that normality assumption holds good.

Another way to visually confirm the assumption of normality is by using qqPlot(model name, simulate = TRUE, envelope = 0.95). The R command used is as follows:

```
> qqPlot(sal_model_1, simulate = TRUE, envelope = 0.95)
```

Figure 9-7 shows the resultant plot.

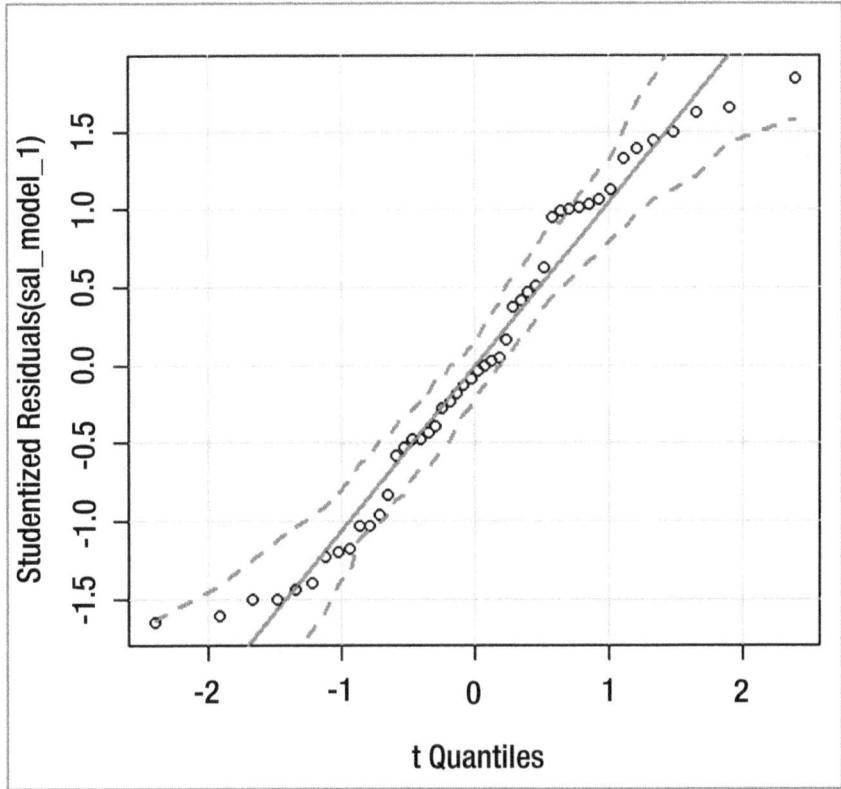

Figure 9-7. *Plot of normality generated through qqPlot(model name, simulate = TRUE, envelope = 0.95)*

As you can see, very few points (only two) are outside the confidence interval. Hence, we can assume that the residuals are normally distributed and that the model has fulfilled the assumption of normality.

The standardized residuals vs. leverage plot shows that most of the standardized residuals are around zero[th] line.

Now, we need to validate the independence of the residuals or the independence of the errors, or lack of autocorrelation. However, in this case, because we know that each data entry belongs to a different employee and is taken at a particular point in time, and that no dependencies exist between the data of one employee and another, we can safely assume that there is independence of the residuals and independence of errors. From an academic-interest point of view, however, you can run a Durbin-Watson test to determine the existence of autocorrelation, or lack of independence of errors. The command in R to do this and the corresponding output is as follows:

```
> durbinWatsonTest(sal_model_1)
 lag Autocorrelation D-W Statistic p-value
   1       0.2987001      1.338564    0.008
Alternative hypothesis: rho != 0
```

As the p-value is < 0.05, the Durbin-Watson test rejects the null hypothesis that there is no autocorrelation. Hence, the Durbin-Watson test holds up the alternate hypothesis that there exists autocorrelation, or the lack of independence of errors. However, as mentioned previously, we know that the data used does not lack independence. Hence, we can ignore the Durbin-Watson test.

As you can see, all the tests of the regression model assumptions are successful.

9.1.5 Multicollinearity

Multicollinearity is another problem that can happen with multiple linear regression methods. Say you have both date of birth and age as predictors. You know that both are the same in a way, or in other words, that one is highly correlated with the other. If two predictor variables are highly correlated with each other, there is no point in considering both of these predictors in a multiple linear regression equation. We usually eliminate one of these predictors from the multiple linear regression model or equation, because multicollinearity can adversely impact the model.

Multicollinearity can be determined in R easily by using the vif(model name) function. *VIF* stands for *variance inflation factor*. Typically, for this test of multicollinearity to pass, the VIF value should be greater than 5. Here is the test showing the calculation of VIF:

```
>
> vif_value <- vif(sal_model_1)
> #VIF stands for Variance Inflation Factor
> #This shows whether there is multicollinearity between the
> #predictor variables
> #By thumb rule if VIF is > 5 then it signifies multicollinearity
> vif_value
 Expe_Yrs Skill_lev
 4.907852  4.907852
>
```

Hence, we can assume that there is no significant multicollinearity. However, we cannot rule out moderate multicollinearity.

Multicollinearity typically impacts the significance of one of the coefficients and makes it nonsignificant. However, in this case, we do not see such an impact. Instead, we see that the coefficients of both predictors are significant. Further, the existence of multicollinearity does not make a model not usable for prediction. Hence, we can use the preceding model for prediction even though we presume multicollinearity according to some schools of statistical thought which suggest multicollinearity when VIF value is greater than 4.

The following shows how to use the model to predict the Annual Salary for the new data of Experience in Years and Skill Level:

```
>
> predictor_New_data <- data.frame(Expe_Yrs = 3, Skill_lev = 3)
> #In the above I have created a new predictor data
> #Through the following command I will chek the predicted
> #value of the response variable Annual Salary
> predict(sal_model_1, newdata = predictor_New_data)
       1
11571.63
> #If we compare this figure with the data we have on hand it seems this
> #value is near to reality
>
```

Now, let's take another set of values for the predictor variables and check what the model returns Annual Salary. The prediction made by sal_model_1 in this case is shown here:

```
>
> predictor_new_data1 <- data.frame(Expe_Yrs = 5, Skill_lev = 5)
> predict(sal_model_1, newdata = predictor_new_data1)
       1
17278.28
> #This is very close to the value of the data we have in our input
> #file for the Experience in Years of 5 and Skill Level of 5
```

If we see significant multicollinearity between the predictor variables, one approach to building the model is to drop one of the predictor variables and proceed with the other. Similarly, you can try leaving out the other predictor and building the model with the first predictor. After both models are built, check which of these models is more significant statistically. One approach to compare the models is to compute the Akaike information criterion (AIC) value. Any model with a lesser AIC value is a more significant model.

In this case, if we eliminate one of the variables (say, Skill Level), we tend to get a regression of only one predictor variable (Experience in Years) against the response variable (Annual Salary), which is nothing but a case of simple linear regression, shown here:

```
> #Let us drop one of the predictor variables Skill_lev as it also
> #normally changes with the experience
> #Let us now get the model of the relationship between the
> #response variable Annual Salary and predictor variable Experience in Years
> sal_model_2 <- lm(Annu_Salary ~ Expe_Yrs, data = sal_data_1)
> summary(sal_model_2)

Call:
lm(formula = Annu_Salary ~ Expe_Yrs, data = sal_data_1)

Residuals:
    Min       1Q   Median       3Q      Max
-1279.40  -591.36   -93.04   584.68  1796.49

Coefficients:
            Estimate Std. Error t value Pr(>|t|)
(Intercept)  4444.63     237.22   18.74   <2e-16 ***
Expe_Yrs     2151.78      47.68   45.13   <2e-16 ***
---
Signif. codes:  0 '***' 0.001 '**' 0.01 '*' 0.05 '.' 0.1 ' ' 1

Residual standard error: 783.9 on 46 degrees of freedom
Multiple R-squared:  0.9779,    Adjusted R-squared:  0.9774
F-statistic:  2037 on 1 and 46 DF,  p-value: < 2.2e-16
```

This is also a significant model with the response variable Annual Salary and the predictor variable Experience in Years (as we know), as the p-value of the model as well as the p-value of the predictor are less than 0.05. Further, the model explains about 97.74 percent of the variance in the response variable.

Alternatively, if we remove the Experience in Years predictor variable, we get the model shown here:

```
> sal_model_3 <- lm(Annu_Salary ~ Skill_lev, data = sal_data_1)
> summary(sal_model_3)

Call:
lm(formula = Annu_Salary ~ Skill_lev, data = sal_data_1)

Residuals:
    Min      1Q  Median      3Q     Max
-5528.9  -597.1   505.6  1389.2  2416.5

Coefficients:
            Estimate Std. Error t value Pr(>|t|)
(Intercept)   1201.2      716.0   1.678      0.1
Skill_lev     4109.2      217.1  18.930   <2e-16 ***
---
Signif. codes:  0 '***' 0.001 '**' 0.01 '*' 0.05 '.' 0.1 ' ' 1

Residual standard error: 1779 on 46 degrees of freedom
Multiple R-squared: 0.8862,    Adjusted R-squared: 0.8838
F-statistic: 358.4 on 1 and 46 DF,  p-value: < 2.2e-16
```

This is also a significant model with the response variable Annual Salary and the predictor variable Skill Level (as we know), as the p-value of the model as well as the p-value of the predictor are less than 0.05. Further, the model explains about 88 percent of the variance in the response variable as shown by the R-squared value.

However, when we have various models available for the same response variable with same predictor variables or different predictor variables, one of the best ways to select the most useful model is to choose the model with the lowest AIC value. Here we have made a comparison of the AIC values of three models: sal_model_1 with both Experience in Years and Skill Level as predictors, sal_model_2 with only Experience in Years as the predictor variable, and sal_model_3 with only Skill Level as the predictor variable:

```
>
> AIC(sal_model_1)
[1] 710.7369
> AIC(sal_model_2)
[1] 858.63
> AIC(sal_model_3)
[1] 858.63
```

If you compare the AIC values as shown, you find that the model with both Experience in Years and Skill Level as predictors is the best model.

9.1.6   Stepwise Multiple Linear Regression

Other ways to build models and select the best model include carrying out a forward stepwise regression or a backward stepwise regression. In the forward stepwise regression, we start with one predictor and at each run keep on adding another predictor variable until we exhaust all the predictor variables. In the case of backward stepwise regression, we start with all the predictors and then start removing the parameters one by one. Both will yield the same result. Let's do a backward stepwise regression now. We will use AIC as shown previously to select the best model. The model with the lowest AIC is the model we'll select.

We need to have the package *MASS* and then use this library to run the `stepAIC(model name)` function from this library. Here is the stepwise multiple linear regression model generation:

```
>
> library(MASS)
> sal_model <- lm(Annu_Salary ~ Expe_Yrs + Skill_lev, data = sal_data_1)
> stepAIC(sal_model, direction = "backward")
Start:  AIC=572.52
Annu_Salary ~ Expe_Yrs + Skill_lev

             Df Sum of Sq       RSS    AIC
<none>                    6411961 572.52
- Skill_lev   1  21857249  28269210 641.73
- Expe_Yrs    1 139199116 145611077 720.41

Call:
lm(formula = Annu_Salary ~ Expe_Yrs + Skill_lev, data = sal_data_1)

Coefficients:
(Intercept)     Expe_Yrs     Skill_lev
       3012         1590          1264

> #In the above you can see that the lowest value of
> #AIC pertains to the starting model with both the predictors
```

This confirms our understanding as per the discussion in the prior section of this chapter. The downside for the effective use of this stepwise approach is that as it drops predictor variables one by one, it does not check for the different combinations of the predictor variables.

9.1.7   All Subsets Approach to Multiple Linear Regression

Another alternative is to use the all subsets regression approach, which evaluates all the possible subsets out of the predictors.

We need the *leaps* package and need to use the `regsubsets(model name)` function. We can use the adjusted R-square option in the plot function as follows to understand which of the predictors we need to include in our model. We should select the model that has the highest adjusted R-square value. How to do this in R is shown here:

```
>
> library(leaps)
> #leaps is the library required to use regsubsets() function
> #this acts similar to the lm() function except that the "lm" is
> #replaced here by regsubsets
> get_leaps <- regsubsets(Annu_Salary ~ Expe_Yrs + Skill_lev, data = sal_data_1, nbest = 2)
> #Normally we have options to use R-Squared or Adjusted R-Squared value to
> #understand which is the best model
> #Best model is the one with highest R-Squared or Adjusted R-Squared value
> plot(get_leaps, scale = "r2")
```

If we use the R-squared value, we get the plot shown in Figure 9-8. We chose the predictor combinations with the highest R-squared value.

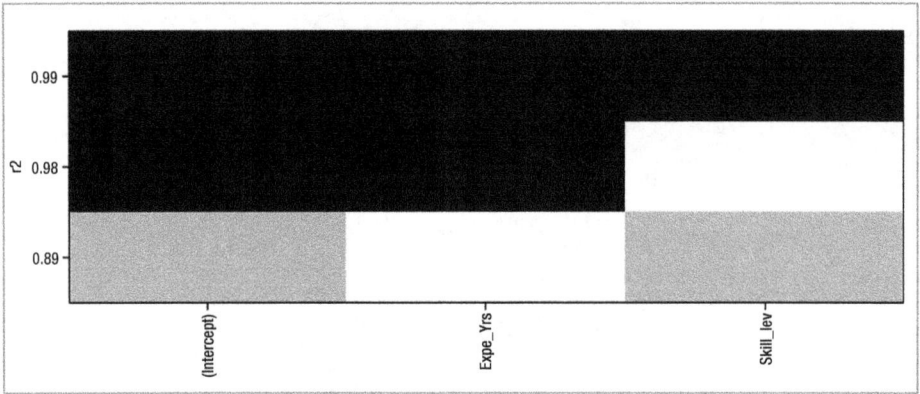

Figure 9-8. *Plot of the multiple regression model generated in R using the all subsets approach scaled with R-squared*

As you can see, we select both the predictors Experience in Years and Skill Level, as this model has the highest R-squared value of 0.99. However, we have seen that the adjusted R-squared is a value that provides better insight than the R-squared value, as it adjusts for the degrees of freedom. If we use the adjusted R-squared instead of R-squared, we get the plot shown in Figure 9-9.

```
>
> plot(get_leaps, scale = "adjr2")
>
```

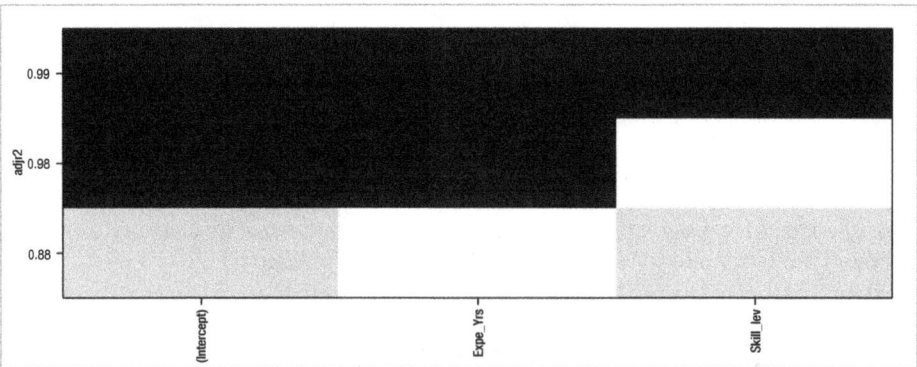

Figure 9-9. *Plot of the multiple regression model generated in R using all subsets approach scaled with adjusted R-squared*

In this example also, the predictors that get selected for the best model is the one with both the predictors selected.

9.1.8   Multiple Linear Regression Equation

The regression line is a smoothed graph of averages. It is basically a smoothing of the averages of the response variable for each value set of the independent variables. The regression line is drawn in such a way that it minimizes the error of the fitted values with respect to the actual values. This method, known as the *least squares method*, minimizes the sum of the squared differences between the actual values of the response variable and the predicted values of the response variable. The multiple linear regression equation takes the following form:

$$Y_i = \beta_0 + \beta_1 x_1 + \beta_2 x_2 + \beta_3 x_3 + \ldots$$

In this equation, β_0 is known the *intercept*, and the β_1 is known as the *slope* of the regression line. The intercept is the value of the response variable when the values of each independent variable are 0. This depicts the point at which the regression line touches the y axis when x_1 and x_2 etc are 0. The slope can be calculated easily by using this formula:

(R × standard deviation of the response variable) / Standard deviation of the independent variable

From this formula, you can see that when the value of the independent variable increases by one standard deviation, the value of the response variable increases by R × one standard deviation of the response variable, where R is the coefficient of correlation.

223

In our example, the multiple linear regression equation is as follows:

```
Annu_Salary = 3011.66 + 1589.68 × Expe_Yrs + 1263.65 × Skill_lev
```

where β_0 = intercept = 3011.66

β_1 = coefficient of Experience in Years = 1589.68

β_3 = coefficient of Skill_levl = 1263.65

9.1.9   Conclusion

From our data, we got a good multiple linear regression model that we validated for the success of the assumptions. We also used this model for predictions.

9.2   Using an Alternative Method in R

As we mentioned in the introduction of this chapter, the expectation for the use of the lm() function is that the response variable is normally distributed. As we know from our sample data, Annual Salary is normally distributed, or follows Gaussian distribution. Hence, we can alternatively use the generalized linear model using the R function glm() with the frequency distribution as belonging to gaussian family with parameter link = "identity", as shown here:

```
> glm_sal_model <- glm(Annu_Salary ~ Expe_Yrs + Skill_lev, data = sal_data_1, family = gaussian(link = "identity"))
> summary(glm_sal_model)

Call:
glm(formula = Annu_Salary ~ Expe_Yrs + Skill_lev, family = gaussian(link = "identity"),
    data = sal_data_1)

Deviance Residuals:
   Min      1Q   Median      3Q      Max
 -605.6  -318.5   -23.8    354.3    666.0

Coefficients:
             Estimate Std. Error t value Pr(>|t|)
(Intercept)   3011.66     162.58   18.52  < 2e-16 ***
Expe_Yrs      1589.68      50.86   31.26  < 2e-16 ***
Skill_lev     1263.65     102.03   12.38 4.25e-16 ***
---
Signif. codes:  0 '***' 0.001 '**' 0.01 '*' 0.05 '.' 0.1 ' ' 1

(Dispersion parameter for gaussian family taken to be 142488)

    Null deviance: 1.280e+09  on 47  degrees of freedom
Residual deviance: 6.412e+06  on 45  degrees of freedom
AIC: 710.74

Number of Fisher Scoring iterations: 2
```

As expected, you will find that the result is the same as that obtained through the lm() function.

9.3 Predicting the Response Variable

The fitted model not only explains the relationship between the response variable and the independent variables but also provides a mechanism to predict the value of the response variable from the values of the new independent variables. This is done as shown here:

```
> predictor <- data.frame(Expe_Yrs = 5, Skill_lev = 4)
> predicted <- predict(glm_sal_model, newdata = predictor)
> predicted
        1
16014.64
```

As you can see from the data used for building the model, the predicted value is almost in tune with the related actual values in our data set.

Please note: we have used glm_sal_model instead of sal_model_1 generated using the lm() function, as there is no difference between the two.

This is done using the function predict(model name, newdata), where model name is the name of the model arrived at from the input data, and newdata contains the data of independent variables for which the response variable has to be predicted.

This model may work in predicting the Annual Salary for Experience in Years and Skill Level beyond those in the data set. However, we have to be very cautious in using the model on such an extended data set, as the model generated does not know or has no means to know whether the model is suitable for the extended data set. We also do not know whether the extrapolated data follows the linear relationship. It is possible that after a certain number of years, while experience increases, the Skill Level and the corresponding Annual Salary may not go up linearly, but the rate of increase in salary may taper off, leading to a slowly tapering down in the slope of the relationship.

9.4 Training and Testing the Model

We can also use separate subsets of the data set for training the model (basically, to arrive at the model) and testing the model. Ideally, such data sets have to be generated randomly. Typically, 75 percent to 80 percent of the data set is taken to train the model, and another 25 percent to 20 percent of the data set is used to test the model.

Let's use the same data set that we used previously to do this. For this, we have to use `install.packages("caret")` and `library(caret)`. The splitting of the data set into two subsets—training data set and test data set—using R is shown here:

```
>
> library(caret)
> set.seed(123)
> #setting seed ensures the repeatability of the results of the different experiments
> #Now we are going to partition the data by using createDataPartition function
> #from caret package
> Data_Partition <- createDataPartition(sal_data_1$Annu_Salary, p = 0.80, list = FALSE)
> #Now Data_Partition actually contains 40 records of the training data
> #However, let us name it correctly as training data
> Training_Data <- sal_data_1[Data_Partition, ]
> summary(Training_Data)
  Annu_Salary        Expe_Yrs         Skill_lev
 Min.   : 4000    Min.   :0.000    Min.   :0.50
 1st Qu.:10000    1st Qu.:2.438    1st Qu.:2.50
 Median :14500    Median :4.750    Median :3.15
 Mean   :13925    Mean   :4.415    Mean   :3.09
 3rd Qu.:18000    3rd Qu.:6.062    3rd Qu.:4.00
 Max.   :22000    Max.   :8.500    Max.   :5.00
> #Let us now create a Test Data subset leaving out the subset of data in Training_Data
> Test_Data <- sal_data_1[-Data_Partition, ]
> #The above has created the Test Data now
> #This will contain 8 records out of the original 48 records (i.e. 20% of the records)
```

This split of the entire data set into two subsets, `Training_Data` and `Test_Data`, has been done randomly. Now, we have 40 records in `Training_Data` and 8 records in `Test_Data`.

We will now train our `Training_Data` using the machine-learning concepts to generate a model. This is depicted as follows:

```
>
> #Now, we will train the Training_Data to arrive at the model
> #We are going to use train() function from the caret package here
> #Alternatively we can use our regular lm() function also
> Trained_Model <- train(Annu_Salary ~ Expe_Yrs + Skill_lev, data = Training_Data, method = "lm")
> summary(Trained_Model)

Call:
lm(formula = .outcome ~ ., data = dat)

Residuals:
    Min      1Q  Median      3Q     Max
-593.19 -228.07  -12.11  315.43  618.50

Coefficients:
            Estimate Std. Error t value Pr(>|t|)
(Intercept)   3057.6      169.2   18.07  < 2e-16 ***
Expe_Yrs      1600.5       56.1   28.53  < 2e-16 ***
Skill_lev     1230.1      110.2   11.16  2.1e-13 ***
---
Signif. codes:  0 '***' 0.001 '**' 0.01 '*' 0.05 '.' 0.1 ' ' 1

Residual standard error: 359.3 on 37 degrees of freedom
Multiple R-squared:  0.9954,    Adjusted R-squared:  0.9951
F-statistic: 3996 on 2 and 37 DF,  p-value: < 2.2e-16
```

As you can see, the model generated, `Trained_Model`, is a good fit with p-values of the coefficients of the predictors being < 0.05 as well as overall model p-value being < 0.05.

We will now use the `Trained_Model` arrived at as previously to predict the values of `Annual_Salary` in respect to Experience in Years and Skill Level from the `Test_Data`. This is shown here, in a snapshot from R:

```
> #Now we will predict the Annual Salary for the records
> #of Experience in Years and Skill Levels from the Test_Data
> #using the model generated using the Training_Data
> pred_annu_salary <- predict(Trained_Model, newdata = Test_Data, interval = "prediction")
> summary(pred_annu_salary)
   Min. 1st Qu.  Median    Mean 3rd Qu.    Max.
   5518    8611   14970   13440   17900   20600
```

Now, let's see whether the values of Annual Salary we predicted using the model generated out of `Training_Data` and actual values of the Annual Salary in the `Test_Data` are in tune with each other. The actual values and the predicted values are shown here:

```
> Test_Data$Annu_Salary
[1]  6000 14000  9000 21000 15000  6000 18000 19000
> pred_annu_salary
         2          8         14         24         26         28         37         46
  5888.267 14380.171  9519.168 20597.088 15550.869  5517.835 17766.453 18307.418
```

You can see here that both the Actual Annual Salary from `Test_Data` and Annual Salary from the model generated out of `Training_Data` (pred_annu_salary) match closely with each other. Hence, the model generated out of `Training_Data` (Trained_Model) can be used effectively.

9.5 Cross Validation

Cross validation like k-fold Cross Validation is used to validate the model generated. This will be very useful when we have limited data and the data is required to be split into small test set (like 20% of data) and relatively bigger training set (like 80% of data) and this makes the validation of the model relatively difficult or not feasible because the data in the training set and test set may be split in such a way that both may not be very representative of the entire data set.

This problem is eliminated by cross validation methods like k-fold Cross Validation. Here, actually we divide the data set into k-folds and use k-1 sets as training data and the remaining 1 set as the test data and repeatedly do this for k times. Each k-fold will have almost equal number of data points (depends upon k-value) randomly drawn from the entire data set. In our case as we have totally 48 records each fold has 4 or 5 records. None of the elements of one fold are repeated in the other fold. For each fold the model is validated and the value predicted by the model (Predicted) and by the cross validation is tabulated as the output along with the difference between actual value and the cross validated prediction (cvpred) as CV residual. Using the difference between the Predicted values and the cvpred we can arrive at the root mean square error of the fit of the linear regression model. This cross validation method is also useful in the case of huge data as every data point is used for the training as well as for testing by rotation and in none of the folds the same data point is taken again for consideration.

Let us take the example of the multiple linear regression we have used earlier. Let us validate this model using the k-fold validation. In our example, we will be using K = 10. This is for convenience sake so that every time we have 90% of the data in the training set and another 10% of the data in the test set. This way the data once in training set will move some other time to the test set. Thus in fact by rotation we will ensure that the all the points are used for model generation as well as the testing. For this cross validation we will use library(DAAG) and we will use either cv.lm(dataset, formula for the model, m=number of folds) or CVlm(dataset, formula for the model, m=number of folds) function. Here m is nothing but the number of folds (i.e. K) we have decided. The result of run of this for our example is provided in the following Figures.

```
> cv_model <- CVlm(sal_data_1, Annu_Salary ~ Expe_Yrs + Skill_lev, m = 10)
Analysis of Variance Table

Response: Annu_Salary
           Df    Sum Sq  Mean Sq F value   Pr(>F)
Expe_Yrs    1 1.25e+09 1.25e+09    8785 < 2e-16 ***
Skill_lev   1 2.19e+07 2.19e+07     153 4.3e-16 ***
Residuals  45 6.41e+06 1.42e+05
---
Signif. codes:  0 '***' 0.001 '**' 0.01 '*' 0.05 '.' 0.1 ' ' 1



fold 1
Observations in test set: 4
               10    41    45    46
Predicted   19826 10163 18399 18334
cvpred      19754 10158 18340 18272
Annu_Salary 20000 10000 19000 19000
CV residual   246  -158   660   728

Sum of squares = 1051795    Mean square = 262949    n = 4

fold 2
Observations in test set: 5
               13    20      37      38    40
Predicted    9350 11103   17767 19988.8 10145
cvpred       9386 11101   17748 19963.1 10172
Annu_Salary  9000 11000   18000 20000.0 10000
CV residual  -386  -101     252    36.9  -172

Sum of squares = 253856    Mean square = 50771    n = 5
```

Figure 9-10. *A partial snapshot of output of k-fold cross validation*

```
fold 10
Observations in test set: 4
               21    26    27    44
Predicted   13451 15546 15383 15383
cvpred      13512 15614 15422 15422
Annu_Salary 13000 15000 15000 15000
CV residual  -512  -614  -422  -422

Sum of squares = 994705    Mean square = 248676    n = 4

Overall (Sum over all 4 folds)
    ms
163893
Warning message:
In CVlm(sal_data_1, Annu_Salary ~ Expe_Yrs + Skill_lev, m = 10) :

 As there is >1 explanatory variable, cross-validation
 predicted values for a fold are not a linear function
 of corresponding overall predicted values.  Lines that
 are shown for the different folds are approximate
```

Figure 9-11. *A partial snapshot of output of k-fold cross validation (last fold)*

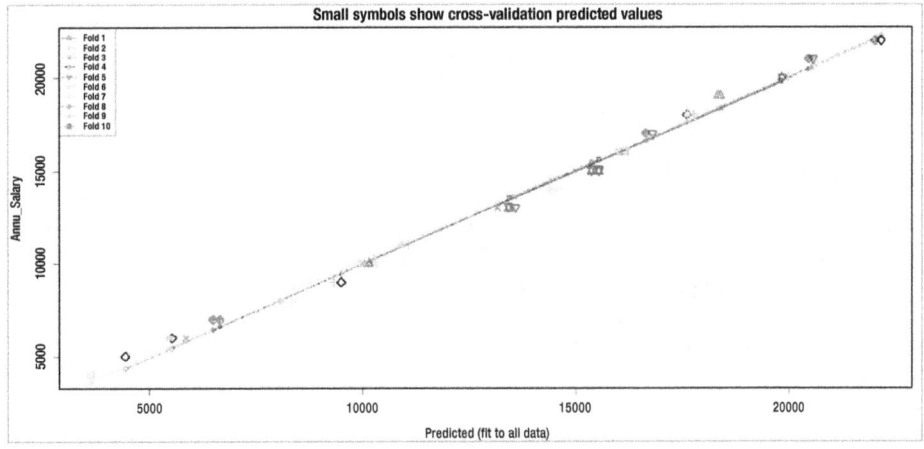

Figure 9-12. *Graphical output of k-fold cross validation showing all the ten folds*

The values predicted by the multiple linear regression model (lm function) and the values predicted by the cross validation are very close to each other. As you can see from above figures, the various points fitted using cross validation are almost mapping on to the regression model we arrived at.

```
> rmse <- sqrt(mean((cv_model$cvpred - cv_model$Predicted)^2))
> rmse
[1] 60
```

Figure 9-13. *Root mean square error calculated between linear regression model and cross validation model*

If we check the root mean square error between the values predicted by multiple linear regression model and cross validation model, as shown in the above Figure, it is very negligible i.e. 60. Hence, k-fold cross validation validates the multiple linear regression model arrived at by us earlier.

Instead of k-fold cross validation we can use other methods like Repeated k-fold cross validation, Bootstrap sampling, leave-one-out cross validation.

9.6 Summary

In this chapter, you saw examples of multiple linear relationships. When you have a response variable that is continuous and is normally distributed with multiple predictor variables, you use multiple linear regression. If a response variable can take discrete values, you use logistic regression.

You also briefly looked into significant interaction, which occurs when the outcome is impacted by one of the predictors based on the value of the other predictor. You learned about multicollinearity, whereby two or more predictors may be highly correlated or may represent the same aspect in different ways. You saw the impacts of multicollinearity and how to handle them in the context of the multiple linear regression model or equation.

You then explored the data we took from one of the entities and the correlation between various variables. You could see a high correlation among all three variables involved (the response variable as well as the predictor variables). By using this data in R, you can arrive at the multiple linear regression model and then validate that it is a good model with significant predictor variables.

You learned various techniques to validate that the assumptions of the regression are met. Different approaches can lead to different interpretations, so you have to proceed cautiously in that regard.

In exploring multicollinearity further, you saw that functions such as vif() enable you to understand the existence of multicollinearity. You briefly looked at handling multicollinearity in the context of multiple linear regression. Multicollinearity does not reduce the value of the model for prediction purposes. Through the example of Akaike information criterion (AIC), you learned to compare various models and that the best one typically has the lowest AIC value.

You then explored two alternative ways to arrive at the best-fit multiple linear regression models: stepwise multiple linear regression and all subsets approach to multiple linear regression. You depicted the model by using the multiple linear regression equation.

Further, you explored how the glm() function with the frequency distribution gaussian with link = "identity" can provide the same model as that generated through the lm() function, as we require normality in the case of a continuous response variable.

Further, you saw how to predict the value of the response variable by using the values of the predictor variables.

Finally, you explored how to split the data set into two subsets, training data and test data. You can use the training data to generate a model for validating the response variable of test data, by using the predict() function on the model generated using the training data.

CHAPTER 10

Logistic Regression

In Chapters 8 and 9, we discussed simple linear regression and multiple linear regression, respectively. In both types of regression, we have a dependent variable or response variable as a continuous variable that is normally distributed. However, this is not always the case. Often, the response variable is not normally distributed. It may be a binary variable following a binomial distribution and taking the values of 0/1 or No/Yes. It may be a categorical or discrete variable taking multiple values that may follow other distributions other than the normal one.

If the response variable is a discrete variable (which can be nominal, ordinal, or binary), you use a different regression method, known as *logistic regression*. If the response variable takes binary values (such as Yes/No or Sick/Heathy) or multiple discrete variables (such as Strongly Agree, Agree, Partially Agree, and Do Not Agree), we can use logistic regression. Logistic regression is still a linear regression. Logistic regression with the response variable taking only two values (such as Yes/No or Sick/Healthy) is known as *binomial logistic regression*. A logistic regression with a response variable that can take multiple discrete values is known as *multinomial logistic regression*. Note that nonlinear regression is outside the scope of this book.

Consider the following examples:

- You want to decide whether to lend credit to a customer. Your choice may depend on various factors including the customer's earlier record of payment regularity with other companies, the customer's credibility in the banking and financial sector, the profitability of the customer's organization, and the integrity of the promoters and management.

- You are deciding whether to invest in a project. Again, your choice depends on various factors, including the risks involved, the likely profitability, the longevity of the project's life, and the capability of the organization in the particular area of the project.

- You are deciding whether to hire a particular candidate for a senior management post. This choice may depend on various factors including the candidate's experience, past record, attitude, and suitability to the culture of your organization.

© Dr. Umesh R. Hodeghatta and Umesha Nayak 2017

U. R. Hodeghatta and U. Nayak, *Business Analytics Using R - A Practical Approach*,

DOI 10.1007/978-1-4842-2514-1_10

233

- You are deciding whether a particular employee is likely to stick with the organization. This choice may depend on various factors including the internal working environment of the organization, whether the employee is deployed on a challenging project, whether the compensation to that employee is commensurate with the industry standard, and whether the employee is technically good enough to be lured by other organizations.

Interactions between predictors as well as multicollinearity may still be issues in logistic regression, and they need to be addressed appropriately. However, the assumption of linearity, normality, and homoscedasticity that generally apply to regressions do not apply to logistic regression.

A starting point for building any logistic regression model is to get your data in a data-frame format, as this is a requirement of the $glm()$ function in R. As you saw in previous chapters, the $glm()$ function with $family = gaussian(link = "identity")$ is equivalent to the $lm()$ function; the requirement is that the response or dependent variable is distributed normally. However, when you use $glm()$ for logistic regression, the response variable takes the binary values $family = binomial(link = "logit")$. Why? Because we want the value to be between 0 and 1, which can be interpreted as a probability. We use the natural logarithm (ln) of the odds ratio:

ln(odds ratio) = ln[probability of success / (1 – probability of success)]

Hence, we use the following bounding function that enables us to determine the probability of success and derive the logistic regression model by combining linear regression with the bounding function:

$$f(a) = 1 / (1 + e^{-a})$$

The following is the logistic regression model obtained:

P(Response = Yes, given Independent Variable$_1$, Independent Variable$_2$, ... Independent Variable$_N$) =

$$1 / (1 + e^{-(\beta_0 + \beta_1 \times \text{Independent Variable}_1 + \beta_2 \times \text{Independent Variable}_2 + ... + \beta_N \times \text{Independent Variable}_N)})$$

and

P(Response = No, given Independent Variable$_1$, Independent Variable$_2$, ... Independent Variable$_N$) =

$$1 - [1 / (1 + e^{-(\beta_0 + \beta_1 \times \text{Independent Variable}_1 + \beta_2 \times \text{Independent Variable}_2 + ... + \beta_N \times \text{Independent Variable}_N)})]$$

which is nothing but

$$1 / (1 + e^{(\beta_0 + \beta_1 \times \text{Independent Variable}_1 + \beta_2 \times \text{Independent Variable}_2 + ... + \beta_N \times \text{Independent Variable}_N)})$$

From these two equations pertaining to P(Response = Yes) and P(Response = No), we get the odds, as follows:

$$P(\text{Response} = \text{Yes}) / P(\text{Response} = \text{No}) =$$

$$e^{(\beta_0 + \beta_1 \times \text{Independent Variable}_1 + \beta_2 \times \text{Independent Variable}_2 + ... + \beta_N \times \text{Independent Variable}_N)}$$

Hence, logit, or log odds, is as follows:

logit(P) = ln[P(Response = Yes) / P(Response = No)] = $\beta_0 + \beta_1 \times$ Independent Variable$_1 + \beta_2 \times$ Independent Variable$_2 + ... + \beta_N \times$ Independent Variable$_N$

We use the maximum likelihood method to generate the logistic regression equation that predicts the natural logarithm of the odds ratio. From this logistic regression equation, we determine the predicted odds ratio and the predicted probability of success:

Predicted probability of success = predicted odds ratio / (1 + predicted odds ratio)

Here, we do not use the dependent variable value as it is. Instead, we use the natural logarithm of the odds ratio.

10.1 Logistic Regression

In this section, we demonstrate logistic regression using a data set.

10.1.1 The Data

Let's start by considering that we have created data with six variables:

- Attrition represents whether the employee has exited the organization or is still in the organization (Yes for exit, and No for currently working in the organization).

- Yrs_Exp represents the experience of the employee at this time (in years).

- Work_Challenging represents whether the work assigned to the employee is challenging.

- Work_Envir represents whether the work environment is Excellent or Low.

- Compensation represents whether the compensation is Excellent or Low.

- Tech_Exper represents whether the employee is technically expert (Excellent or Low).

The data covers the last six months and pertains only to those employees with two to five years of experience. The data is extracted from the CSV text file Attri_Data_10.txt by using the read.csv() command:

```
> attrition_data <- read.csv("Attri_Data_10.txt", header = TRUE, sep = ",")
> summary(attrition_data)
 Attrition      Yrs_Exp      Work_Challenging     Work_Envir       Compensation        Tech_Exper
 No :24     Min.   :2.000    No :28           Excellent:28    Excellent:21    Excellent:44
 Yes:28     1st Qu.:2.500    Yes:24           Low      :24    Low      :31    Low      : 8
            Median :4.000
            Mean   :3.519
            3rd Qu.:4.500
            Max.   :5.000
>
```

This code also presents a summary of the data. As you can see, the Attrition field has 28 Yes values: that means that these employees have exited the organization. The 24 No values represent employees who are still continuing in the organization. You can also observe from the preceding summary that 28 employees have not been assigned challenging work (Work_Challenging), and 24 employees have. Furthermore, 28 employees are working in teams where the work environment (Work_Envir) is considered excellent, whereas 24 are working in teams where the work environment is not that great (here marked Low). Finally, 21 employees have excellent compensation, at par or above the market compensation (shown here as Excellent); but 31 have compensation that is below the market compensation or low compensation (shown here as Low). Out of the total employees, 44 have excellent technical expertise, whereas 8 others have low technical expertise. The data set contains 52 records.

Ideally, when the organization is providing challenging work to an employee, the work environment within the team is excellent, compensation is excellent, and technical expertise of the employee is low, then the chance for attrition should be low.

Here is a glimpse of the data:

```
> head(attrition_data)
  Attrition Yrs_Exp Work_Challenging Work_Envir Compensation Tech_Exper
1       Yes     2.5               No        Low          Low  Excellent
2        No     2.0              Yes  Excellent    Excellent  Excellent
3        No     2.5              Yes  Excellent          Low  Excellent
4       Yes     2.0               No  Excellent          Low  Excellent
5        No     2.0              Yes        Low          Low        Low
6       Yes     2.0               No        Low          Low  Excellent
> tail(attrition_data)
   Attrition Yrs_Exp Work_Challenging Work_Envir Compensation Tech_Exper
47        No     4.0              Yes  Excellent    Excellent  Excellent
48        No     4.5               No  Excellent          Low        Low
49       Yes     5.0               No  Excellent    Excellent  Excellent
50        No     5.0               No  Excellent    Excellent  Excellent
51       Yes     2.0              Yes  Excellent    Excellent  Excellent
52        No     4.0              Yes  Excellent    Excellent  Excellent
```

10.1.2   Creating the Model

Now, let's build a logistic regression model by using the glm() function of R. We need to use family = binomial(link="logit") along with glm() because our response variable is binary. To start, let's generate the model by using all the parameters, since they have Attrition as binary response (or dependent) variable; furthermore, we want to use this model to predict the possibility of any employee resigning later (in tune with this model and other variables Yrs_Exp, Work_Challenging, Work_Envir, Compensation, and Tech_Exper). The command in R to generate the logistic regression model is shown here:

```
> attri_logit_model <- glm(Attrition ~ Yrs_Exp + Work_Challenging + Work_Envir + Compensation + Tech_Exper, data = attrition_data, family = binomial(link="logit"))
```

The model created by using the glm() function is shown here, along with the summary (generated by using summary(model name)):

```
> summary(attri_logit_model)

Call:
glm(formula = Attrition ~ Yrs_Exp + Work_Challenging + Work_Envir +
    Compensation + Tech_Exper, family = binomial(link = "logit"),
    data = attrition_data)

Deviance Residuals:
    Min       1Q   Median       3Q      Max
-1.37759  -0.20326  0.04508  0.22389  2.95410

Coefficients:
                      Estimate Std. Error z value Pr(>|z|)
(Intercept)           -1.1964     2.4077  -0.497   0.6193
Yrs_Exp                0.1320     0.5102   0.259   0.7959
Work_ChallengingYes   -3.4180     1.4091  -2.426   0.0153 *
Work_EnvirLow          4.6118     1.6783   2.748   0.0060 **
CompensationLow        2.8160     1.3513   2.084   0.0372 *
Tech_ExperLow         -3.9598     1.7030  -2.325   0.0201 *
---
Signif. codes:  0 '***' 0.001 '**' 0.01 '*' 0.05 '.' 0.1 ' ' 1

(Dispersion parameter for binomial family taken to be 1)

    Null deviance: 71.779  on 51  degrees of freedom
Residual deviance: 26.018  on 46  degrees of freedom
AIC: 38.018

Number of Fisher Scoring iterations: 7
```

Only one value among the categorical variables is shown here. This is because each variable has two levels, and one level is taken as a reference level by the model. An example is the categorical variable Work_Challenging, which has two levels: Work_ChallengingYes and Work_ChallengingNo. Only Work_ChallengingYes is shown in the model, as Work_ChallengingNo is taken as the reference level.

■ **Note** The Weights of Evidence transformation technique can be used if each factor variable has many levels. This ensures that only one combined variable represents multiple levels of each variable, thus reducing the coefficients of the model. This is useful because categorical variables with many levels can create issues in logistic regression.

You can see in the preceding summary of the logistic regression model that except for Yrs_Exp, all other variables are significant to the model (as each p-value is less than 0.05). Work_ChallengingYes, Work_EnvirLow, Compensation_Low, and Tech_ExperLow are the significant variables. Yrs_Exp is not a significant variable to the model, as it has a high p-value. It is quite obvious from even a visual examination of the data that Yrs_Exp will not be significant to the model, as attrition is observed regardless of the number of years of experience. Furthermore, you can see that the model has converged in seven Fisher's scoring iterations, which is good because ideally we expect the model to converge in less than eight iterations.

We can now eliminate Yrs_Exp from the logistic regression model and recast the model. The formula used for recasting the logistic regression model and the summary of the model are provided here:

```
> attri_logit_model_2 <- glm(Attrition ~ Work_Challenging+Work_Envir+Compensation+Tech_Exper,data=attrition_data,family=binomial(link="logit"))
```

```
> summary(attri_logit_model_2)
Call:
glm(formula = Attrition ~ Work_Challenging + Work_Envir + Compensation +
    Tech_Exper, family = binomial(link = "logit"), data = attrition_data)

Deviance Residuals:
    Min       1Q    Median        3Q       Max
-1.36759  -0.20050   0.05191   0.22273   2.86409

Coefficients:
                      Estimate Std. Error z value Pr(>|z|)
(Intercept)           -0.6216     0.9101  -0.683   0.4946
Work_ChallengingYes   -3.4632     1.4025  -2.469   0.0135 *
Work_EnvirLow          4.5215     1.5995   2.827   0.0047 **
CompensationLow        2.7090     1.2542   2.160   0.0308 *
Tech_ExperLow         -3.8547     1.6065  -2.400   0.0164 *
---
Signif. codes:  0 '***' 0.001 '**' 0.01 '*' 0.05 '.' 0.1 ' ' 1

(Dispersion parameter for binomial family taken to be 1)

    Null deviance: 71.779  on 51  degrees of freedom
Residual deviance: 26.086  on 47  degrees of freedom
AIC: 36.086

Number of Fisher Scoring iterations: 7
```

As you can see, the model parameters are significant because the p-values are less than 0.05.

The degrees of freedom for the data is calculated as n minus 1 (the number of data points − 1, or 52 − 1 = 51). The degrees of freedom for the model is n minus 1 minus the number of coefficients (52 − 1 − 4 = 47). These are shown in the preceding summary of the model. *Deviance* is a measure of lack of fit. Null deviance is nothing but the deviance of the model with only intercept. *Residual deviance* is the deviance of the model. Both are part of the preceding summary of the model. The following shows that the residual deviance reduces with the addition of each coefficient:

```
> anova(attri_logit_model_2, "PChiSq")
Analysis of Deviance Table

Model: binomial, link: logit

Response: Attrition

Terms added sequentially (first to last)


                   Df Deviance Resid. Df Resid. Dev
NULL                                51      71.779
Work_Challenging   1  15.6908        50      56.089
Work_Envir         1  17.4619        49      38.627
Compensation       1   3.3265        48      35.300
Tech_Exper         1   9.2142        47      26.086
```

Let's compare both the models—attri_logit_model (with all the predictors) and attri_logit_model_2 (with only significant predictors) and check how the second model fares with respect to the first one:

```
> anova(attri_logit_model_2, attri_logit_model, test = "Chisq")
Analysis of Deviance Table

Model 1: Attrition ~ Work_Challenging + Work_Envir + Compensation + Tech_Exper
Model 2: Attrition ~ Yrs_Exp + Work_Challenging + Work_Envir + Compensation +
    Tech_Exper
  Resid. Df Resid. Dev Df Deviance Pr(>Chi)
1        47     26.086
2        46     26.018  1 0.067459   0.7951
>
```

This test is carried out by using the anova( ) function and checking the chi-square p-value. In this table, the chi-square p-value is 0.7951. This is not significant. This suggests that the model attri_logit_model_2 without Yrs_Exp works well compared to the model attri_logit_model with all the variables. There is not much difference between the two models. Hence, we can safely use the model without Yrs_Exp (that is, attri_logit_model_2).

From this model (`attri_logit_model_2`), we can see that the coefficient of `Work_ChallengingYes` is –3.4632, `Work_EnvirLow` is 4.5215, `CompensationLow` is 2.7090, and `Tech_ExperLow` is –3.8547. These coefficient values are the natural logarithm of the odds ratio. A coefficient with a minus sign indicates that it decreases the potential for `Attrition`. Similarly, a coefficient with a plus sign indicates that it increases the potential for `Attrition`. Hence, the odds of having `Attrition` = `Yes` is exp(4.5215) = 91.97 times higher than not having any `Attrition` with all other variables remaining the same (ceteris paribus) when `Work_Envir` = `Low` compared to when the `Work_Envir` = `Excellent`. This means that if `Work_Envir` = `Excellent`, the chance of `Attrition` = `Yes` is 5 percent, or 0.05, then the odds for `Attrition` = `No` under the same conditions are (0.05 / (1 – 0.05)) × 91.97 = 4.8376. This corresponds to a probability of `Attrition` = `No` of 4.8376 / (1 + 4.8376) = 0.8286, or about 82.86 percent. The odds of having `Attrition` = `Yes` is exp(2.7090) = 15.02 times higher than not having any `Attrition` with all other variables remaining the same when `Compensation` = `Low` compared to when the `Compensation` = `High`. Both `Work_Envir` = `Low` and `Compensation` = `Low` increase the possibility of `Attrition` = `Yes`.

However, other two variables, `Work_Challenging` = `Yes` and `Tech_Exper` = `Low` with negative signs to the respective coefficients means that they reduce the possibility of `Attrition` = `Yes`. `Work_Challenging` = `Yes` with the coefficient value of –3.4632 lowers the possibility of `Attrition` = `Yes` by exp(–3.4632) = 0.0313 with all other variables remaining the same compared to when `Work_Challenging` = `No`. Similarly, `Tech_Exper` = `Low` with the coefficient value of –3.8547 lowers the possibility of `Attrition` = `Yes` by exp(–3.8547) = 0.0211 with all other variables remaining the same compared to when `Tech_Exper` = `High`.

From this, you can see that the major impact to `Attrition` is influenced mainly by `Work_Envir` and `Compensation`.

10.1.3   Model Fit Verification

It is important for us to verify the model fit. This can be done by computing the pseudo R-squared value. This value is calculated by using the formula 1 – (`model$deviance` / `model$null.dev`). This tells us the extent that the model explains the deviance. The following code shows how to compute this value using R:

```
> pseudo_R_Squared <- 1 - (attri_logit_model_2$deviance / attri_logit_model_2$null.dev)
> pseudo_R_Squared
[1] 0.6365818
```

This calculation shows that the model explains 63.65 percent of the deviance. You can also compute the value of pseudo R-square by using `library(pscl)` and `pR2(model_name)`.

Another way to verify the model fit is by calculating the p-value with the chi-square method as follows:

p-value <- pchisq[(model_deviance_diff),(df_data – df_model),lower.tail=F]

Here, df_data can be calculated by nrow(data_set) - 1, or in our case, nrow(attrition_data) - 1; df_model can be calculated by model$df.residual; and model_deviance_diff can be calculated as model$null.dev - model$deviance. These calculations are shown here:

```
>
> deviance_diff <- attri_logit_model_2$null.dev - attri_logit_model_2$deviance
> deviance_diff
[1] 45.6934
> df_data <- nrow(attrition_data) - 1
> df_data
[1] 51
> df_residual <- attri_logit_model_2$df.residual
> df_residual
[1] 47
> p_value <- pchisq(deviance_diff, (df_data - df_residual), lower.tail = FALSE)
> p_value
[1] 2.852542e-09
>
```

Because the p-value is very small, the reduction in deviance cannot be assumed to be by chance. As the p-value is significant, the model is a good fit.

10.1.4   General Words of Caution

The following warning message could be thrown while generating the logistics model:

```
Warning message:
glm.fit: fitted probabilities numerically 0 or 1 occurred
```

This may be due to data or a portion of data predicting the response perfectly. This is known as the *issue of separation* or *quasi-separation*.

Here are some general words of caution with respect to the logistic regression model:

- We have a problem when the null deviance is less than the residual deviance.

- We have a problem when the convergence requires many Fisher's scoring iterations.

- We have a problem when the coefficients are large in size with significantly large standard errors.

In these cases, we may have to revisit the model to look again at each coefficient.

10.1.5   Multicollinearity

We talked about multicollinearity in Chapter 9. Multicollinearity can be made out in R easily by using the vif(model name) function. *VIF* stands for *variance inflation factor*. Typically, a rule of thumb for the multicollinearity test to pass is that the VIF value should be greater than 5. The following test shows the calculation of VIF:

```
> vif(attri_logit_model_2)
Work_Challenging        Work_Envir      Compensation        Tech_Exper
        1.984868          2.461992          1.611694          1.562850
```

As you can see, our model does not suffer from multicollinearity.

10.1.6   Dispersion

Dispersion (variance of the dependent variable) above the value of 1 (as mentioned in the summary of the logistic regression dispersion parameter for the binomial family to be taken as 1) is a potential issue with some of the regression models, including the logistic regression model. This is known as *overdispersion*. Overdispersion occurs when the observed variance of the dependent variable is bigger than the one expected out of the usage of binomial distribution (that is, 1). This leads to issues with the reliability of the significance tests, as this is likely to adversely impact standard errors.

Whether a model suffers from the issue of overdispersion can be easily found using R, as shown here:

```
> #If the ratio of the Residual Deviance of a model to
> #its Residual Degrees of Freedom is greater than 1 then
> #the model suffers from the issue of Overdispersion
> #Let us now check whether our Logistic Regression Model
> #suffers from this issue
> overdisp_indicator <- attri_logit_model_2$deviance / attri_logit_model_2$df.residual
> overdisp_indicator
[1] 0.5550193
> #As you can see the value is less than 1.  Hence, our
> #model does not suffer from the issue of Overdispersion
```

The model generated by us, attri_logit_model_2, does not suffer from the issue of overdispersion. If a logistic regression model does suffer from overdispersion, you need to use quasibinomial distribution in the glm() function instead of binomial distribution.

10.1.7   Conclusion for Logistic Regression

For our data, we created a good logistic regression model that we have verified for significance and goodness of fit. The model does not suffer from multicollinearity or overdispersion.

■ **Note** Using `family=binomial(link="probit")` in the `glm()` function also works similarly to `family=binomial(link="logit")` in most of the circumstances. For `logit`, you may use `family=binomial()` directly in `glm()` without using `link="logit"`, as both produce the same result.

10.2 Training and Testing the Model

We can also use separate subsets of the data set for training the model (basically to create the model) and testing the model. Ideally, such data sets have to be generated randomly. Typically, 75 percent to 80 percent of the data set is used to train the model, and another 25 percent to 20 percent of the data set is used to test the model.

Let's use the same data set as we used previously to do this. We have to run `install.packages("caret")` and use `library(caret)`. Here we split the data set into two subsets (training data set and test data set) using R:

```
> library(caret)
> set.seed(1234)
> #Setting seed ensures the repeatability of the results
> #of the different trials
> #Now we are going to partition the data using
> #createDataPartition function from the caret package
> Data_Partition <- createDataPartition(attrition_data$Attrition, p = 0.80, list = FALSE)
> #Now Data_Partition has 80% of the records of data set as training data
> #However, let us name it correctly as Training Data
> Training_Data <- attrition_data[Data_Partition, ]
> summary(Training_Data)
 Attrition      Yrs_Exp      Work_Challenging   Work_Envir      Compensation      Tech_Exper
 No :20    Min.   :2.000   No :24            Excellent:24   Excellent:17     Excellent:37
 Yes:23    1st Qu.:2.500   Yes:19            Low      :19   Low      :26     Low      : 6
           Median :4.000
           Mean   :3.581
           3rd Qu.:4.500
           Max.   :5.000
> #Let us now create a Test_Data subset leaving out the subset of data
> #in the Training_Data
> Test_Data <- attrition_data[-Data_Partition, ]
> summary(Test_Data)
 Attrition      Yrs_Exp      Work_Challenging   Work_Envir      Compensation      Tech_Exper
 No :4     Min.   :2.000   No :4             Excellent:4    Excellent:4      Excellent:7
 Yes:5     1st Qu.:2.000   Yes:5             Low      :5    Low      :5      Low      :2
           Median :3.000
           Mean   :3.222
           3rd Qu.:4.500
           Max.   :5.000
```

This split of the entire data set into two subsets (Training_Data and Test_Data) has been done randomly. Now, we have 43 records in Training_Data and 9 records in Test_Data.

We now train our `Training_Data` by using the machine-learning concepts to generate a model:

```
> #Now let us create the Logistic Regression Model from Training_Data
> #I am leaving out the Yrs_Exp as it does not make sense to include
> #in the model
> train_logit_model <- glm(Attrition ~ Work_Challenging+Work_Envir+Compensation+Tech_Exper, data=Training_Data, family=binomial("logit"))
> summary(train_logit_model)

Call:
glm(formula = Attrition ~ Work_Challenging + Work_Envir + Compensation +
    Tech_Exper, family = binomial("logit"), data = Training_Data)

Deviance Residuals:
    Min       1Q    Median        3Q       Max
-1.55513  -0.25104   0.06228   0.17532   2.63557

Coefficients:
                      Estimate Std. Error z value Pr(>|z|)
(Intercept)           -0.3566     0.9389  -0.380   0.7041
Work_ChallengingYes   -3.0850     1.4052  -2.195   0.0281 *
Work_EnvirLow          4.2964     1.7184   2.500   0.0124 *
CompensationLow        2.3046     1.2715   1.812   0.0699 .
Tech_ExperLow        -21.2770  3853.0689  -0.006   0.9957
---
Signif. codes:  0 '***' 0.001 '**' 0.01 '*' 0.05 '.' 0.1 ' ' 1

(Dispersion parameter for binomial family taken to be 1)

    Null deviance: 59.401  on 42  degrees of freedom
Residual deviance: 19.397  on 38  degrees of freedom
AIC: 29.397

Number of Fisher Scoring iterations: 18
```

As you can see, the model generated (`train_logit_model`) has taken 18 Fisher's scoring iterations to converge, and `Tech_ExperLow` has a huge coefficient and standard error. Hence, this model may not be useful. For this reason, we cannot proceed with using the training model to predict `Attrition` with respect to the records of `Test_Data`. However, if we could successfully come up with a training model, we could proceed with our further analysis as follows:

1. Use the model generated out of the training data to predict the response variable for the test data and store the predicted data in the test data set itself.

2. Compare the values generated of the response variable with the actual values of the response variable in the test data set.

3. Generate the confusion matrix to understand the true positives (TP), true negatives (TN), false positives (FP), and false negatives (FN).

    - True positives are the ones that are actually positives (1) and are also predicted as positives (1).

    - True negatives are the ones that are actually negatives (0) but are also predicted as negatives (0).

    - False positives are the ones that are predicted as positives (1) but are actually negatives (0).

    - False negatives are the ones that are predicted as negatives (0) but are actually positives (1).

4. Check for accuracy, specificity, and sensitivity:

- Accuracy = (TP + TN) / Total Observations

- Specificity = True Negative Rate = TN / (FP + TN)

- Sensitivity = Recall = True Positive Rate = TP / (FN + TP)

    In addition, Precision = TP / (FP + TP) and F1 Score = 2TP / (2TP + FP + FN) may be considered.

Higher accuracy, higher sensitivity, and higher specificity are typically expected. Check whether these values are appropriate to the objective of the prediction in mind. If the prediction will affect the safety or health of people, we have to ensure the highest accuracy. In such cases, each predicted value should be determined with caution and further validated through other means, if required.

10.2.1 Predicting the Response Variable

The originally fitted model (`attri_logit_model_2`) not only explains the relationship between the response variable and the independent variables but also provides a mechanism to predict the value of the response variable from the values of the new independent variables. This is done as shown here:

```
> predictor <- data.frame(Yrs_Exp=3, Work_Challenging="Yes", Work_Envir="Excellent", Compensation="Excellent", Tech_Exper="Low")
> #The above creates a new data
> #Ideally the output for Attrition when we use the model attri_logit_model_2 to predict
> #should be representing "No"
> predicted <- predict(attri_logit_model_2, newdata=predictor, type="response")
> predicted
         1
0.0003562379
> #The probability value generated is very low which represents "No"
> #Hence the model has predicted well in this case
```

We take the value of Attrition as Yes if the probability returned by the prediction is > 0.5, and we take the same as No if the probability returned by the prediction is not > 0.5. As you can see in the preceding code, the value is far below 0.5 so we can safely assume that Attrition = No.

The preceding prediction is determined by using the function predict(model name, newdata=dataframe_name, type="response"), where model name is the name of the model arrived at from the input data, newdata contains the data of independent variables for which the response variable has to be predicted, and type="response" is required to ensure that the outcome is not logit(y).

10.2.2 Alternative Way of Validating the Logistic Regression Model

As we have said, we could not generate a valid model using the training data and so could not validate the same using the test data. However, we generated a model (attri_logit_model_2) using the full data set (attrition_data) and validated it. Another way of validating such a model is as follows:

1. We use the model generated to predict the dependent variable values (logit) using the predicted_value <- predict(model, type="response") on the full data set that we used to generate the model:

```
>
> #We use the original data set and run the generated model on it
> #only to predict the value of the dependent variable i.e. Attrition
> predicted_value <- predict(attri_logit_model_2, type = "response")
```

2. Then we generate a confusion matrix:

```
>
> #We are now going to generate Confusion Matrix
> table(attrition_data$Attrition, predicted_value > 0.5)

       FALSE TRUE
  No     22    2
  Yes     3   25
> #We have taken predicted_value > 0.5 above as we take any
> #probability value above 0.5 as 1 (True) and any probability
> #otherwise as 0 (False)
>
```

We can clearly see from the confusion matrix that the model generates very high true positives and true negatives.

3. Now we use the ROCR package and the prediction() function from it as follows: prediction_object <-prediction(predicted_value, dataset$dependent_variable). With this, we now create a prediction_object:

```
>
> #Generating the prediction object using the ROCR package
> library(ROCR)
Loading required package: gplots

Attaching package: 'gplots'

The following object is masked from 'package:stats':

    lowess

> prediction_object <- prediction(predicted_value, attrition_data$Attrition)
>
```

4. Using the performance() function from the ROCR package on the prediction_object, we obtain TPR = TP / (FN + TP) = TP / (All Positives) and FPR = FP / (FP + TN) = FP / (All Negatives) and plot TPR against the FPR to obtain a receiver operating characteristic (ROC) curve. This is done using plot(performance(prediction_object, measure = "tpr", x.measure = "fpr"). Alternatively, we can use sensitivity/specificity plots by using plot(performance(prediction_object, measure = "sens", x.measure = "spec") or precision/recall plots by using plot(performance(prediction_object, measure = "prec", x.measure = "rec"). The first of these R commands used to generate the ROC curve is shown here, followed by the curve generated (see Figure 10-1):

```
>
> #Now we generate performance measures from the prediction
> #object
> perf_1 <- performance(prediction_object, measure = "tpr", x.measure = "fpr")
> plot(perf_1)
```

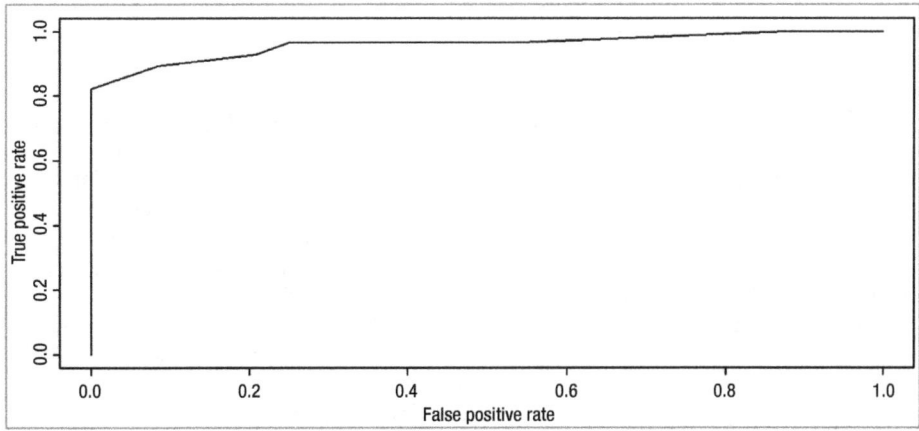

Figure 10-1. *Generated ROC curve*

This ROC curve clearly shows that the model generates almost no false positives and generates high true positives. Hence, we can conclude that the model generated is a good model.

10.3   Multinomial Logistic Regression

Multinomial logistic regression is used with categorical or discrete dependent variables that have more than two levels. The independent variables can be categorical variables or continuous variables. However, the methods to generate and evaluate these models are not straightforward and are tedious. These require lots of understanding of the underlying mathematics and statistics. Hence, we are not covering this in this book.

However, the `mlogit()` function from the `mlogit` package or the `multinom()` function from the `nnet` package are used to generate multinomial logistic regression for dependent variables with more than two unordered levels.

For dependent variables with more than two ordered levels, the `lrm()` function from the `rms` package is used to generate the multinomial logistic regression.

10.4   Regularization

Regularization is a complex subject that we won't discuss thoroughly here. However, we provide an introduction to this concept because it is an important aspect of statistics that you need to understand in the context of statistical models.

Regularization is the method normally used to avoid overfitting. When we keep adding parameters to our model to increase its accuracy and fit, at some point our prediction capability using this model decreases. By taking too many parameters, we are overfitting the model to the data and losing the value of generalization, which could have made the model more useful in prediction.

Using forward and backward model fitting and subset model fitting, we try to avoid overfitting and hence make the model more generalized and useful in predicting future values. This will ensure less bias as well as less variance when relating to the test data.

Regularization is also useful when we have more parameters than the data observations in our data set and the least squares method cannot help because it would lead to many models (not a single unique model) that would fit to the same data. Regularization allows us to find one reasonable solution in such situations.

Shrinkage methods are the most used regularization methods. They add a penalty term to the regression model to carry out the regularization. We penalize the loss function by adding a multiple (λ, also known as the *shrinkage parameter*) of the regularization norm, such as Lasso or Ridge (also known as the *shrinkage penalty*), of the linear regression weights vector. We may use cross-validation to get the best multiple (λ value). The more complex the model, the greater the penalty. We use either L_1 regularizer (Lasso) or L_2 regularizer (Ridge). Regularization shrinks the coefficient estimates to reduce the variance.

Ridge regression shrinks the estimates of the parameters but not to 0, whereas the Lasso regression shrinks the estimates of some parameters to 0. For Ridge, the fit will increase with the value of λ, and along with that the value of variance also increases. This can lead to a huge increase in parameter estimates, even for small changes in the training data, and get aggravated with the increase in the number of parameters. Lasso creates less-complicated models, thus making the predictability easier.

248

Let's explore the concept of regularization on our data set `attrition_data` without `Yrs_Exp`. We don't take `Yrs_Exp` into consideration because we know that it is not significant.

We use the `glmnet()` function from the `glmnet` package to determine the regularized model. We use the `cv.glmnet()` function from the `glmnet` package to determine the best lambda value. We use `alpha=1` for the Lasso and use `alpha=0` for the Ridge. We use `family="binomial"` and `type="class"` because our response variable is binary and we are using the regularization in the context of logistic regression, as required. The `glmnet()` function requires the input to be in the form of a matrix and the response variable to be a numeric vector. This fits a generalized linear model via penalized maximum likelihood. The regularization path is computed for the Lasso or elasticnet penalty at a grid of values for the regularization parameter lambda.

The generic format of this function as defined in the `glmnet` R package is as follows:

glmnet(x, y, family=c("gaussian", "binomial", "poisson", "multinomial", "cox", "mgaussian"),

weights, offset=NULL, alpha = 1, nlambda = 100,

lambda.min.ratio = ifelse(nobs<nvars,0.01,0.0001), lambda=NULL,

standardize = TRUE, intercept=TRUE, thresh = 1e-07, dfmax = nvars + 1,

pmax = min(dfmax × 2+20, nvars), exclude, penalty.factor = rep(1, nvars),

lower.limits=-Inf, upper.limits=Inf, maxit=100000,

type.gaussian=ifelse(nvars<500, "covariance", "naive"),

type.logistic=c("Newton", "modified.Newton"),

standardize.response=FALSE,   type.multinomial=c("ungrouped", "grouped"))

As usual, we will not be using all the parameters. We will be using only the absolutely required parameters in the interest of simplicity. Please explore the `glmnet` package guidelines for details of each parameter.

We will first prepare the inputs required. We need the model in the format of a matrix, as the input for the `glmnet()` function. We also require the response variable as a vector:

```
>
> library(glmnet)
> #converting the model into a matrix as required for the input
> x <- model.matrix(Attrition ~ Work_Challenging + Work_Envir + Compensation + Tech_Exper, data = attrition_data)
> y <- attrition_data$Attrition
> glmnet_fit <- glmnet(x, y, family = "binomial", alpha = 1, nlambda = 100)
> summary(glmnet_fit)
            Length Class     Mode
a0          68     -none-    numeric
beta        340    dgCMatrix S4
df          68     -none-    numeric
dim         2      -none-    numeric
lambda      68     -none-    numeric
dev.ratio   68     -none-    numeric
nulldev     1      -none-    numeric
npasses     1      -none-    numeric
jerr        1      -none-    numeric
offset      1      -none-    logical
classnames  2      -none-    character
call        6      -none-    call
nobs        1      -none-    numeric
>
```

Explaining the contents of the summary is beyond the scope of this book, but we will show how the regularization is carried out primarily using the graphs. We use the plot() function for this purpose. As we are using the binary data and logistic regression, we use xvar="dev" (where dev stands for *deviance*) and label = TRUE to identify the parameters in the plot as inputs to the plot() function:

```
> plot(glmnet_fit, xvar = "dev", label = TRUE)
```

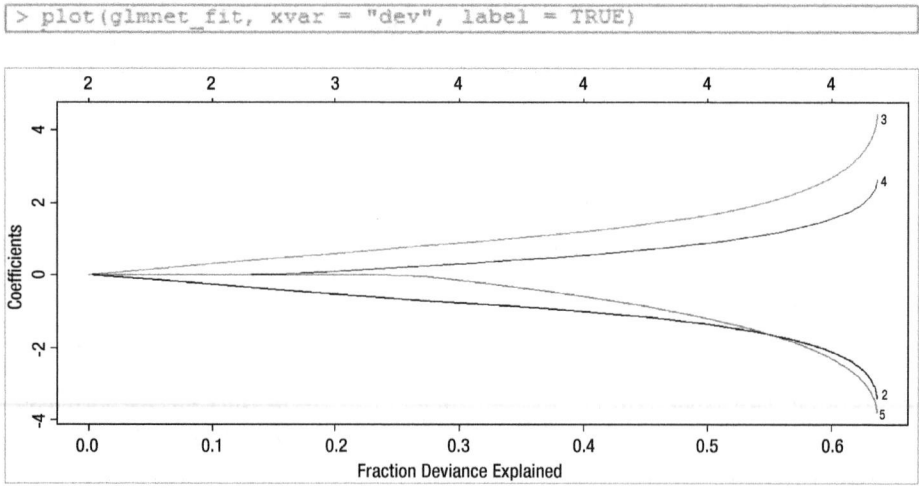

Figure 10-2. *Shows the deviance of each variable: two have + coefficients, and two have – coefficients*

The output of the glmnet_fit using the print() function is shown here:

```
>
> print(glmnet_fit)

Call:  glmnet(x = x, y = y, family = "binomial", alpha = 1, nlambda = 100)

        Df      %Dev     Lambda
 [1,]    0 -3.217e-16 0.2730000
 [2,]    2  5.564e-02 0.2487000
 [3,]    2  1.091e-01 0.2266000
 [4,]    3  1.561e-01 0.2065000
 [5,]    3  1.994e-01 0.1882000
 [6,]    3  2.369e-01 0.1715000
 [7,]    4  2.720e-01 0.1562000
 [8,]    4  3.109e-01 0.1423000
 [9,]    4  3.451e-01 0.1297000
[10,]    4  3.754e-01 0.1182000
[11,]    4  4.024e-01 0.1077000
[12,]    4  4.265e-01 0.0981100
[13,]    4  4.481e-01 0.0893900
[14,]    4  4.674e-01 0.0814500
[15,]    4  4.849e-01 0.0742200
[16,]    4  5.006e-01 0.0676200
[17,]    4  5.148e-01 0.0616200
[18,]    4  5.276e-01 0.0561400
[19,]    4  5.391e-01 0.0511500
[20,]    4  5.496e-01 0.0466100
[21,]    4  5.590e-01 0.0424700
```

```
[39,]    4  6.296e-01 0.0079580
[40,]    4  6.306e-01 0.0072510
[41,]    4  6.315e-01 0.0066070
[42,]    4  6.322e-01 0.0060200
[43,]    4  6.329e-01 0.0054850
[44,]    4  6.334e-01 0.0049980
[45,]    4  6.339e-01 0.0045540
[46,]    4  6.343e-01 0.0041490
[47,]    4  6.347e-01 0.0037810
[48,]    4  6.349e-01 0.0034450
[49,]    4  6.352e-01 0.0031390
[50,]    4  6.354e-01 0.0028600
[51,]    4  6.356e-01 0.0026060
[52,]    4  6.358e-01 0.0023740
[53,]    4  6.359e-01 0.0021630
[54,]    4  6.360e-01 0.0019710
[55,]    4  6.361e-01 0.0017960
[56,]    4  6.362e-01 0.0016370
[57,]    4  6.362e-01 0.0014910
[58,]    4  6.363e-01 0.0013590
[59,]    4  6.363e-01 0.0012380
[60,]    4  6.364e-01 0.0011280
[61,]    4  6.364e-01 0.0010280
[62,]    4  6.364e-01 0.0009365
[63,]    4  6.365e-01 0.0008533
[64,]    4  6.365e-01 0.0007775
[65,]    4  6.365e-01 0.0007084
[66,]    4  6.365e-01 0.0006455
[67,]    4  6.365e-01 0.0005882
[68,]    4  6.365e-01 0.0005359
>
```

This primarily shows the degrees of freedom (number of nonzero coefficients), the percentage of null deviance explained by the model, and the lambda value. As you can see, the lambda value keeps on decreasing. As the lambda value decreases, the percent of deviance explained by the model increases, as does the significant number of nonzero coefficients. Even though we supplied nlambda = 100 for the function (this is the default), the lambda value is shown only 68 times. This is because the algorithm ensures that it stops at an optimal time when it sees there is no further significant change in the percent deviation explained by the model.

Now we will make the prediction of the class labels at lambda = 0.05. Here type = "class" refers to the response type:

```
> predict(glmnet_fit, newx = x[1:4,], type = "class", s = 0.05)
  1
1 "Yes"
2 "No"
3 "No"
4 "Yes"
```

As you can see, all four values are predicted accurately, as they match the first four rows of our data set.

Now we will do the cross-validation of the regularized model by using the cv. glmnet() function from the glmnet package. This function does k-fold cross-validation for glmnet, produces a plot, and returns a minimum value for lambda. This also returns a lambda value at one standard error. This function by default does a 10-fold cross-validation. We can change the k-folds if required. Here we use type.measure = "class" as we are using the binary data and the logistic regression. Here, class gives the misclassification error:

```
>
> cv.fit <- cv.glmnet(x, y, family = "binomial", type.measure = "class")
> summary(cv.fit)
            Length Class  Mode
lambda      67     -none- numeric
cvm         67     -none- numeric
cvsd        67     -none- numeric
cvup        67     -none- numeric
cvlo        67     -none- numeric
nzero       67     -none- numeric
name        1      -none- character
glmnet.fit  13     lognet list
lambda.min  1      -none- numeric
lambda.1se  1      -none- numeric
>
```

We now plot the output of cv.glmnet()—that is, cv.fit—by using the plot() function:

```
> plot(cv.fit)
```

Figure 10-3 shows the cross-validated curve along with the upper and lower values of the misclassification error against the log(lambda) values. The cross-validated curve here is depicted by red dots.

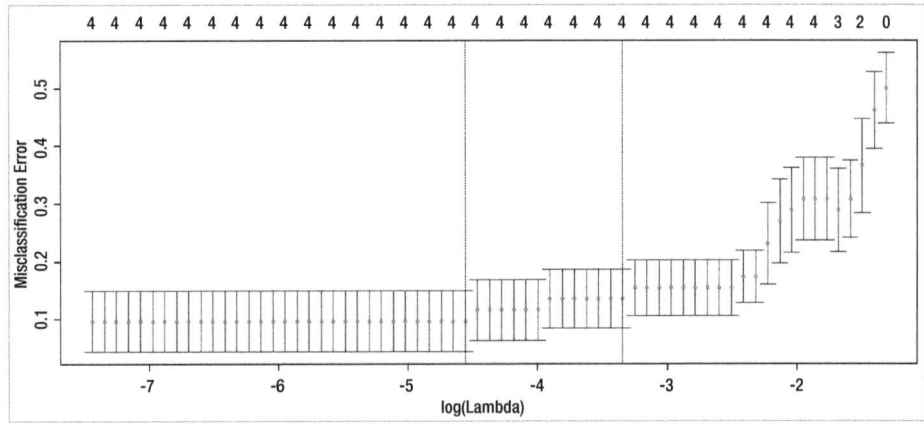

Figure 10-3. *Output of the plot(cv.fit)*

The following shows some of the important output parameters of the cv.fit model, including lambda.min or lambda.1se:

```
>
> #We will now read some of the important outputs of cv.fit
> cv.fit$lambda.min
[1] 0.01052007
> cv.fit$lambda.1se
[1] 0.03525908
>
> #In the above lambda.min is the value of lambda that gives minimum cvm
> #cvm is nothing but minimum cross validated error
> #lambda.1se is the largest value of lambda such that the error is
> #within 1 standard error of the minimum
>
```

We can view the coefficient value at the lambda.min value using the coef(cv.fit, s = "lambda.min") command in R. The output is a sparse matrix with the second levels shown for each independent factor:

```
>
> coef(cv.fit, s = "lambda.min")
6 x 1 sparse Matrix of class "dgCMatrix"
                                1
(Intercept)            -0.4770243
(Intercept)                   .
Work_ChallengingYes   -2.6311567
Work_EnvirLow          3.4122989
CompensationLow        1.9985559
Tech_ExperLow         -2.9425308
```

Let's now see how this regularized model predicts the values by using the predict() function and the s = "lambda.min" option. We will check this for the first six values of our data set. The results are shown here:

```
>
> predict(cv.fit, newx = x[1:6,], s = "lambda.min", type = "class")
  1
1 "Yes"
2 "No"
3 "No"
4 "Yes"
5 "No"
6 "Yes"
>
```

All six values are predicted properly by the predict() function. However, please note that we have not validated the results for our entire data set. The accuracy of the model may not be 100 percent, as our objective of regularization was to provide a generalized model for future predictions without worrying about an exact fit (overfit) on the training data.

10.5 Summary

In this chapter, you saw that if the response variable is a categorical or discrete variable (which can be nominal, ordinal, or binary), you use a different regression method, called logistic regression. If you have a dependent variable with only two values, such as Yes or No, you use *binomial logistic regression*. If the dependent variable takes more than two categorical values, you use multinomial logistic regression.

You looked at a few examples of logistic regression. The assumptions of linearity, normality, and homoscedasticity that generally apply to regressions do not apply to logistic regression. You used the glm() function with "family = binomial(link="logit") to create a logistic regression model.

You also looked at the underlying statistics and how logit (log odds) of the dependent variable is used in the logistic regression equation instead of the actual value of the dependent variable.

You also imported the data set to understand the underlying data. You created the model and verified the significance of the predictor variables to the model by using the p-value. One of the variables (Yrs_Exp) was not significant. You reran the model without this predictor variable and arrived at a model in which all the variables were significant.

You explored how to interpret the coefficients and their impact on the dependent variable. You learned about deviance as a measure of lack of fit and saw how to verify the model's goodness of fit by using the p-value of deviance difference using the chi-square method.

You need to use caution when interpreting the logistic regression model. You checked for multicollinearity and overdispersion.

You then split the data set into training and test sets. You tried to come up with a logistic regression model out of the training data set. Through this process, you learned that a good model generated from such a training set can be used to predict the dependent variable. You can use a confusion matrix to check measures such as accuracy, specificity and sensitivity.

By using the prediction() and performance() functions from the ROCR package, you can generate a ROC curve to validate the model, using the same data set as the original.

You learned how to predict the value of a new data set by using the logistic regression model you developed. Then you had a brief introduction to multinomial logistic regression and the R packages that can be used in this regard.

Finally, you learned about regularization, including why it's required and how it's carried out.

CHAPTER 11

Big Data Analysis—Introduction and Future Trends

Data is power. Data is going to be another dimension of value in any enterprise. Data is the decision driver going forward. All organizations and institutions have woken up to the value of data and are trying to collate data from various sources and mine it for its value. Businesses are trying to understand consumer/market behavior in order to get the maximum out of each consumer with the minimum effort possible. Fortunately, these organizations and institutions have been supported by the evolution of technology in the form of increasing storage power and computing power, as well as the power of the cloud, to provide infrastructure as well as tools. This has driven the growth of data analytical fields including descriptive analytics, predictive analytics, machine learning, deep learning, artificial intelligence, and the Internet of Things. Organizations are collecting data without the need for thinking the value of it and use it to tell them the value the data has for them. Data is made to learn from itself and thus throw light on many that have been hitherto unknown or possibly a logically thinking person may not think of or accept at face value.

This chapter does not delve into the various definitions of big data. Many pundits have offered many divergent definitions of big data, confusing people more than clarifying the issue. However, in general terms, big data means a huge amount of data that cannot be easily understood or analyzed manually or with limited computing power or limited computer resources; analyzing big data requires the capability to crunch data of a diverse nature (from structured data to unstructured data), from various sources (such as social media, structured databases, unstructured databases, and the Internet of Things).

In general, when people refer to big data, they are referring to data with three characteristics: variety, volume, and velocity, as shown in Figure 11-1.

© Dr. Umesh R. Hodeghatta and Umesha Nayak 2017
U. R. Hodeghatta and U. Nayak, *Business Analytics Using R - A Practical Approach*,
DOI 10.1007/978-1-4842-2514-1_11

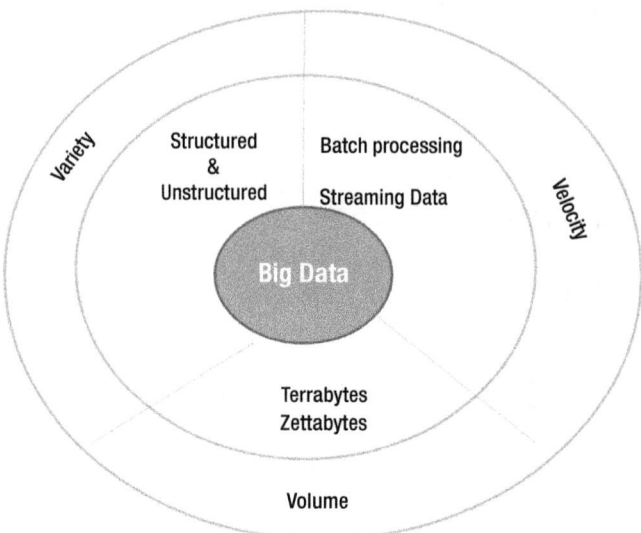

Figure 11-1. *Characteristics of big data*

Variety refers to the different types of data that are available on the Web, the Internet and various databases, etc. This data can be structured or unstructured and can be from various social media. *Volume* refers to the size of the data that is available for you to process. Its size is *big*—terabytes and petabytes. *Velocity* refers to how fast you can process and analyze data, determine its meaning, arrive at the models and use the models that can help business.

The following have aided the effective use of big data:

- Huge computing power of clusters of computing machines extending the processing power and the memory power by distributing the load over several machines

- Huge storage power distributing the data over various storage resources

- Significant development of algorithms and packages for machine learning

- Developments in the fields of artificial intelligence, natural language processing, and others

- Development of tools for data visualization, data integration, and data analysis

11.1   Big Data Ecosystem

Over the past ten years or so, organizations such as Google, Yahoo, IBM, SAS, SAP, and Cloudera have made significant efforts to design and develop a substantial system of tools to facilitate the collating and integrating of huge amounts of data from diverse sources, mine the data to reveal patterns or truth hidden in the data, visualize the data, present the learning from the data, and suggest proactive actions.

No doubt, R has emerged as a strong open source language and has been adopted by a very large community of users particularly because of its ease of use, its packaged and validated algorithms available, and the documentation existing on the same. However, the Apache Hadoop ecosystem—with its Hadoop Distributed File System coupled with various tools/mechanisms such as MapReduce, YARN, Pig, Mahout, Hive, HBase, Storm, and Oozie—has strengthened the drive of big data analysis, along with commercial tools including SAP and SAS. The Hadoop framework is shown in Figure 11-2.

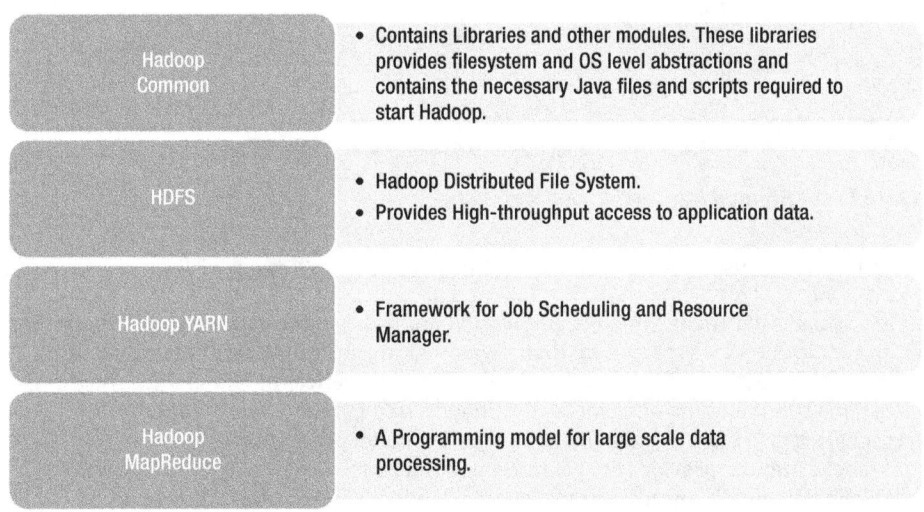

Figure 11-2. *Hadoop ecosystem*

Hadoop Distributed File System (HDFS) allows data to be distributed and stored among many computers. Further, it allows the use of the increased processing power and memory of multiple clustered systems. This has overcome the obstacle of not being able to store huge amounts of data in a single system and not being able to analyze that data because of a lack of required processing power and memory. The Hadoop ecosystem consists of modules that enable us to process the data and perform the analysis.

A user application can submit a job to Hadoop. Once data is loaded onto the system, it is divided into multiple blocks, typically 64 MB or 128 MB. Then the Hadoop Job client submits the job to the JobTracker. The JobTracker distributes and schedules the individual tasks to different machines in a distributed system; many machines are clustered together to form one entity. The tasks are divided into two phases: Map tasks are done on small portions of data where the data is stored, and Reduce tasks combine data to produce the final output. The TaskTrackers on different nodes execute the tasks as per MapReduce implementation, and the reduce function is stored in the output files on the file system. The entire process is controlled by various smaller tasks and functions. The full Hadoop ecosystem and framework are shown in Figure 11-3.

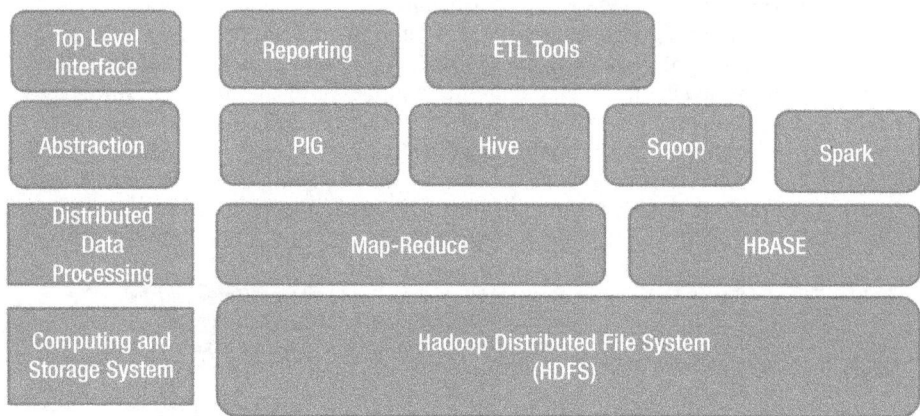

Figure 11-3. *Hadoop framework and ecosystem*

Apache Hadoop YARN is a tool used for resource provisioning as well as management and job scheduling/monitoring activities.

Apache Pig can analyze a huge amount of data. This platform uses a simple scripting language that allows users to create their own programs to complement the capability of predefined functions of Pig. Pig's compiler produces sequences of MapReduce programs. Hence, this eliminates the need for writing lengthy and cumbersome MapReduce programs. Pig also has the capability to carry out parallel processing.

Apache Mahout provides the environment and programming capability to write scalable machine-learning algorithms and applications. Today, Mahout includes Samsara, a vector math experimentation environment.

Apache Hive provides the capability to read, write, and manage data by providing SQL capability.

Apache HBase is the Hadoop distributed database, with high scalability and a huge storage capability. It provides real-time access to data. HBase is a NoSQL database for Hadoop.

Apache Storm enables distributed real-time processing of streams of data in the same way that Hadoop MapReduce does batch processing. Storm is a computation engine that performs continuous computation, real-time analytics, online machine learning, and many other related capabilities such as distributed RPC.

Apache Oozie enables effective workflow scheduling to manage Apache Hadoop jobs. It is extremely well integrated with other tools in the Apache Hadoop ecosystem.

In addition to these tools, NoSQL (originally referring to *not only SQL*) databases such as Cassandra, ArangoDB, MarkLogic, OrientDB, Apache Giraph, MongoDB, and Dynamo have supported or complemented the big data ecosystem significantly. These NoSQL databases can store and analyze multidimensional, structured or unstructured, huge data effectively. This has provided significant fillip to the consolidation and integration of data from diverse sources for analysis.

Currently Apache Spark is gaining momentum in usage. Apache Spark is a fast, general engine for big data processing, with built-in modules for streaming, SQL, machine learning, and graph processing. Apache Spark, an interesting development in recent years, provides an extremely fast engine for data processing and analysis. It allows an easy interface to applications written in R, Java, Python, or Scala. Apache Spark has a stack of libraries such as MLib (Machine Learning), Spark Streaming, Spark SQL, and GraphX. It can run in stand-alone mode as well as on Hadoop. Similarly, it can access various sources such as HBase to Cassandra to HDFS. Many users and organizations have shown interest in this tool and have started using it, resulting in it becoming very popular in a short period of time. This tool provides significant hope to organizations and users of big data.

Tools such as Microsoft Business Intelligence and Tableau provide dashboards and the visualization of data. These have enabled organizations to learn from the data and leverage this learning to formulate strategies or improve the way they conduct their operations or their processes.

The following are some of the advantages of using Hadoop for big data processing:

- Simple parallel architecture on any cheap commodity hardware

- Built-in fault-tolerance system, and application-level failure detection and high availability

- Dynamic cluster modification without interruption

- Easy addition or removal of machines to / from the cluster

- Java based and platform independent

Microsoft Azure, Amazon, and Cloudera are some of the big providers of cloud facilities and services for effective big data analysis.

11.2   Future Trends in Big Data Analytics

The applications of big data and areas in which big data analytics are used is increasing year by year. This section provides some of the trends that are going to be accelerating in the years to come.

11.2.1   Growth of Social Media

Over a short period of time, social media has created a significantly large amount of data, and the trend is growing almost exponentially. This data, related to people across the globe, is bringing an understanding to organizations of hitherto unknown facts and figures. This is driving those organizations to think differently and formulate their strategies differently.

11.2.2   Creation of Data Lakes

Organizations are getting data from diverse sources. But often they don't know the value of the data. They dump the data into data *lakes* without even looking at the value it provides. Once the data is inside the data lake, organizations look for patterns and/or allow data to "discover itself." This attitude is of immense value going ahead.

11.2.3   Visualization Tools at the Hands of Business Users

The delay that has occurred between the analysis of data by data analysts and the presentation of that data to the business is no longer acceptable in the context of increasing competitiveness. Businesses are required to take quick action to use the knowledge gained from the data effectively. Tools such as Microsoft Business Intelligence, Tableau, and SAS Visual Analytics have provided significant utility to business users. More visualization helps business users quickly understand the patterns and trends and make effective and timely decisions. The tool capabilities are trending toward being dynamic, to depict additional aspects evidenced by the data in such visualization charts or dashboards.

11.2.4   Prescriptive Analytics

Data analysis is no longer focused on understanding the patterns or value hidden in the data. The future trend is to prescribe the actions to be taken, based on the past and depending on present circumstances, without the need for human intervention. This is going to be of immense value in fields such as healthcare and aeronautics.

11.2.5   Internet of Things

The *Internet of Things* is a driving force for the future. It has the capability to bring data from diverse sources such as home appliances, industrial machines, weather equipment, and sensors from self-driving vehicles or even people. This has the potential to create a huge amount of data that can be analyzed and used to provide proactive solutions to potential future and current problems. This can also lead to significant innovations and improvements.

11.2.6   Artificial Intelligence

Neural networks can drive artificial intelligence—in particular, making huge data learn from itself without any human intervention, specific programming, or the need for specific models. *Deep learning* is one such area that is acting as a driver in the field of big data. This may throw up many of the whats which we are not aware of. We may not understand the whys for some of them but the whats of those may be very useful. Hence, we may move away from the perspective of always looking for cause and effect. The speed at which the machine-learning field is being developed and used drives significant emphasis in this area. Further, natural language processing (NLP) and property graphs (PG) are also likely to drive new application design and development, to put the capabilities of these technologies in the hands of organizations and users.

11.2.7   Whole Data Processing

With the current infrastructure and the current level of tool support available, particularly in the cloud, it is possible in most cases to analyze a complete set of data rather than sample out the data for analysis. This avoids the downsides of sampling. Using huge amounts of data drives us in the right direction, even though the data may not be complete or perfect. We need not be always looking for perfect data.

11.2.8   Vertical and Horizontal Applications

Analytics is moving in the direction of consolidating vertical moves specific to industries such as healthcare, banking, and automotive. On the other hand, horizontal moves cut across industry spheres including consumer purchasing behavior, transaction monitoring for prevention of fraud and money laundering, and understanding the exits of the customers from a particular brand or a particular organization.

11.2.9   Real-Time Analytics

Organizations are hungry to understand the opportunities available to them. They want to understand in real time what is happening—for example, what a particular person is purchasing or what a person is planning for—and use the opportunity appropriately to offer the best possible solutions or discounts or cross-sell related products or services. Organizations are no longer satisfied with a delayed analysis of data that results in missed business opportunities because they were not aware of what was happening in real time.

11.2.10   Putting the Analytics in the Hands of Business Users

It is consistently observed that a delay occurs before data analysts bring the results of their data analysis to the attention of business users. Because of this time loss, the analysis, even though wonderful, may not be useful and may not lead organizations to create effective strategies. Instead, making tools more useful and directly usable by business users who can then make decisions on a timely basis will put business users in an advantageous position. The world is moving toward making this a reality to a large extent.

11.2.11   Migration of Solutions from One Tool to Another

The diversity of tools means that solutions provided for one tool are not easily migrated to other systems. This is primarily because of the different programming languages and environments used. The world is moving toward an effort to make the solutions from one tool easily implemented or migrated to other tools. Efforts in Predictive Model Markup Language (PMML) are already moving in this direction. The Data Mining Group (DMG) is working in this regard.

11.2.12   Cloud, Cloud, Everywhere the Cloud

Both data and tools in the cloud have provided a significant boost to big data analysis. More and more organizations and institutions are using cloud facilities for their data storage and analysis. Organizations are moving from the private cloud to the public or hybrid cloud for data storage and data analysis. This has provided the organizations cost-effectiveness, scalability, and availability. Of course, security may be a concern, and significant efforts to increase security in the cloud are in progress.

11.2.13   In-Database Analytics

In-database analytics have increased security, and reduced privacy concerns, in part by addressing governance. Organizations, if required, can do away with intermediate requirements for data analysis such as data warehouses. Organizations that are more conscious about governance and security concerns will provide significant fillips to in-database analytics. Lots of vendor organizations have already made their presence felt in this space.

11.2.14   In-Memory Analytics

The value of in-memory analytics is driving transactional processing and analytical processing side by side and in memory. This may be very helpful in fields where immediate intervention based on the results of analysis is essential. Systems with Hybrid Transactional/Analytical Processing (HTAP) are already being used by some organizations. However, using HTAP for the sake of using it may not be of much use, even when the rate of data change is slow and you still need to bring in data from various diverse systems to carry out effective analysis. Instead it may be overkill, leading to higher costs to the organization.

11.2.15   Autonomous Services for Machine Learning

More and more organizations may reach out to autonomous services for machine learning (such as Microsoft Azure Machine Learning Studio, Amazon Machine Learning, or Google Prediction API) if they can't get reliable and experienced data scientists who can help them out effectively.

11.2.16   Addressing Security and Compliance

There is an increased awareness of information security and compliance requirements with consumers as well as organizations. This is leading to significant efforts to increase security in data analytical environments. This trend is going to continue to make the tools and systems more secure. Diverse requirements of different countries may put certain restrictions on how the data will be used and protected. Compliance is likely to be a strain on the organizations using data for analysis.

11.2.17   Healthcare

Big data in healthcare can be used to predict epidemics, prevent diseases, and improve value-based healthcare and quality of living. An abundance of data is generated from various modern devices such as smartphones, Fitbit products, and pedometers that measure, for example, how far you walk in a day or the number of calories you burn. This data can be used to create diet plans or prescribe medicines. Other unstructured data—such as medical device logs, doctor's notes, lab results, x-ray reports, and clinical and lab data—can be big enough data to analyze and improve patient care and thus increase efficiency. Other data that can be generated and processed for big data analytics includes claims data, electronic health/medical record data (EHR or EMR), pharmaceutical R&D data, clinical trials data, genomic data, patient behavior and sentiment data, and medical device data.

References

1. BAESENS, BART. (2014). Analytics in a Big Data World, The Essential Guide to Data Science and Its Applications. Wiley India Pvt. Ltd.

2. MAYER-SCHONBERGER, VIKTOR & CUKIER KENNETH. (2013). Big Data, A Revolution That Will Transform How We Live, Work and Think. John Murray (Publishers), Great Britain.

3. LINDSTROM, MARTIN. (2016). Small Data – The Tiny Clues That Uncover Huge Trends. Hodder & Stoughton, Great Britain.

4. FREEDMAN, DAVID; PISANI, ROBERT & PURVES, ROGER. (2013). Statistics. Viva Books Private Limited, New Delhi.

5. LEVINE, DAVID.M. (2011). Statistics for SIX SIGMA Green Belts. Dorling Kindersley (India) Pvt. Ltd., Noida, India.

6. DONNELLY, JR. ROBERT.A. (2007). The Complete Idiot's Guide to Statistics, 2/e. Penguin Group (USA) Inc., New York 10014, USA.

7. TEETOR, PAUL. (2014). R Cookbook. Shroff Publishers and Distributors Pvt. Ltd., Navi Mumbai.

8. WITTEN, IAN.H.; FRANK, EIBE & HALL, MARK.A. (2014). Data Mining, 3/e – Practical Machine Learning Tools and Techniques. Morgan Kaufmann Publishers, Burlington, MA 01803, USA.

9. HARRINGTON, PETER. (2015). Machine Learning in Action. Dreamtech Press, New Delhi.

10. ZUMEL, NINA & MOUNT, JOHN. (2014). Practical Data Science with R. Dreamtech Press, New Delhi.

11. KABACOFF, ROBERT.I. (2015). R In Action – Data analysis and graphics with R. Dreamtech Press, New Delhi.

© Dr. Umesh R. Hodeghatta and Umesha Nayak 2017

U. R. Hodeghatta and U. Nayak, *Business Analytics Using R - A Practical Approach*, DOI 10.1007/978-1-4842-2514-1

12. [Online] www.quora.com.

13. [Online] www.r-bloggers.com.

14. [Online] www.stackexchange.com.

15. [Online] https://cran.r-project.org/.

16. [Online] www.r-project.org/.

17. COMPUTERWORLD FROM IDG. (2016). 8 big trends in big data analysis. [Online] Available from: http://www.computerworld.com/article/2690856/big-data/8-big-trends-in-big-data-analytics.html

18. WELLESLEY INFORMATION SERVICES, MA 02026, USA. (2016). Big Data Analytics Predictions for 2016. Available from: http://data-informed.com/big-data-analytics-predictions-2016/

19. COMPUTERWORLD FROM IDG. (2016). 11 Market Trends in Advanced Analytics. [Online] Available from: http://www.computerworld.com/article/2489750/it-management/11-market-trends-in-advanced-analytics.html#tk.drr_mlt

20. WELLESLEY INFORMATION SERVICES, MA 02026, USA. (2016). 5 Big Trends to Watch in 2016. [Online] Available from: http://data-informed.com/5-big-data-trends-watch-2016/.

21. ZHANG, NANCY.R. Ridge Regression, LARS, Logistic Regression. [Online] Available from: http://statweb.stanford.edu/~nzhang/203_web/lecture12_2010.pdf

22. QIAN, JUNYANG & HASTIE, TRAVOR. (2014). Glmnet Vignette. [Online] Available from: http://web.stanford.edu/~hastie/glmnet/glmnet_alpha.html

23. USUELLI, MICHELE. (2014). R Machine Learning Essentials. Packt Publishing.

24. BALI, RAGHAV & SARKAR, DIPANJAN. (2016). R Machine Learning By Example. Packt Publishing.

25. DAVID, CHIU & YU-WEI. (2015). Machine Learning with R Cookbook. Packt Publishing.

26. LANTZ, BRETT. (2015). Machine Learning with R, 2/e. Packt Publishing.

27. Data Mining - Concepts and Techniques By Jiawei Han, Micheline Kamber and Jian Pei, 3e, Morgan Kaufmann

28. S. Agarwal, R. Agrawal, P. M. Deshpande, A. Gupta, J. F. Naughton, R. Ramakrishnan, and S. Sarawagi. On the computation of multidimensional aggregates. VLDB'96

29. D. Agrawal, A. E. Abbadi, A. Singh, and T. Yurek. Efficient view maintenance in data warehouses. SIGMOD'97

30. R. Agrawal, A. Gupta, and S. Sarawagi. Modeling multidimensional databases. ICDE'97

31. S. Chaudhuri and U. Dayal. An overview of data warehousing and OLAP technology. ACM SIGMOD Record, 26:65-74, 1997

32. E. F. Codd, S. B. Codd, and C. T. Salley. Beyond decision support. Computer World, 27, July 1993.

33. J. Gray, et al. Data cube: A relational aggregation operator generalizing group-by, cross-tab and sub-totals. Data Mining and Knowledge Discovery, 1:29-54, 1997.

34. Swift, Ronald S. (2001) Accelerating Customer Relationships Using CRM and Relationship Technologies, Prentice Hall

35. Berry, M. J. A., Linoff, G. S. (2004) Data Mining Techniques. Wiley Publishing.

36. Ertek, G. Visual Data Mining with Pareto Squares for Customer Relationship Management (CRM) (working paper, Sabancı University, Istanbul, Turkey)

37. Ertek, G., Demiriz, A. A framework for visualizing association mining results (accepted for LNCS)

38. Hughes, A. M. Quick profits with RFM analysis. http://www.dbmarketing.com/articles/Art149.htm

39. Kumar, V., Reinartz, W. J. (2006) Customer Relationship Management, A Databased Approach. John Wiley & Sons Inc.

40. Spence, R. (2001) Information Visualization. ACM Press.

41. Dyche, Jill, The CRM Guide to Customer Relationship Management, Addison-Wesley, Boston, 2002.

42. Gordon, Ian. "Best Practices: Customer Relationship Management" Ivey Business Journal Online, 2002, pp. 1-6.

43. Data Mining for Business Intelligence: Concepts, Techniques, and Applications in Microsoft Office Excel with XLMiner [Hardcover] By Galit Shmueli (Author), Nitin R. Patel (Author), Peter C. Bruce (Author)

44. A. Gupta and I. S. Mumick. Materialized Views: Techniques, Implementations, and Applications. MIT Press, 1999.

45. J. Han. Towards on-line analytical mining in large databases. ACM SIGMOD Record, 27:97-107, 1998.

46. V. Harinarayan, A. Rajaraman, and J. D. Ullman. Implementing data cubes efficiently. SIGMOD'96

47. C. Imhoff, N. Galemmo, and J. G. Geiger. Mastering Data Warehouse Design: Relational and Dimensional Techniques. John Wiley, 2003

48. W. H. Inmon. Building the Data Warehouse. John Wiley, 1996

49. R. Kimball and M. Ross. The Data Warehouse Toolkit: The Complete Guide to Dimensional Modeling. 2ed. John Wiley, 2002

50. P. O'Neil and D. Quass. Improved query performance with variant indexes. SIGMOD'97

51. Microsoft. OLEDB for OLAP programmer's reference version 1.0. In http://www.microsoft.com/data/oledb/olap, 1998

52. A. Shoshani. OLAP and statistical databases: Similarities and differences. PODS'00.

53. S. Sarawagi and M. Stonebraker. Efficient organization of large multidimensional arrays. ICDE'94

54. OLAP council. MDAPI specification version 2.0. In http://www.olapcouncil.org/research/apily.htm, 1998

55. E. Thomsen. OLAP Solutions: Building Multidimensional Information Systems. John Wiley, 1997

56. P. Valduriez. Join indices. ACM Trans. Database Systems, 12:218-246, 1987.

57. J. Widom. Research problems in data warehousing. CIKM'95.

58. Kurt Thearling. Data Mining. http://www.thearling.com, kurt@thearling.com

59. "Building Data Mining Applications for CRM", By Alex Berson, Stephen Smith and Kurt Thearling

60. Building Data Mining Applications for CRM by Alex Berson, Stephen Smith, Kurt Thearling (McGraw Hill, 2000).

61. Introduction to Data Mining, By Pang-Ning, Michael Steinbach, Vipin Kumar, 2006 Pearson Addison-Wesley.

62. Data Mining: Concepts and Techniques, Jiawei Han and Micheline Kamber, 2000 (c) Morgan Kaufmann Publishers

63. Data Mining In Excel, Galit Shmueli Nitin R. Patel Peter C. Bruce, 2005 Galit Shmueli, Nitin R. Patel, Peter C. Bruce

64. Principles of Data Mining by David Hand, Heikki Mannila and Padhraic Smyth ISBN: 026208290x The MIT Press © 2001 (546 pages)

65. http://scikit-learn.org/stable/modules/generated/sklearn.tree.DecisionTreeClassifier.html

66. http://paginas.fe.up.pt/~ec/files_1011/week%2008%20-%20Decision%20Trees.pdf

67. http://www.quora.com/Machine-Learning/Are-gini-index-entropy-or-classification-error-measures-causing-any-difference-on-Decision-Tree-classification

68. http://www.quora.com/Machine-Learning/Are-gini-index-entropy-or-classification-error-measures-causing-any-difference-on-Decision-Tree-classification

69. https://rapid-i.com/rapidforum/index.php?topic=3060.0

70. http://stats.stackexchange.com/questions/19639/which-is-a-better-cost-function-for-a-random-forest-tree-gini-index-or-entropy

71. Creswell, J. W. (2013). Research design: Qualitative, quantitative, and mixed methods approaches. Sage Publications, Incorporated.

72. http://www.physics.csbsju.edu/stats/box2.html

73. Advance Data Mining Techniques, Olson, D.L, Delen, D, 2008 Springer

74. Phyu, Nu Thair, "Survey of Classification Techniques in Data Mining", Proceedings of the International MultiConference of Engineers and Computer Scientists 2009 Vol I IMECS 2009, March 18 - 20, 2009, Hong Kong

75. Myatt, J. Glenn, "Making Sense of Data – A practical Guide to Exploratory Data Analysis and Data Mining", 2007, WILEY-INTERSCIENCE A JOHN WILEY & SONS, INC., PUBLICATION

76. Fawcett, Tom, "An Introduction to ROC analysis", Pattern Recognition Letters 27 (2006) 861–874

77. Sayad, Saeed. "An Introduction to Data Mining", Self-Help Publishers (January 5, 2011).

78. Delmater, Rhonda, and Monte Hancock. "Data mining explained." (2001).

79. Alper, Theodore M. "A classification of all order-preserving homeomorphism groups of the reals that satisfy finite uniqueness." *Journal of mathematical psychology* 31.2 (1987): 135-154.

80. Narens, Louis. "Abstract measurement theory." (1985).

81. Luce, R. Duncan, and John W. Tukey. "Simultaneous conjoint measurement: A new type of fundamental measurement." *Journal of mathematical psychology* 1.1 (1964): 1-27.

82. Provost, Foster J., Tom Fawcett, and Ron Kohavi. "The case against accuracy estimation for comparing induction algorithms." *ICML*. Vol. 98. 1998.

83. Hanley, James A., and Barbara J. McNeil. "The meaning and use of the area under a receiver operating characteristic (ROC) curve." *Radiology* 143.1 (1982): 29-36.

84. Ducker, Sophie Charlotte, W. T. Williams, and G. N. Lance. "Numerical classification of the Pacific forms of Chlorodesmis (Chlorophyta)." *Australian Journal of Botany* 13.3 (1965): 489-499.

85. Kaufman, Leonard, and Peter J. Rousseeuw. "Partitioning around medoids (program pam)." *Finding groups in data: an introduction to cluster analysis*(1990): 68-125.

Index

A

Affinity analysis, 182
Aggregate() function, 182
Akaike information criterion (AIC)
        value, 219
Amazon, 261
Apache Hadoop ecosystem, 259
Apache Hadoop YARN, 260
Apache HBase, 260
Apache Hive, 260
Apache Mahout, 260
Apache Oozie, 260
Apache Pig, 260
Apache Spark, 261
Apache Storm, 260
Apply() function, 49
Arrays, R, 31
Artificial intelligence, 262
Association-rule analysis, 182
        association rules, 185–186
        if-then, 183
        interpreting results, 186
        market-basket
                analysis, 182–183
        rules, 183
        support, 183
Association rules/affinity analysis, 118

B

Bar plot, 77–78
Bayes theorem, 132
Bias-variance erros, 147
Big data, 257
        analysis, 257

analytics, future trends, 261
        addressing security and
                compliance, 264
        artificial intelligence, 262
        autonomous services for machine
                learning, 264
        business users, 263
        cloud, 264
        data lakes, 262
        growth of social media, 261
        healthcare, 265
        in-database analytics, 264
        in-memory analytics, 264
        Internet of Things, 262
        migration of solutions, 263
        prescriptive analytics, 262
        real-time analytics, 263
        vertical and horizontal
                applications, 263
        visualization at business
                users, 262
        whole data processing, 263
        characteristics, 258
        ecosystem, 259–261
        use of, 258
Big data analytics, 5
Binomial distribution, 87
Bivariate data analysis, 110
Bootstrap aggregating/bagging, 152
Boxplots, 78–79
Business analytics, 5
        applications of
                customer service and
                        support areas, 9
                human resources, 9
                marketing and sales, 8

© Dr. Umesh R. Hodeghatta and Umesha Nayak 2017
U. R. Hodeghatta and U. Nayak, *Business Analytics Using R - A Practical Approach*,
DOI 10.1007/978-1-4842-2514-1

Business analytics (*cont.*)
   product design, 9
   service design, 9
  computer packages
   and applications, 6
  consolidate data from various
   sources, 7
  drivers for, 5
  framework for, 14
  infinite storage and computing
   capability, 7
  life cycle of project, 11–13
  programming tools and platforms, 7
  required skills for business analyst, 10
   data analysis techniques and
    algorithms, 10
   data structures and storage/
    warehousing techniques, 11
   programming knowledge, 11
   statistical and mathematical
    concepts, 11
Business Analytics and
  Statistical Tools, 17–20
Business analytics process
  data collection and integration, 95
   data warehouse, 95
   HR and finance functions, 95
   IT database, 95
   manufacturing and production
    process, 95
   metadata, 95
   NoSQL databases, 95
   operational database, 95
   primary source, 95
   sampling technique, 96
   secondary source, 95
   variable selection, 97
  definition, 94
  deployment, 129–130
  functions
   collection and integration, 92
   deployment, 94
   evaluation, 93
   exploration and visualization, 92
   management and review report, 94
   modeling techniques and
    algorithms, 93
   preprocessing, 92
   problem, objectives, and
    requirements, 91

historical data, 91
identifying and understanding
  problem, 94
life cycle, 91
management report and review
  data cleaning carried out, 128
  data set use, 128
  deployment and usage, 129
  issues handling, 129
  model creation, 128
  prerequisites, 128
  problem description, 128
model evaluation
  confusion matrix, 123
  gain/lift charts, 125
  holdout partition, 122
  k-fold cross-validation, 123
  ROC chart, 126
  test data, 122
  validation, 122
model evaluationt
  training, 122
preprocessing (*see* Preprocessing data)
real-time data, 91
regression model, 127
root-mean-square error, 127
sequence of phases, 91, 93
techniques and algorithms
  data types, 121
  descriptive analytics, 118
  machine learning, 119
  predictive analytics, 118

C

Classification techniques, 131
  decision tree (*see* Decision tree
   structure)
  disadvantage, 150
  k-nearest neighbor (K-NN), 150
  probabilistic models, 132
   advantages and limitations, 136
   bank credit-card approval
    process, 133
   Naïve Bays, 134
  R
   cross-validation error, 160
   CSV format, 154
   functions, 154–155
   misclassification error, 155

plotting deviance vs. size, 158–159
school data set, 153
testing model, 156–157
training set and test set, 155
tree() package, 155
random forests, 152
step process, 132
types, 150
Cloud, 264
Cloudera, 261
Clustering analysis, 118
average linkage (average distance), 167
categorical variable, 164
centroid distance, 168
complete linkage (maximum
distance), 167
Euclidean distance, 163
finance, 162
hierarchical clustering
algorithm, 168
dendrograms, 169
limitations, 169
hierarchical method, 163
HR department, 162
Manhattan distance, 164
market segmentation, 161
measures distance (between
clusters), 166
mixed data types, 165
n records, 163
nonhierarchical clustering
(see K-means algorithm)
nonhierarchical method, 163
overview, 161
pearson product correlation, 164
purpose of, 162
single linkage (minimum
distance), 166–167
Coefficient of determination, 196
Comma-Separated Values (CSV), 38–41
Computations on data frames
analyses, 79
EmpData data, 81
in R, 80
scatter plots, 81–84
Continuous data, 98
Control structures in R, 45
for loops, 46–47
if-else, 46

looping functions, 48–49
apply() function, 49
cut() function, 53–54
lapply() function, 50
sapply() function, 51
split() function, 54
tapply() function, 51, 53
while loops, 47–48
writing functions, 55–56
Correlation, 210
Correlation coefficient, 189–192
Correlation graph, 115
Cross-Industry Standard Process for Data
Mining (CRISP-DM), 94
Cut() function, 53–54
Cutree() function, 179

■ D

Data, 257
Data aggregation, 118
Data analysis, R
reading and writing data, 37
from Microsoft Excel file, 42–44
from text file, 38, 40–42
from web, 44
Data analysis tools, 17, 21
Data analytics, 4
Data exploration and visualization, 104
descriptive statistics, 106
goal of, 104
graphs
box/whisker plot, 107
correlation, 115
density function, 107, 116
histograms, 107
notched plots, 109–110
registered users vs.
casual users, 112
scatter plot matrices, 112
scatter plots, 110
trellis plot, 114
types of, 106
univariate analysis, 107
normalization techniques, 117
phase, 104
tables, 105
transformation, 117
View() command, 105

Data frames, R, 32
Data lakes, 262
Data Mining Group (DMG), 263
Data science, 5
Data structures
   in R, 29
      arrays, 31
      data frames, 32
      factors, 35
      lists, 34
      matrices, 30–31
Decision tree structure, 136
   bias and variance, 147
   classification rules, 145
   data tuples, 140
   entropy/expected information, 140
   generalization errors, 145
   gini index, 139
   impurity, 139
   induction, 142
   information gain, 138
   overfitting and underfitting, 146
   overfitting errors, 148
      CART method, 150
      pruning process, 150
      regression trees, 150
      tree growth, 149
   recursive divide-and-conquer
      approach, 138
   root node, 136
Deep learning, 262
Dendrograms, 169
Density function, 116
Descriptive analytics, 118
   computations on dataframes
      (see Computations on data frames)
   graphical (see Graphical
      description of data)
   Maximum depth of river, 60
   mean depth of the river, 59
   median of the depth of river, 61
   notice, sign board, 59
   percentile, 62
   population and sample, 62–63
   probability, 84, 86–88
   quartile 3, 61
   statistical parameters (see Statistical
      parameters)
Discrete data types, 98
Durbin-Watson test, 198

E

Economic globalization, 8
Ecosystem, big data, 259–261
Euclidean distance, 163
Extensible Markup Language (XML), 37

F

Factors, R, 35
for loops, 46–47

G

Graphical description of data
   bar plot, 77–78
   boxplot, 78, 79
   histogram, 77
   plots in R
      code, 74
      creation, simple plot, 74
      plot(), 75
      variants, 76
Gross domestic product (GDP), 96

H

Hadoop Distributed File
      System (HDFS), 259
Hadoop ecosystem, 260
   advantages, 261
Hadoop framework, 259
Healthcare, big data, 265
Hierarchical clustering
   algorithm, 168
   closeness, 168
   dendrograms, 169
   limitations, 169
Histograms, 77, 107
Huge computing power, 258
Huge storage power, 258
Hybrid Transactional/Analytical
      Processing (HTAP), 264
Hypothesis testing, 192

I

If-else structure, 46
In-database analytics, 264
In-memory analytics, 264

Integrated development environment
    (IDE), 23
Internet of Things, 262
Interquartile Range (IQR) method, 173
Interval data types, 98

J

JavaScript Object Notation (JSON) files, 38
JobTracker, 259

K

k-fold cross-validation, 123
K-means algorithm
    case study
        outliers verification, 173
        relevant variables, 173
        scores() function, 173
        standardized values, 174
        test data set, 172
    data points (observations), 175
        aggregate() function, 180
        cutree() function, 179
        data observations, 179–180
        dendrogram, 178
        dist() function, 175
        hclust() function, 175
        hierarchical partitioning
            approach, 175
        library(NbClust) command, 176
        NbClust() command, 176
        observations, 175
        plot() function, 178
        rect.hclust() function, 178
        rent and distances, 180
        selected approaches, 175
    goal, 169
    k-means algorithm, 170
    limitations, 172
    objective of, 170
    partition clustering methods, 180
kmeansruns() function, 181
k-nearest neighbor (K-NN), 150

L

lapply() function, 50
Lasso Regression method, 193
Linear regression
    assumptions, 193
    correlation

attrition, 189
cause-and-effect relationship, 188
coefficient, 189–190, 192
customer satisfaction, 189
employee satisfaction index, 189
sales quantum, 189
strong/weak association, 189
data frame creation, 194
degrees of freedom, 196
equal variance, variable, 199
equation, 196
F-statistic, 197
function, 194
independent and dependent
    variable, 188
innovativeness, 187
intercept, 194, 204
least squares method, 193
linear relationship, 188
marketing efforts, 187
multiple R-squared, 196
predict() function, 203
profitability, 188
properties, 188
p-value, 196
quality-related statistics, 196
R command, 195
residuals, 195
residual standard error, 196
sales personnel, 194–195
standard error, 196
testing
    independence errors, 198
    linearity, 197
    normality, 198–199
validation
    crPlots(model name) function, 202
    gvlma() function, 200–201
    scale-location plot, 201–202
value of significance, 196
work environment, 187
Lists, R, 34
Logistic regression
    binomial distribution, 233
    data creation, 235
    glm() function, 234
    lm() function, 234
    logistic regression model, 234
    model creation
        comparison, 239
        conclusion, 242
        deviance, 238

Logistic regression (*cont.*)
    dispersion, 242
    glm() function, 236
    model fit verification, 240
    multicollinearity, 242
    residual deviance, 238
    summary of, 238
    variables, 240
    warning message, 241
  multinomial logistic regression, 248
  read.csv() command, 235
  regularization (*see* Regularization)
  training and testing, 243
    prediction() function, 246
    response variable, 245
    validation, 245
Looping functions, 48–49
  apply() function, 49
  cut() function, 53–54
  lapply() function, 50
  sapply() function, 51
  split() function, 54
  tapply() function, 51, 53

M

Machine learning, 119, 258
Manhattan distance, 164
MapReduce, 260
Market-basket analysis (MBA). *See* Affinity
    analysis
Matrices, R, 30–31
Measurable data. *See* Quantitative data
Microsoft Azure, 261
Microsoft Business Intelligence and
    Tableau, 261
Microsoft Excel file, reading data, 42–44
Microsoft SQL Server database, 5
Minkowski distance, 164
Min-max normalization, 117
Mtcars Data Set, 52
Multicollinearity, 218
Multinomial logistic regression, 233, 248
Multiple linear regression, 207
  assumptions, 208
  components, 207
  correlation, 210
  data, 209
  data-frame format, 208
  discrete variables, 207
  equation, 223

  lm() function, 212, 224
  multicollinearity, 208, 218
  predictors, 208
  response variable, 225
  R function glm(), 224
  stepwise, 221
  subsets approach, 221
  training and testing model, 225
  validation
    crPlots, 215
    Durbin-Watson test, 217
    ncvTest(model name), 216
    normal Q-Q plot, 214
    qqPlot, 217
    residuals *vs.* fitted, 213
    residuals *vs.* leverage plot, 215
    scale-location plot, 214
    Shapiro-Wilk
      normality test, 216
multiple linear regression equation.
    See Multiple linear regression
Multiple regression, 188
myFun() function, 56

N

Naïve Bays, 134
Natural language processing (NLP), 262
NbClust() function, 181
Nominal data types, 98
Nonhierarchical clustering. *See* K-means
    algorithm
Non-linear regression, 188
Normal distribution, 86
Normalization techniques, 117
NoSQL, 261
Null hypothesis, 192

O

Online analytical processing (OLAP), 95
Open Database Connectivity
    (ODBC), 42–43
Ordinal data types, 98
Overdispersion, 242

P

Packages and libraries, R, 56–57
Partition clustering methods, 180
Poisson distribution, 88

Prediction, 131
Predictive analytics
    classification, 118
    regression, 119
Predictive Model Markup Language
        (PMML), 263
Preprocessing data
    preparation, 99
        duplicate, junk, and null
            characters, 100
        empty values, 100
        handling missing values, 99
        R
            as.numeric() function, 103
            complete.cases() function, 103
            data types, 100
            factor levels, 103
            factor() type, 102
            head() command, 101
            methods, 100
            missing values, 103
            names() and c() function, 102
            table() function, 103
            vector operations, 101
        types, 97
Probabilistic classification, 132
    advantages and limitations, 136
    bank credit-card approval process, 133
    Naïve Bays, 134
Probability
    concepts, 84
    distributions (see Probability
        distributions)
    events, 85
    mutually exclusive events, 85
    mutually independent events, 85
    mutually non-exclusive events, 86
Probability distributions
    binomial, 87
    normal, 86–87
    poisson, 88
Probability sampling, 96
Property graphs (PG), 262

■ Q

Qualitative data, 97
Quantitative data, 97

■ R

R
    advantages, 21
    console, 22
    control structures, 45
        for loops, 46–47
        if-else, 46
        looping functions, 48–51, 53–54
        while loops, 47–48
        writing functions, 55–56
    data analysis
        reading and writing data, 37–38,
            40–44
    data analysis tools, 17, 21
    data structures, 29
        arrays, 31
        data frames, 32
        factors, 35
        lists, 34
        matrices, 30–31
    glm() function, 224
    installation, 21–22
        RStudio interface, 23–24
    interfaces, 38
    library(NbClust) command, 176
    lm() function, 212, 224
    Naïve Bays, 134
    objects types, 27–28
    packages and libraries, 56–57
    pairs() command, 112
    programming, basics, 25–26
        assigning values, 26–27
        creating vector, 27
    View() command, 105
Random forests, 152
Random sampling, 96
Ratio data types, 98
read.csv() function, 38
read.table() function, 38
Receiver operating characteristic (ROC), 247
rect.hclust() function, 178
Regularization
    cv.fit() model, 253
    cv.glmnet() function, 249
    generic format, 249
    glmnet() function, 249
    glmnet_fit command, 252

Regularization (*cont.*)
  methods, 248
  plot() function, 250, 252
  plot(cv.fit), 253
  predict() function, 254
  print() function, 250, 252
  shrinkage methods, 248
  variable, 250
Ridge Regression method, 193
RODBC package, 42
Root-mean-square error (RSME), 127
RStudio
  installation error, 23
  installing, 23
  interface, 23–24
  output, 25
  window, 24

S

sapply() function, 51
Scatter plot matrices, 112
Scatter plots
  analysis of data, 81
  changes, relationship, 83–84
  Coding, 81
  created in R, 82
  EmpData1, 82–83
seq_along() function, 47
Shrinkage methods, 248
Simple regression, 188
split() function, 54
Standard deviations, 70–72
Statistical parameters
  mean
    data set, 64
    downside of, 66
    in R, 64–65
    limitations, 64
    profit and effective, 65
    single parameter, 65
    usage of, 64
  median, 66–67
  mode, 68
  quantiles, 69
  range, 68
  standard deviation, 70–72

summary(dataset), 73
  variance, 73
Storm, 260
Stratified sampling, 96
Supervised machine learning, 119
Systematic sampling, 96

T

tapply() function, 51, 53
Text file, reading data, 38, 40–42
Transformation, 117
Trellis graphics, 114

U

Univariate analysis, 107
Unsupervised machine learning, 120
  association-rule analysis, 161, 182
    association rules, 185–186
    if-then, 183
    interpreting results, 186
    market-basket analysis, 182–183
    rules, 183
    support, 183
  clustering (*see* Clustering analysis)

V

Variance errors, 147
Variance inflation factor (VIF), 218
Variety, 258
Velocity, 258
Visualization
  Workflow, 104
Visualization. *See* Data exploration and
    visualization

W, X, Y

Web, reading data, 44
while loops, 47–48
Whole data processing, 263

Z

Z-score normalization, 117

Get the eBook for only $4.99!

Why limit yourself?

Now you can take the weightless companion with you wherever you go and access your content on your PC, phone, tablet, or reader.

Since you've purchased this print book, we are happy to offer you the eBook for just $4.99.

Convenient and fully searchable, the PDF version enables you to easily find and copy code—or perform examples by quickly toggling between instructions and applications.

To learn more, go to http://www.apress.com/us/shop/companion or contact support@apress.com.

CPSIA information can be obtained
at www.ICGtesting.com
Printed in the USA
LVHW030215130120
643322LV00005B/68/P

9 781484 225134